FIRST THESSALONIANS

THE HIDDEN HISTORY OF THE PAULINE CHURCHES

FIRST THESSALONIANS

THE HIDDEN HISTORY OF THE PAULINE CHURCHES

by

HARRY SHAEFER

Kephalos Publishing LLC
Johnson City, Tennessee

Published by Kephalos Publishing LLC,
407 Highland Ave
Johnson City Tennessee

Library of Congress Control Number: 2013905726
ISBN: 978-0-9889151-0-7

Author photo by Becca Davis Photography
In transliterated Greek words, ê represents eta and ô represents omega.
The Index was prepared by R.J.Powell.
Interior layout: Jonathan Gullery

Translations are my own. For text and critical apparatus, I used the Seventh Edition of Alfred Rahlfs' *Septuaginta* and the 27th revision of Nestle-Aland *Novum Testamentum Graece*.

The SymbolGreekII font used to print this work is available from Linguist's Software, Inc., PO Box 580, Edmonds, WA 98020-0580, USA. (Telephone (425) 775-1130. www.linguistsoftware.com.)

CONTENTS

I especially want to acknowledge the influence of John Knox, of Charles Buck and Greer Taylor, whose book on St. Paul helped me identify St. Paul's writings as my primary interest, and of John Hurd, for sorting out the levels of the correspondence hidden in I Corinthians. The contributions of these scholars have been greatly undervalued.

My first readers, Anne Koehler, the Rev. Edward J. Mills, Saundra Gerrell Kelley, and James E. Morgan, have done me and my readers great service. David Hendricksen read an early version of the complete manuscript and helped me clarify the relationship between faith, which is an inner attitude, and its outward expression. I am especially indebted to Joseph Tyson, PhD; John C. Hurd, Jr., PhD; and Charles W. Swain, PhD, for their critical comments. Mark Matson, Ph.D, helped me approach ancient rhetoric.

My dear Marjorie has been an enthusiastic supporter of this work all the way through; her encouragement has been indispensable assistance.

PART I

PRELIMINARIES

CHAPTER 1

THE NEED FOR A NEW HISTORY OF THE VERY EARLY CHURCH

S INCE very early in the history of the Christian Church, people have read the Acts of the Apostles first, and then Paul's letters, beginning with Romans and then the two letters to the Thessalonians much later. This has given us a traditional version of the history of the early church. If, however, we read the letters first without Acts and try to tease out the historical events that lie behind them, we get a very different picture of that history.

St. Paul's letters are the earliest historical evidence for the movement that became the Christian Church, and, as far as New Testament scholars agree, First Thessalonians is the oldest of the letters.[1] I have long wanted to thoroughly mine the Pauline letters for their evidence of history, beginning with the earliest letter. To my knowledge, the historical evidence of the letters has not yet been exhaustively examined.

In the twentieth century, six scholars in particular made cases for a history based on Paul's letters: John Knox, Donald Riddle, Charles Buck and Greer Taylor, John Hurd, and Gerd Luedemann. Together they have created a scenario of how we would construct the history of Paul's ministry if Acts did not exist. (See Appendix 1 for a positive presentation of their work).

However, those scholars worked primarily on the events where Acts and Paul's letters differ. They did not start from the earliest letter and attempt to exhaust it. In order to see this picture, we must creatively forget everything

---

1. The other candidates are Galatians and Second Thessalonians. Some scholars see Galatians as the oldest, and a very few scholars conclude that Second Thessalonians was written before First Thessalonians. Nevertheless, there is a substantial agreement that First Thessalonians is the oldest of Paul's letters and the oldest document in the New Testament.

we "know" and read First Thessalonians as if it were the only document of the Christian Church that has survived until modern times. This is where a different picture emerges.

These six scholars examined the letters to evaluate their evidence for a chronology of Paul's ministry as it would contribute to a study of Paul, particularly as that study would shed light on his biography. Their work is valuable because it gives us insight regarding what was going on with Paul when he wrote the letters. However, in addition to Paul's statements regarding his own activities, Paul made statements about other events and situations at the time of his writing. None of these six scholars examine those statements in a thorough fashion.

Riddle is more interested in Paul's character than his chronology or history. To be sure, he describes Paul's character in a biographical frame, but he does not make a big issue of the events of the chronology. Riddle achieves his goal by ignoring the history as presented in Acts, and by not over-worrying the history in Paul. Riddle did not mine the letters for other history of the circumstances in which they were written. Riddle's book is a biography of Paul, not a history of the early church. As an overall result, the work on the history is still missing.

Other than Gal 1:13-2:10, Knox did not attempt to draw out all of the historical allusions in Paul's letters.[2] His focus was on Paul's personal story rather than on the history of the very early church. Knox did not attempt to use Paul's letters to write a history of the movement.

Buck's focus was on three specific trajectories[3] of change in Paul's thought. Beyond that, Buck did not attempt to establish a chronology for Paul's life or a history of the very early church. Buck and Hurd make a considerable attempt to set First Corinthians into its historical context. The result is signifi-

---

2. John Coolidge Hurd, Jr., *The Earlier Letters of Paul – and Other Studies* (Frankfurt am Main, Berlin, Bern, New York, Paris, Wien: Peter Lang, 1998), 23, commented that Knox depended on a small selection of passages from the letters: Gal. 1:13-2:10; 1 Cor. 16:1-4; and Rom. 15:23-32. These sections all refer, he maintained, to the Collection.

3. The three trajectories are Christology, Eschatology, and the Law. In the earliest letter, God raised Jesus from the dead; in the latest, Jesus was the agent of his own resurrection. In the earliest letter, the dead and the living will be gathered into Christ's *parousia* without a transformation; in a mid-trajectory letter, the dead and the living will be transformed at their resurrection; in late-trajectory letters, Christians are being transformed during their lifetimes. In the earliest letters, Paul continued to approve the Jewish law; in later letters, the law was superseded by grace.

cant and tantalizing insight into the meaning of the letter. However, similar work has not yet been done for the other letters.

Hurd was primarily interested in detailing the conversation that preceded the writing of First Corinthians. Hurd focused his examination on First Corinthians. He did not begin with First Thessalonians, nor did he attempt to discover everything it can tell us about the very early Jesus movement.

In his book best known to English readers, Luedemann developed a chronology for Paul's ministry. He did not, however, exhaustively mine the letters for everything else we might learn about history. Like Knox, he focused on Paul's statements in the first two chapters of Galatians.

Therefore the work of examining the other letters, beginning with the earliest letter, with a purpose of evaluating the evidence about the history of the very early ecclesia, remains to be done. This book will attempt to make that beginning.

It may be that when we finish, readers will say, "Well, we always knew that." However, since there has not yet been a clear statement of what these primary sources can tell us, such knowledge does not qualify as knowledge under the most rigorous standards. Our objective, then, is rigorous knowledge of the historical situations in which Paul's letters were written.

There is a second part to this task; namely, the letters need to be set into their historical contexts and re-interpreted according to those contexts. It is important for us to set the letters into the historical situations of their recipients, as far as it is possible for us to do so, so that we understand the situations to which Paul was speaking. It is equally important for us to understand the situation of the writer. What were his hopes as he wrote, what were his anxieties, what pressures were placed upon him? As Hurd says, we need to be aware of "his interests, insights, needs, hopes, fears, and his maturing experience as an ambassador for Christ."[4] We also need to know how his writing fitted into the context of social communication. We are limited by the reality that we may never be able to know what he was thinking, but we need nevertheless to do the best job we possibly can.[5] Our need to recognize both the situations of the readers and of the writer is a corollary of recognizing that the epistles

---

4. John Coolidge Hurd, Jr. *The Origin of I Corinthians* (New York: Seabury Press 1965), 6.

5. Hurd, *Origin*, xi, 5, 5-6: Hurd's intention was to revive interest in how Paul's writings have a context in "the events of his most eventful life." particularly noting that it is questionable to use Paul's letters to explain each other, because they all have different historical, emotional, and social

really are letters.

This is important because these are letters, not essays. Hurd opened the first chapter of his book with this distinction, developed by Adolf Deissmann and others, between letters and essays.[6] Essays are addressed to a general audience, but letters are addressed to an individual or a group in a specific historical situation. In a letter, both the sender and the receiver know the details, so that the sender does not have to explain; but in an essay, details have to be explained for general readers. Consequently, letters are often obscure to later readers. Later readers have to reconstruct the unmentioned details of the historical situation in order to understand the conversation. Paul's letters, then, need to be interpreted on the basis of the best possible historical reconstruction.

In the recent past, we have interpreted the letters as if they were essays without historical contexts. This is a mistake. We cannot tell, however, how much of a mistake it is, until we have an alternative. When the historical exposition of the letters shall give us historical contexts for the letters, we will then be able to see how those contexts modify our interpretation of the letters.

We have interpreted the letters as if they were timeless theological essays, while at the same time we have adopted an Acts-based history of Paul's ministry. That brings up the question of the extent to which our understanding of the theology of the letters is influenced by reading them in the context of that history. Again, I believe we cannot really answer that question until we have produced an alternative to which we can compare our current understanding.

The place to begin is with First Thessalonians. So far as scholars agree, it is our earliest evidence of the very early ecclesia.

As we begin, we need to take time to discuss the authenticity of 2:14-16. In those three verses, Paul makes a digression from his topic and blames the crucifixion of Jesus, and much else, on "the Jews."[7] There are good and im-

contexts; he differentiates the interests, needs, questions, and misunderstandings of the church being addressed from Paul's interests, intentions, fears and experiences at the time when he wrote. *Earlier Letters*, 22: He notes that Riddle's putting the letters into a sequence related to the Circumcision Crisis went some distance to set the letters into their historical contexts.
Earlier Letters, 29: he notes that Paul dealt foremost with problems, and to understand him, we must recognize those problems.

6. Hurd, *Origin*, 1.

7. The Greek term *Ioudaioi* might be translated "Judaeans," suggesting people who lived in a

portant reasons why most New Testament scholars regard these verses to be an interpolation. However, there are also answers for each of those reasons, and these verses play very well with a proposed analysis of the difficulties that were threatening the ecclesia when Paul wrote.

Then the four chapters of Part II take up topics that are presented in the letter as assumed or agreed upon material. Paul presents these topics as statements on which he does not expect opposition or question. These statements, then, give us a clear view of the gospel as Paul originally preached it in Thessalonica.

In addition to the topics on which Paul expected agreement, there are also two topics that were new, on which he expected disagreement, resistance, and perhaps argument. These two topics came to my attention through a very careful process of analyzing the function of each coherent segment of the letter. Part III begins with the development of that discovery. From there, it is a straightforward matter to discuss these two issues and how they might have come to be.

particular place at a particular ancient time. I have chosen to translate *Ioudaioi* as "the Jews" precisely because these words capture the offensive and emotional character of Paul's words.

CHAPTER 2

THE AUTHENTICITY
OF THE DIGRESSION

THE majority of contemporary scholars have concluded that verses
2:15-16 are an interpolation. There are several reasons why they think
so: 2:16 refers to an event later than the writing of First Thessalonians; the
position taken in these verses is at odds with the position Paul took in his
later letters; the position taken in these verses is appropriate to a later time;
at least one word appears in a sense too unusual for Paul; Second Thessalonians, which copied much of First Thessalonians, does not copy these verses;
if these verses are omitted, it does not detract from the flow of thought; and
the thought is particularly offensive to modern ears.

Verse 16 refers to a catastrophe that has happened to the people of Judaea, and most scholars think it refers to the destruction of the Temple by the
Roman Empire in 70 c.e. This was a cataclysmic loss for Judaism, leaving the
worldwide network of dispersed Jews without a national center and without
the Temple worship that had been part of their experience for centuries. The
destruction of the Temple might well have looked like an end-time event to
followers of Jesus who were looking for the end time. The majority of contemporary scholars agree that verse 2:16, "The wrath of the end-time has
already begun for them," refers to the destruction of the Jerusalem Temple.[8]

By any measure, First Thessalonians was written before 52 c.e.[9] and per-

---

8. Richard I. Pervo, *The Making of Paul: Constructions of the Apostle in Early Christianity*
(Minneapolis: Fortress, 2010), 48-49, suggests that this identification is commonly accepted
today.

9. Abraham J. Malherbe, *The Letters to the Thessalonians: A New Translation with Introduction
and Commentary* (New Haven and London:Yale University Press, The Anchor Yale Bible, 2000),

haps as early as 41 c.e.[10] If this phrase about the "wrath of the end-time" refers to the destruction of the Temple, which happened eighteen to twenty-four years later, it could only have been written after 70 and by someone other than Paul. If someone, then, had written this last phrase, or perhaps all of 14-16, in the margin of the letter, a later copyist would, as was customary, copy it into the text.

Paul taught the equality of Jews and others in many places, saying that the two become one in Christ (Gal 3:28), saying circumcision does not make a difference (1 Cor 7:19; Gal 5:6), what makes a difference is whether or not people obey God's commandments (1 Cor 7:17-24), describing how he acted like a Jew in order to win Jews (1 Cor 9:19-23), and sharing his vision that it was part of God's plan for most Jews not to respond to Christ now, in order that the gospel might be offered to others (Rom 9-11). None of this suggests that Paul blamed the Jews for the crucifixion. Paul's anger elsewhere was aimed at highfaluting prophets who would require gentile converts to be circumcised and keep kosher kitchens (2 Cor 11-13, Phil 3:2-3, Gal 1:6-7, 3:1, 5:2-6, 12). Scholars thus think these verses are so distant from the rest of Paul's thought that they must be an interpolation.

There are passages in the Gospels that parallel this expression blaming the Jews for crucifying Jesus and killing the prophets (Mat 23:29-39 and parallel Luke 13:34-35). These expressions date from the last decade of the First Century, when the Jesus movement was separating itself from the synagogue. Probably that withdrawal included animosity and hostile commentary on both sides; we know from evidence only the harsh things that nascent Christians said about the Jews. These verses from First Thessalonians mirror them and express a sentiment that is more appropriate to the last decade of the First Century than to the Fourth or Fifth Decades, and therefore scholars tend to see these verses as an interpolation written at that later time.

Some of the words in these two verses are not words that Paul used regu-

---

13, asserts that Paul arrived in Thessalonica in A.D. 49; 71-72, he confirms that there was only a brief passage of time before he wrote the letter.
Arthur J. Dewey, Roy W. Hoover, Lane G. McGaughy, and Daryl D. Schmidt, *The Authentic Letters of Paul: A New Reading of Paul's Rhetoric and Meaning: The Scholar's Version* (Salem, Oregon: Polebridge Press, 2010), 17, suggest 50 or early 51 C.E. for the date for the letter.

10. Gerd Luedemann, *Paul, Apostle to the Gentiles: Studies in Chronology* (Philadelphia: Fortress Press) German text © 1980; English translation by F. Stanley Jones © 1984), 238.
Hurd has suggested 46 C.E., in an unpublished encyclopedia article.

larly. In particular, he used the word *mimêtai* ("imitators") in a different way than he customarily used it. Usually, Paul used the word *mimêtai* positively to refer to believers' praiseworthy imitation of himself and of Christ Jesus, as he does in 1:6. Here, in 2:14, the meaning of their being imitators is a bad thing, in that the same sort of bad thing has happened to them as has happened to others. The argument suggests that Paul would not have used this word in such a radically different sense from the way he used it in the previous chapter.

Second Thessalonians, which most contemporary scholars think was written by someone other than Paul at a later time than First Thessalonians, copies many phrases from First Thessalonians. Second Thessalonians, however, does not include a copy of these verses. Perhaps First Thessalonians did not include these verses when Second Thessalonians was copied.

The omission of these verses does not cause any loss of sense. Verse 2:17 can follow after 2:13 with as much continuity of thought as it has following 2:16; indeed, verse 2:17 follows perfectly well after 2:12. There is no problem with the intelligibility of the text if we regard any part of 2:13-16 as an interpolation.

Finally, this sentiment is offensive to the modern ear. Since World War II, with its extreme expression of prejudice against Jews, there has been revulsion against anti-Semitism. Studies of the variety of Judaisms of the centuries surrounding the life of Jesus of Nazareth have been carried to new depths. The unpleasantness involved in Christianity's separation has been studied and described as a historical phenomenon. The global judgment of the Jews expressed in these verses is false; the Jews did not kill Jesus, nor did they kill the prophets whom God sent to them. The sentiment of these verses is distasteful and offensive to sensitive people and contrary to the best that is Christianity.

Each of these arguments, however, can be answered convincingly. Then, in addition, there are further arguments in favor of regarding this passage as authentic.

From any time after 70 C.E. the destruction of the Temple has great appeal as "the wrath of the end time." However, it is entirely possible for Paul to have used this phrase before 70 C.E. to refer to some other cataclysmic event. What would qualify as a catastrophe of eschatological wrath? The Gospel of Mark names wars, rumors of wars, earthquake, fire, and famine (Mark 13:7-8.). There were such events in the forties and fifties; we know of some such events, and there were others. Paul could have been thinking of any such disaster, known or unknown to us, when he wrote this phrase.

Probably, however, Paul was thinking of an event in Judaea. Whether it was an earthquake, fire, or famine, it probably happened only a short time before Paul wrote the letter. One such event was the famine in Judaea in 46 C.E. That famine has been suggested as the event that Paul meant here.[11]

Most scholars today agree that there is very little or no development in Paul's thinking, based in part on the view that Paul's letters were written when his thought was already mature and in too brief a span for there to have been time for further growth. This view also is based in part on taking Paul's four major letters[12] as the model for Paul's thought; passages which are not consistent with the major letters are suspected of being inauthentic. Based on the evidence of the letters themselves, there is an important argument that they were written over a longer span of time than is commonly supposed (see the chapter on Historical Analysis).

First Thessalonians, however, is very different from Romans. In First Thessalonians Paul wrote to people he knew well, who knew him well. He wrote amidst a crisis which caused him to be concerned for the continued existence of his ecclesia. In his concern, perhaps Paul let slip an emotional outburst. In particular, we might consider that this passage in First Thessalonians represents an emotional immaturity. It was one which he would later regret and try to overcome with wiser words.

The letter has been focused on the event when Paul's Thessalonian hearers became a faith community. The repetition of the word *kenos* in 2:1 and 3:5 suggests that Paul's concern for the continued existence of the ecclesia was emotionally strong. The curse in 2:15-16 came out of that emotional context, so that the singleness of Paul's concern throughout this section and its emotional depth tends to authenticate these verses as appropriate to the letter and probably authentic.

Since the members of the ecclesia in Rome did not know him, it was important to him to make a good first impression. In Romans, he addressed some passages to gentiles and some to Jews, so that it appears that the church

---

11. Charles Buck and Greer Taylor, *St. Paul: A Study of the Development of His Thought* (Charles Scribner's Sons. 1969), 148-50, 212.

12. Romans, First and Second Corinthians, and Galatians are the longest and most mature of Paul's letters. They are widely considered his major works.

in Rome was composed of both Jews and others. Thus there was every reason for him to be collected, wise, and irenic in his words and in particular in what he said about his fellow Jews. This vision of Romans as collected and calm raises the possibility that Romans represents Paul's maturity.

The contrasts between the two letters, that the ecclesia of Thessalonians was an all-gentile congregation while the ecclesia in Rome included both Jews and others, that Paul could rely on previous knowledge in the former situation but needed to make a good first impression in the latter, provide an explanation for the differences between 1 Thess 2:14-16 and Romans. This replacement of an intemperate view by a mature wisdom does explain how a man might have expressed himself differently, and it does leave open the possiblity that his thinking changed and developed.

It is indeed the case that this sentiment is echoed in the Gospels and that it is a sentiment appropriate to the time when the Gospels were written. However, rather than seeing it as a sentiment that belongs only to the end of the First Century, we are also able to see that in his concern for the continued existence of his ecclesia, Paul might have expressed the same sentiment that was expressed later. If there is any direction of influence here, it is that the negative connotations of what Paul intemperately said here struck a chord with later feelings and reinforced them.[13]

Paul's use of *mimêtai* here sets the recent difficulties experienced by the ecclesia of the Thessalonians into the context of what is common and predictable for followers of Jesus. Paul has been building in the first two chapters of the letter towards discussion of these recent difficulties. It is a brilliant rhetorical stroke for him to associate his first reference to those difficulties with the experience of others. Indeed, he will continue this theme of setting the difficulties into the context of what was predicted, in 1 Thess 3:3-4. (See the discussion of the functions of the segments in Part III, chapter 1.)

The fact that Second Thessalonians did not copy these verses is interesting and might possibly be evidence that these verses were not in First Thessalonians when Second Thessalonians was written. However, it is not conclusive evidence. Second Thessalonians is selective in what it copied; by the same logic, Paul's statements about his preaching and their response to it in

---

13. Hurd, *Earlier Letters*, Chapter VII passim, 133, observed that Paul's blaming the crucifixion on the Jews anticipated later development.

1 Thess 1:2-10 and 2:1-13 are not repeated in Second Thessalonians, and Second Thessalonians thus is equal evidence that they were not part of the original letter.

The strongest evidence that 2:14-16 is authentic to First Thessalonians is the absence of manuscript evidence that it is an interpolation. We now know that the existing ancient manuscripts derive from a plurality of copies that were even more ancient. There were a significant number of copies of this letter circulating in the First and Second Centuries, just as there were for every other letter which was selected to be included in the New Testament.[14] If this passage were an interpolation, then it is likely that there would be at least one manuscript tradition either omitting these verses or showing some marginal notation that these verses were interpolated, as is the case for 1 Cor 11:33-35.[15] The lack of evidence is a strong indication that these verses are authentic to the original letter.

These verses participate in some level of exaggeration.[16] Even if we take the saying about the Jews as restrictive, deciding that it refers only to **some** Jews, the statement cannot be true. It was in fact the Roman government that crucified Jesus. Some Jews brought pressure on the government, but from a literal point of view, they were not the executors. However, if the verse is not restrictive, then all Jews are responsible for the deaths of the prophets and of Jesus and are the ones who drove Paul out and attempt to prevent him from preaching. Since this likewise cannot be true, it does not appear to be a calm and reasonable statement. Instead, it appears to be a highly emotional outburst. As such we might consider that it serves to humanize Paul. Sometimes his emotions ran away with him! He was not always perfect. He was subject to human frailty, as are we all.[17]

This questioned passage exhibits a quirk that is typical of Paul's style: the three verses reproduce in sequence the thoughts of an earlier passage. The

14. Harry Gamble, "The Redaction of the Pauline Letters and the Formation of the Pauline Corpus," *Journal of Biblical Literature* 94 (1975): 403-418.

15. Philip B. Payne, *Man and Woman, One in Christ: An Exegetical and Theological Study of Paul's Letters* (Grand Rapids, Mi: Zondervan, 2009).

16. Malherbe, *Letters*, 169, says that the comma printed in the Greek text and in many modern translations is wrong, giving a false impression that Paul meant all Jews rather than some of them.

17. Perhaps his temper is what he meant by his "thorn in the flesh" (2 Cor 12:7); however 1 Thess 2:14-17 is the only indication of a temper in this letter.

parallels between 1 Thess 1:2-10 and 2:13-16 are so intricate that they must represent something about how the author's mind worked.[18] See Table 1.

- Both passages begin with *eucharistoumen*, ("we give thanks").
- Both passages give thanks *adialeiptôs*, ("without fail").
- Both passages use a form of *logos*. Verse 1:4 refers to their *eklogên*, their ("election"); verse 2:13 refers to *logon* three times.
- Both passages develop the sense of *logos* as "word." Verse 1:5 says that the gospel did not come to them as **mere words**. Verse 2:13 says that they received the **word** of preaching not as a human **word** but as the **word** of God.
- Both passages speak of their response to the gospel. Verse 1:5 says that they responded in power and holy spirit and great conviction. Verse 2:13 says that they accepted the preached word as what it is, the true word of God.
- Both passages speak of their response as God working in them. Verse 1:5 refers to the holy spirit. Verse 2:13 says that God—or the word of God—"is at work in you, the believers."
- Both passages speak of imitation. Verse 1:6 says that they have become imitators of Paul and of the Lord. Verse 2:14 says that they have become imitators of the ecclesiae of Jesus in Judaea.
- Both passages speak of difficulty or conflict. Verse 1:6 says that they received the word in much conflict, using the word *thlipsis* ("trouble"). Verse 2:14 says that they endured the same thing as the ecclesiae of Jesus in Judaea, using the word *epathete* ("experience" or "endure").
- Both passages speak of ministries. Verse 1:7 speaks of the result of their ministry. Verse 2:15 speaks of the suffering of missionaries, being driven out and hindered.

---

18. John Hurd and other scholars have shown that it is a characteristic of Paul's way of thinking to develop one thought as a parallel to or an expansion of a previous thought. Sequence 1 goes A, B, C, D, E and then sequence 2 goes A′, B′, C′, D′, E′ (where A′ is a variation of A, etc.). In this case, the tightness of thought, the ways in which 2:13-16 parallels 1:2-10, ties chapters 1-3 together as one long unified section.

1 Thess. 1:2-10	1 Thess. 2:13-16
A. 2 Εὐχαριστοῦμεν . . .	A. 13 καὶ ἡμεῖς εὐχαριστοῦμεν . . .
B. 2 ἀδιαλείπτως . . .	B. 13 ἀδιαλείπτως . . .
C. 4 εἴδοτες . . . τὴν ἐκλογήν. . .	C. 13 ὅτι παραλαβόντες λόγον ἀκοῆς παρ' ἡμῶν
D. 5 ὅτι τὸ εὐαγγέλιον οὐκ ἐγενήθη εἰς ὑμᾶς. . .	D. 13 τοῦ θεοῦ ἐδέξασθε
E. 5 ἐν λόγῳ μόνον. . .	E. 13 οὐ λόγον ἀνθρώπων
F. 5 ἀλλὰ καὶ ἐν δυνάμει. . .	F. 13 ἀλλὰ καθώς ἐστιν ἀληθῶς λόγον θεοῦ
G. 5 καὶ ἐν πνεύματι ἁγιῳ καὶ ἐν πληροφορίᾳ. . .	G. 13 ὃς καὶ ἐνεργεῖται ἐν ὑμῖν τοῖς πιστεύουσιν.
H. 6 Καὶ ὑμεῖς μιμηταὶ ἡμῶν ἐγενήθητε καὶ τοῦ κυρίου,. . .	H. 14 Ὑμεῖς γὰρ μιμηταὶ ἐγενήθητε . . . τῶν ἐκκλησιῶν
I. 6 δεξάμενοι τὸν λόγον ἐν θλίψει πολλῇ	I. 14 ὅτι τὰ αὐτὰ ἐπάθετε
J. 7	J. 14
K. 9 ἐπεστρέψατε πρὸς τὸν θεὸν ἀπὸ τῶν εἰδώλων. . .	K. 16 κωλυόντων ἡμᾶς τοῖς ἔθνεσιν λαλῆσαι
L. 9 δουλεύειν θεῷ ζῶντι καὶ ἀληθινῷ καὶ ἀναμένειν τὸν υἱὸν. . .	L. 16 ἵνα σωθῶσιν . . .
M. 10 τὸν ῥυόμενον ἡμᾶς ἐκ τῆς ὀργῆς τῆς ἐρχομένης.	M. 16 ἔφθασεν δὲ ἐπ' αὐτοὺς ἡ ὀργὴ εἰς τέλος.

This table is adapted from the version in Hurd, *Earlier Letters*, pages 69 and 125. Hurd's version shows the parallels in English. I wanted to show the parallels in the Greek text.

Table 1. Parallelism in word and thought in 1:2-10 and 2:13-16

- Both passages speak of conversion from idolatrous religion. Verse 1:9 speaks of their turning from idols. Verse 2:16 speaks of preaching to the non-Jews.
- Both passages speak of conversion to a true religion. Verse 1:9 speaks of serving a living and true God. Verse 2:16 speaks of saving the non-Jews.
- Both passages speak of the coming wrath. Verse 1:10, the end of the passage, speaks of the coming *orgê* ("rage"). Verse 2:16 speaks of the *orgê* that has come in anticipation of the end.

These parallels are much too intricate to be the creation of a copyist; it stands to reason that a poet might try to make a subsequent stanza to be an exact re-expression of an earlier stanza, and that might not be formidably difficult to do. However, to create an extensive parallel development in a later passage, where it is not obvious that the subjects are the same, would not be a casual matter, and it is not easy to come up with a reason why an imitator would do so in this particular case. The intricacy of the parallels suggests that 2:14-16 is integral to the letter.

The parallels in 2:14-16 to 1:2-10 strongly suggest that this passage is an integral part of the letter. Furthermore, the use of "imitators" as an opening phrase in Paul's statement of the facts of the situation is a profound way of introducing the subject of the recent difficulties in Thessalonica and speaking to them both at once; Paul has moved into the story of recent events in a skillful way, while at the same time he confronted his particular anxieties about this ecclesia.

We may regard verses 2:13-16 as authentic to the letter: because 2:13 completes the thought of 2:1-12 as the complete parallel of 1:2-10 (see Part III, chapter 1), because it is a brilliant approach to the story of recent events, because it is as meaningful to consider that the "wrath of the end time" may refer to some event prior to 51 as to the later destruction of the Temple, and because the blaming expression of 2:14-16, unpleasant as it is to modern ears, can be understood as an emotional outburst, in relation to which Paul was later able to express a wiser and more balanced view.

PART II

EXISTING AGREEMENTS

CHAPTER 1

SPIRITUAL AGREEMENTS

SINCE First Thessalonians is not a direct statement of theology, which might be a teaching vehicle, its statements on theology, ethics, and spirituality are side comments. Paul states them in passing, referring to these issues while he is in the process of saying something else. They represent topics that are already agreed. The casualness of these references indicates not only that Paul did not expect any disagreement on these issues, but also indicates that they are a lower archeological layer. They represent the *status quo ante*, the gospel as Paul preached it prior to the writing of this letter.

The essence of the religious movement was attitude. Attitude is a characteristic of an inner, secret self. We have a choice to reveal our inner thoughts, lie about them, or keep silent. Skilled observers may be able to follow these inner processes, but in most of the experience of our lives, those processes are shielded. The early form of Christianity expected a change in the quality of these secret thoughts.

The dimensions of this inner religion are faith, love, and hope, sobriety and vigilance, rejoicing and praying. In these dimensions, First Thessalonians charts new ground in religion. Judaism has focused on correctness of behavior and is technically orthopractic; later Christianity focused on correctness of belief, and by the same technicality is orthodox. First Thessalonians, distinctively, presents a religion of the heart.

Faith, love, and hope, vigilance, and rejoicing

Paul's use of faith, love, and hope seems to come out of nowhere.[19] Paul

---

19. Malherbe, *Letters*, 109, thinks Paul may have originated this triad, particularly since it does not appear anywhere prior to Paul's use.

repeats this trio in First Corinthians, but he does not appear to have found
the trio in an earlier source. When they appear in 1 Cor 13:13, they have not
been prepared for in the two preceding chapters. The trio appears to just pop
up, fully formed, without gestation. Nevertheless, their influence on First
Thessalonians is pervasive.

In First Corinthians Paul put them in the sequence faith, hope, and love,
and he added, "and the greatest of these is love," suggesting that the sequence
"faith, hope, and love" places the most important of the trio last. Yet in First
Thessalonians, the sequence is "faith, love, and hope." He stated them in this
order for rhetorical reasons, because he wanted to discuss hope last of the
three (see Part III, chapter 1).

Paul's words

1:3 remembering your work of faith
and your labor of love
and your steadfastness of the hope

and

5:8 . . . putting on the breastplate of faith and love
and the headgear of hope for salvation.

Spiritual analysis

Paul began the letter by giving thanks for their faith, love, and hope. He
ended the body of the letter by urging them to put on faith, love, and hope
as armor. This use of the triad at the beginning and at the ending is a common wrap-around rhetorical technique. It signals the content of the letter by
marking the beginning and ending of the substantial discussion. The topic of
the letter is faith, love, and hope.

All three pertain to the secret inner person. People are able to keep their
hope a secret; people are able to keep their love unexpressed in words; people
are able to keep their faith a secret. These three virtues perfectly illustrate the
inner nature of this new religion.

While the military gear may seem surprising, it is appropriate to the
context. Paul has maintained a military image throughout the letter by his
references to the *parousia* and the *apantêsis* ("meeting" or "a going out to
welcome"). He has made the military image vivid with the audible references

in a mini-apocalypse (1 Thess 4:16). His use of "breastplate" and "headgear," continues the same image. Here, in the context of being sober and vigilant for the day of the Lord, it is particularly appropriate, since the military spend a great deal of their time having to be alert when there is no apparent danger.[20] While Paul organized this letter around faith, love, and hope, this vigilance also stands out as their spiritual character and ours.

In the closing of the letter, Paul states the theme of a life of prayer so strongly, that it is imperative that we recognize prayer as a predominant feature of this nascent religion. Paul presents prayer as a combination of thanksgiving and rejoicing. These closing words are a high point in the spirituality of the letter.

Faith

Paul named faith first in sequence. Many of his phrases refer to this virtue.

Paul's words

1:7 . . . an example to all the believers . . .

1:8 . . . your faith . . .

2:4 . . . God who trusts us to preach . . .

2:10 . . . you the believers,

2:13 . . .you, the believers.

3:2 . . . to steady you and to encourage you in your faith

3:6 . . . your faith and your love

3:7 . . . to create your faith . . .

3:10 . . . and make up what is lacking in your faith.

Spiritual analysis

Faith and its consequences organize the first three sub-sections of the letter. In 1:5-10, Paul celebrated the fact that these Thessalonians responded to the gospel, received the word, and became believers. Their response became

---

20. Paul probably used a military image in the overarching *inclusio* and in the reference to the trumpet in 4:16 at the *parousia* because some members of the Thessalonian ecclesia identified with the military. Thessalonica was a veteran colony. However, Malherbe thinks that the presence of soldiers in the community is sufficient to make the metaphor pertinent: Malherbe, *Letters*, 297.

The difference, of course, is between seeing the military armor on someone else and being able to imagine it on oneself.

an example for others throughout Macedonia and Achaia as their faith became known far abroad.

In 2:1-13 Paul spoke again of his preaching and their response. The emphasis in this passage is on the manner in which Paul and his team offered the gospel. Even more important, they responded to this offer by accepting it as what it really is, the word of God. Faith, then, refers to the response to the gospel.

The passage 2:14-16 began with a consequence of faith: difficulties that are caused by others. It then was distracted into a strong outburst concerning consequences. The digression underscores the point that there are consequences to faith, and some of them are negative.

These three passages, then, constitute the treatment of faith in this letter.

In 1:8, 3:2, 6, 7, and 10, "faith" translates the Greek word *pistis*, which encompasses both belief and trust. Paul used a word formed on the same root in 2:4 when he spoke of being "entrusted" with the gospel. He used another cognate in 1:7, 2:10, and 13 to refer to the members of the ecclesia as "the believers."[21]

Paul's use of the word *pisteuoi* ("believers") to refer to the members of the ecclesia is another clue that he intended a religion of people's personal thoughts.[22] Paul has characterized them as having a particular attitude.

What one thinks intellectually can be revealed or kept secret. Whether or not one feels confident in God can be revealed or kept secret. Both belong to the private self, the inner attitude. When Paul spoke of the members of the ecclesia as "the believers" he confirms that belief is of the essence of this early form of Christianity.

Paul expressed a vision of faith despite consequences in two passages.

---

21. Many scholars have read 2:1-12 as *apologia*, because Paul appears to be defending himself against comparisons with some unidentified opponents; in distinction from them, whoever they were, he was sincere, did not use flattery, and did not seek to please human beings. Other scholars have seen this section as Paul's autobiography, his statement of the meaning and purpose of his own life. The passage, nevertheless, illustrates the correct manner for the presentation of this gospel as faith, and therefore, it seems to me that it fits appropriately in the discussion of faith and its consequences.

22. The available contrasts are instructive: Daniel 7 explains that the everlasting kingdom is given to the "holy" ones, that is, to people characterized by something other than their attitude. The name given to the Pharisees, that is, the Separatists, characterizes them according to their purity of living standards. Therefore, to characterize the followers of Jesus as "believers" represents a step in a different direction.

Paul's words

1:3 . . . and your steadfastness of the hope
before our Lord Jesus Christ in the presence of God our Father,

and

3:3 . . . that you not be shaken in these current difficulties,
for you know that we can expect troubles;
4 we kept on telling you so ahead of time, when we were with
you,
that we were going to have difficulties,
just as has happened and as you know.

Spiritual analysis

Since Paul also said in 3:4 that he had told them in advance that there
would be *thlipses*, what they have suffered is a consequence of faith. It is a
normal course of events.

Since there are consequences to faith, it is an essential part of faith to
continue through difficulties. Paul later developed the concept of continuing
faith as a separate concept: *hypomonês* ("steadfastness") (Rom 5:3). In 1 Thess
1:3, Paul joined the word *hypomonês* with hope. In 3:3-4, he showed that he
meant faith that was not shaken by difficulties.

Faith that is steadfast despite the difficulties that it causes is still a function of the inner, private self.

Love

The second virtue is love, and most of the discussion of love is in a second section of the letter. While in 2:1-12 Paul was describing the manner
in which he presented the gospel, which is properly part of his discussion of
faith, he also used this segment to begin his discussion of love, by pointing to
his love for them.

Paul's words

2:3 For our proclamation came
not to deceive, not to trick, not to manipulate
4 but just as we have been known by God who trusts us to preach,

> just so we speak,
> not pleasing humans but God who discerns our hearts.
> 5   We never spoke in flattering words, as you know,
> nor as a pretext for greed, God is my witness,
> 6   and we were not seeking to impress people, neither you nor
> others.

and

> 7   . . . we were gentle among you
> as a nursing woman nourishes her own children.

and

> 11   . . . we were to each one of you like a father to his own children,

and

> 2:8   Yearning, we chose to give you not only God's good news
> but our own selves, so dear had you become to us.

and

> 2:16   . . . preaching to save the gentiles . . .

Spiritual analysis

These expressions commend love for each other and for everyone in the form of sincere openness to God and to each other.

Paul saw the issue of what pleases God as an issue of what is in one's heart. While he was speaking of acting in such a way as to please God rather than pleasing human beings, he said, almost as an aside, in 2:4: "not pleasing human beings but God who *dokimazonti* ("discerns") our hearts." The statement that God trusted Paul implies that God perceived Paul's heart correctly. Although *dokimazonti* could be translated "examines" or "tests," in this context it implies a true perception. God knows the secrets of the heart. Therefore it is the heart, the inner secret attitude of the person that pleases or displeases God.

Paul commended a certain open straightforwardness in the five claims about his own ministry. He did not preach to them to deceive or trick them or manipulate them (2:3).[23] He did not, he says, seek to please human beings (2:4). He did not ever, he says, use flattering words (2:5a). He did not preach as a pretext for personal enrichment (2:5c). He did not seek to impress people with his own importance (2:6a; literally "not seeking glory from people"). Rather, he says, he was gentle[24] with them just as a nursing mother is gentle with her own children (2:7). Each of these statements is a claim about Paul and the apostolic team, about his behavior while he was founding the ecclesia of the Thessalonians, and about his attitude from which that behavior arose. These statements make the claim that his outward appearance reflected his inner sincerity.

To the extent that these claims are a letter writing convention, they really represent an encouragement for his hearers to behave in the same way.[25] Paul expected that these Thessalonians would respond to the gospel with a similar integrity of mind and behavior. He expected their behavior to match the love in their hearts, and the love in their hearts to be sincere. Frankly what Paul said transcends the paraenetic convention. He was really talking about personal openness and sincerity, a dimension of love that was to be the cornerstone of this new religion.

Two verses later, Paul expressed himself in a way that reveals how fond he was of these Thessalonians. He came to care so much for them, in both the senses of nurturing (2:7) and of emotional feeling (2:8c), that he was willing to entrust himself.

The gift of himself meant an emotional openness. People give themselves by sharing what they think and feel, by making the decision to reveal precisely those thoughts that they are able to hide. The gift of oneself is an open sharing, in contrast with secret-keeping. This gift is an essential part of the

---

23. *Ek planês* means without deceit or deception, and *en dolôi* means without deceit or trick. I have applied these two in the sense of an attempt to deceive to the third phrase in the clause, *ex akatharsias* literally, "out of uncleanness" to the uncleanness that is part of deceit, i.e. manipulation.

24. Malherbe, *Letters*, 145-146: The best textual evidence suggests reading "infants" rather than "gentle," reading a second letter *nu*: *nêpioi* rather than *êpioi*. However, even the ancient translations use "gentle." Therefore, it is good to omit the second *nu*, even though the best texts have it.

25. Malherbe, *Letters*, 221.

gospel, creating an environment for others to be open in the same way, and therefore become support for one another.

That has to mean that Paul became open about his own feelings. Such open sharing of his inner and secret processes is a dimension of intimacy. This verse leads us to the insight that personal intimacy was a characteristic of this developing religion. For Paul to be open about and not guard his own inner thoughts created an atmosphere where others might find the courage to be similarly open.

Furthermore, Paul understood that he proclaimed the gospel in order that his gentile hearers *sôthôsin* ("might be saved") (2:16), doing them a great kindness. The orientation that he preached in order to give a benefit identifies the orientation as loving. Paul's ministry, then, was based on the concept of doing something good for people by preaching to them.

In 2:17-3:10, Paul talked about his love for these Thessalonians and their love for him. In the context of Timothy's report, 3:8, that they were steadfast and that they still loved him, Paul said, "Now we can live," implying that the good news about them revived his spirits. In the next few verses Paul expressed how much he wanted to see them and prayed that they might overflow with grace.

Paul's words

2:17 . . . we . . . became exceedingly eager to see you in person,
with a great desire.

and

3:6 . . . Timothy . . . and has announced to us your faith and your love
and that you always have a good memory of us,
wanting to see us just as we want to see you.

and

3:12 the Lord fill and make you overflow
with love for one another and for everyone,
just as we love you . . .

and

> ^{4:9} . . . for you are God-taught to love one another.
> ¹⁰ For you are doing this towards all the dear ones
>   in all of Macedonia. . .

Spiritual analysis

By these statements he declared his feelings. The fact that he felt this way about them is not an irrelevant corollary to the gospel; the gospel became what it really is: an outpouring of love.

When Paul rejoiced at their love for him, having learned that they wanted to see him as much as he wanted to see them, it was a statement of a core value as well as a statement of fact. Paul, however, was saying more than that. It was more than the simple proposition that it is life-giving to be loved. It is not a mere part of the early Jesus movement for members to love one another; it was the essence of this developing religion. Their love for Paul and each other was a basic qualifier. If members of the Jesus movement did not love one another, they were not really followers of Jesus. If they did not love Paul and each other, they would not qualify, and Paul's work would indeed have been in vain.

Likewise, in the prayer in 3:12 that is the transition between the two sections of this epistle, Paul prayed that this inner quality of love for each other will naturally express itself in kindness; kind behavior is a natural result of the inner attitude. Its essence, however, is not the outward behavior, but a quality of the inner experience.

Paul spoke in 3:11 of their *agapê eis* ("love for each other") and in 4:9 of their knowing how *eis to agapan allêlous* ("to love one another"). The implication is that love for one another in the ecclesia is not selective, allowing a member to love only some of the others. It really means that each of the members is expected to love all of the other members. Furthermore, it is not only love for the other members of the ecclesia. It is also love for people outside the ecclesia—that is, everyone inside and outside the ecclesia.

The word *theodidaktoi* ("God-taught") in 4:9, however, is a real puzzle.[26]

---

26. Malherbe, *Letters*, 244, suggests that *theodidaktos* might mean a teaching of Jesus, or a prophet in their ecclesia, or Paul's teaching.

What did Paul mean that they are God-taught? Could he have meant what he himself taught them? Probably not, because elsewhere he is very clear about what he taught or commanded.[27] Throughout this letter Paul said to his hearers that they already know what he is talking about. The expressions, *oidate* ("you know") and *kathôs oidate* ("just as you know") are repeated over and over again as Paul indicated over and over again that he was discussing memories and subjects that were common to himself and to them. It would be easy to take *theodidaktoi* as equivalent to "you know." The prefix *theo-*, however, introduces something to the discussion that is not present in "you know." It affirms a specific source of their knowledge; they know because God has taught them. It is not clear exactly to what act of God Paul was referring, but it does seem that *theodidaktoi* is not a simple equivalent of Paul's frequent *oidate* expression.

Does he mean they are taught by sayings of the Lord Jesus that had been given them? Could sayings such as Matthew 5:43-48 (and parallels Luke 6:27 and 32) about loving enemies as well as friends, and Matthew 19:19 about loving your neighbor as yourself, have been part of the core teaching of the kerygma? There is some possibility that it was, for the same tradition appears in 1 John 4:7 as "love one another, for love is of God."

Perhaps *theodidaktoi* is a reference to Jesus' summary of the law.[28] In response to a question as to which is the most important commandment, Matthew and Mark both quote a saying of Jesus that the greatest commandment is to love God with all of your heart, all your soul, and all your mind, and that the second is to love the person nearby as yourself (Mark 12:31, Matthew 22:39, and Luke 10:27; Luke attributes the saying to the person questioning Jesus). It is possible that this summary of the law was already in circulation when Paul first preached in Thessalonica. It is reasonable to assume that these Thessalonians had heard these words. Is it reasonable to assume that Paul and the Thessalonians regarded these words with religious awe, that is, as coming from God? Did they think of this commandment to love one another as being taught by God?

We can read the clause, "you are God-taught to love one another" as a

---

27. Paul used a form of *parangelô* ("I command"), for example, in 4:2.

28. Hurd, *Earlier Letters*, 176, thought *theodidaktoi* referred to the summary of the law as in Mark 12:31.

statement of fact. These Thessalonians already love one another. If they already love one another, part of the experience of this love is that it is a gift. It is a gift of God. So, therefore, they love one another; the gift has been given; they are God-taught. This is exactly what Paul was speaking of as love for one another. Love for one another comes from the inner person.

The pivotal prayer in 3:11-13 offers the petition that they abound in love and the loving petition that they be found blameless in the arrival of Jesus Christ.

Hope

The two passages 4:13-18 and 5:1-11 are about hope. The first of these actually mentions hope only in the first sentence.

Paul's words

4:13 I do not want you not to know, dear ones,
   about those who are sleeping,
   so that you do not grieve like others who do not have hope.

The second, ostensibly about *chronos* ("time") and *kairos* ("opportunity"), incorporates a positive attitude towards the future in 5:4.

5:4 But you, dear ones, you are not in the dark,
   such that the day might take you by surprise, like a thief.

Spiritual analysis

Hope is a positive attitude towards the future. As such, it is an attribute of the inner, secret consciousness. A person who is hopeful has the choice whether or not to admit being hopeful to others. In some circumstances, people might prefer to keep their hope or lack of hope to themselves.

The passage in 4:13-18 offers a ground for a specific hope, namely, the hope that members of the ecclesia who have died will nevertheless have an opportunity to participate in the kingdom of our Lord Jesus when he arrives. They will not be left behind simply because of the unfortunate circumstance that they have died. Likewise, the passage in 5:1-11 gives us the ground for hope that when that day comes, even though it will be wrath and destruction for some others, it will not be a disaster for us, because we already belong to the day and can hope for the acquisition of salvation.

Sobriety and vigilance

In 5:5-8 Paul commended a state of watchful sobriety. Like the other characteristics, sobriety and alertness are states of mind, qualities of the inner, secret self.

Paul's words

5:5 By belonging, you have become daylight.
    We are not of the night or of the dark;

6 Therefore let us not sleep like others,
    but be sober and alert.

7 For those who sleep sleep at night,
    and those who get drunk drink at night;

8 but we being of the day stay sober,
    putting on the breastplate of faith and love
    and the headgear of hope for salvation.

Spiritual analysis

The section 5:1-5:11 begins as a discussion of when the *parousia* will happen, and then it digresses briefly to call down destruction on those who announce "Peace and Security." The middle portion of the passage is about being sober and vigilant, and the passage ends with a pair of verses that integrate it with the preceding passage.

Paul developed this section around the images of night and day. It is at night that people sleep. Sleep, of course, is a state in which one is not alert, not prepared for surprising events. Sleep, then, is similar, in terms of this passage, to saying that we have waited long enough for Jesus to come back and that we are not going to maintain the alert. Being awake, therefore, is a metaphor for continuing alertness.[29] People, he says, are awake in the daylight. His point is to make the connection between the daylight and the mode of being alert and ready to take action.

Likewise Paul associated getting drunk with nighttime and being sober with the day. People, he says, get drunk at night. Drunkenness entails a diminution of one's faculties. People are not at their best when drunk. We need to

---

29. Since followers of Jesus have taken many of his sayings in an overly-literal sense, it is something to celebrate that Paul's rejection of sleep has not been abused. Apparently we like sleep too much to consider such a heresy, or perhaps the body knows its own limitations.

be alert and at our best, sober and ready to respond intelligently.

Sobriety and vigilance may seem to be curious attributes in this description of Christian consciousness. They do fit together with the inner nature of the kerygma. Paul was urging these Thessalonians to be alert: the character of this religion is inner awareness of what is going on.

Rejoicing and praying

The blessing in 5:16-22 seems to be rather a set piece. It may be that Paul was quoting an existing poem or the form of a benediction that he used regularly.

Paul's words

16 Rejoice always,

17 Pray without ceasing,

18 Give thanks for all things – for this is God's will for you in
    Christ,

19 Do not quench the spirit,

20 Do not belittle prophecy.

21 Look for the true character of all things: hold tight what is good,

22 and hold apart from every appearance of evil.

Spiritual analysis

Each of the instructions of this piece has a reference to people's inner attitude. Rejoicing is a personal attitude. One could pretend to rejoice, but what would be the point? Constant prayer is an internal attitude; one could give an outward appearance of continuous prayer, so it is not absolutely certain that Paul meant the inward attitude. Thanksgiving for all things could be faked, but what would be the point of behaving as if one were thankful, if one were not? It seems more likely that Paul was asking his hearers to feel thankful rather than to fake it.

Not quenching the spirit is different; it might be a command not to do something to others, when those others are being moved by the spirit. It can, however, also be applied to ourselves. We should no more set aside the spirit that speaks to us than we should belittle the spirit that speaks to others. We need to open ourselves to the possibility of following the leading of the spirit. Both of these interpretations represent a decision, an internal, secret choice to respect the promptings of the spirit. So this injunction also fits the pattern of being addressed to people's attitudes. Likewise the command not to belittle prophecy could mean not to discount other people who were prophesying, but instead amounts to a decision to respect prophecy.

"Look for the true character of all things: hold tight what is good," implies that the decision whether things are good or evil lies within the community. All the members of the ecclesia are here urged to discern for themselves, which, again, is a characteristic of people's private thoughts.

The surprise is finding this clear statement of Christianity as concerned with inner thoughts so early in the New Testament documentation.

We find that faith was understood as a response to the gospel. Their attitudes were expected to be changed to a high standard of vigilance, faith, love, and hope. That attitude was the essential nature of the gospel.

CHAPTER 2

ETHICAL AGREEMENTS

FIRST Thessalonians called for and expected the members of the ecclesia to live morally, and by "living morally," the letter made it clear that it meant change. Paul expressed the call to a change in behavior in three passages.

Paul's words

> 2:12 encouraging you and cajoling you and giving you an example
> how to walk worthily of God
> who is calling you to his kingdom and glory.

and

> 4:1b that just as you have received from us
> how it is necessary for you to walk and to please God,
> that you walk in that way,
> so that you please God abundantly.

and

> 4:12 in order that you should walk worthily of respect from outsiders
> . . .

Ethical analysis

Paul used *peripatein* ("to walk") four times in these three verses. His choice of the word *peripatein* is significant. Hebrew has a similar verb *halak* ('to walk'). Judaism uses the cognate *halakha* to mean "commandment," i.e., that which is binding under the *Torah/Law*. By emphasizing the distinction between *halakha* and *haggadah,* meaning an edifying story that does not impose behavioral restraints and standards, Judaism came to be a religion where correctness was defined as correct behavior. Paul's choice of the word *peripatein* suggests that he thinks of his instructions as commandments, as being a similar standard of behavior.

While there is no indication in these three verses that Paul was thinking of any set of specific commandments, it does appear that he expected his believers to meet a standard. The new religion expected a change of behavior, a new life-style, a new way of walking.

The three participles *parakalountes, paramythoumenoi,* and *martyromenoi* have a buffeting effect. These words keep after them and keep after them to change their behavior. The cumulative effect of such repetition is a very powerful stress. As such, this buffeting suggests that *to walk worthily of God* is no small matter, no small change in behavior. If it were a small change, then any one of these three entreaties would be sufficient. Here we have encouraging, cajoling, **and** setting an example piled up on one another. The overall effect of the three participles is to emphasize how thorough and giving was Paul's presentation of the gospel.

The emphasis is on behaving in such a way as to please God. The expressions "walk" and "please" in 4:1b are grammatically parallel; the implication is that some behaviors please God, but some do not. The members of the ecclesia are being exhorted in this verse to choose those behaviors that please God. Paul's phrase, "that your behavior please God abundantly" may couch, in an ingratiating way, the fact that he expects their behavior to change.

Three of the uses of *peripatein* qualify the change in behavior as "worthily of God," as "pleasing to God," and as "worthily of respect," but beyond that, they do not specify the exact changes in behavior that will be required. Nevertheless, he calls for a change in objective, outward behavior.

The final phrase of 2:12, "who is calling you to his kingdom and glory," identifies which God it is.[30] Paul was urging and exhorting and encouraging them to walk worthily of the God who was calling them to his kingdom and

---

30. Identifying which God we serve is pertinent, because it is not always clear that Paul believed that demons and the satan did not exist. In addition to 2 Cor 6:14-7:1 with its reference to Belial and the craziness of 2 Thess 2, there are references to satan scattered throughout the letters. Paul denies the existence of idols in 1 Cor 8:5-6 but urges against the cup of demons in 1 Cor 9:14-22. Of course he lived at a time when the populace worshipped many different gods.

glory. To reverse the order of the thought, what happened first is that God called them to his kingdom and glory. Now it is their turn to respond to this call. Acting worthily, then, temporally and logically, comes second, as a response.

It is of the greatest importance that this change of behavior be seen as a product rather than a cause of the new relationship with God. Christians have argued from ancient times to the present whether religionists are justified by their righteous behavior or justified by the sacrifice of Christ. In these words in this epistle, Paul urged those who already belong to the Jesus-movement to walk worthily. They are not expected to walk worthily as a qualification for belonging to God; they already belong to God and have no need to qualify. However, because they belong to God, they are now being called to walk worthily. They have not been chosen because of their fine morals. Because they have been chosen, they are now, subsequently, called upon, urged, and exhorted to have morals worthy of their call.

The ethics of a true God who executes justice

Paul's words

> 1:9 . . . you turned towards God away from idols
> to serve a living and true God,

and

> 4:6b for the Lord carries out justice for all these things,

Ethical analysis

The phrase from 1:9, "you turned from idols to serve a living and true God," indicates a change. We today might consider a change in loyalty from one divinity to another as a strictly mental change; but that would be true neither to the ancient world nor to the Judaeo-Christian God. Changing one's affiliation from Athena to Zeus, for example, involved changing to a different set of ceremonies. Otherwise, life would be unchanged. However, this particular God was known to have standards for people's behavior. In the context of what Paul preached of God, a change of loyalty strongly implied a change in behavior, in order to meet those standards.

There is a big difference between Greek morality and Hebrew religious morality. Angering Greek gods was a matter of doing something that disturbed that god or goddess personally, but did not really involve a set of moral principles.[31] Greek morality had nothing quite like the Ten Commandments, although communities had legal sanctions against murder, theft, adultery, and perjury; Greek divinities participated in various ways in support of those sanctions. Greek communities likewise had no tradition like the prophets' denunciations of greed and injustice, even though the Greeks of classical Athens, for one example, took great care to make their criminal justice system fair and equitable, for citizens. Furthermore, the Jews regarded themselves as moral people and they regarded the gentiles as immoral. Even without the enforcement of the Jewish dietary standard, for a Greek to convert to Judaism meant a radical change of behavior, to having to live according to a moral standard.

Therefore, as Paul described their conversion toward the living and true God, he meant a conversion to a God to whom ethical behavior mattered.

Paul also mentioned that God carries out justice. Verse 6b is not entirely explicit against whom God exacts justice. Nevertheless, the threat of retribution is clearly stated, and that raises the bar on the importance of ethical behavior.

The standard of holiness

He was more specific that holiness was the objective in 3:12-13 and in 4:3-7.

Paul's words

> [12] the Lord fill and make you overflow
> with love for one another and for everyone,
> just as we love you,
> [13] in order to steady your hearts
> to be without fault in holiness
> before God our Father
> when our Lord Jesus arrives with all his saints.

and

---

31. Malherbe, *Letters*, 133, says that paganism included cultic requirements but did not specify morality.

4:3   For the will of God is this: your sanctification, . . .

4   that each of you know how to acquire his own wife
      in holiness and honor, . . .

7   For God has not called us for uncleanness
      but for holiness.

Ethical analysis

The words translated "without fault in holiness" in 3:13b are *amemptos* ("blameless" or "without fault") and *hagiosynê* ("holiness"). The word *hagiosynê* has the same root as the word *hagios* ("saint" or "holy one"), meaning those who will arrive with Jesus. They are his troops, who belong to him, who are committed to him. Taking this sense from the word "saints," *hagiosynê* can be understood as the quality of being owned by or belonging to God. The sense of "holy" is that the thing or person is suitable to be owned by God. This sense fits with the verb *stêrizô* ("to steady"). People can be "steadied" into a commitment. It means becoming confirmed and thoroughly comfortable with a committed relationship to God. It means aligning one's life with what is appropriate for a person who belongs to God.

The holiness into which these Thessalonians were being called was their being membered with God. "Member" has become a relatively weak term. One can become a member of many groups by indicating a desire to join and paying a fee. Other groups have a stronger membership boundary; to become a member of a family, one must be born into it, be adopted, or marry into it. The word "member" also means part of the body; hands, feet, eyes, and ears are all members of the body. In Paul's ecclesia, since his converts had probably broken ties with their past associates in order to join, membership had a strong meaning. It was not a little thing to be a member of the ecclesia.

Paul's ecclesia, judging by First Thessalonians, attempted to balance the difficulty of joining with a closeness among the members: he stressed love for one another, and he used the language and metaphor of a family, the language of closeness to one another. Membership, however, also involved their self-concept. How did they think of themselves? Did they primarily think of themselves as members of this ecclesia? Did they primarily think of themselves as belonging to God? This self-identification is one that could develop over time; they could be steadied, like increasing the speed of the gyroscope, into knowing that they belonged to the moral God of heaven.

A related word, *hagiasmos* ("sanctification" or "holiness") is used in 4:3 and 4:4. I used both translation-words because it seems almost impossible to translate both instances with the same English word. Verse 4:3 seems to demand "your sanctification," while 4:4 is better translated as "holiness." Both English words refer to the process of becoming or of being made holy. Being made holy implies a change in behavior.

Paul also used the word *akatharsia* ("uncleanness") in 4:7. Here Paul contrasted *akatharsia* with *hagiasmos*, so that we do well to interpret "uncleanness" as immoral behavior, behavior inappropriate to those who belong to God. It is a call, not just to any change in behavior but a change to holiness as is appropriate for those who belong to God. Paul has used the word *hagiosyne* once and the word *hagiasmos* three times in this brief passage. These uses echo the use of *hagios*, the saints or holy ones who will accompany the Lord Jesus when he arrives. They are to be as moral in their behavior as those who will arrive with Christ.

Blameless in his arrival

In two phrases, Paul sets a very high standard for behavior.

Paul's words

3:13 . . . to be blameless in holiness
    . . . when our Lord Jesus arrives with all his saints.

and

5:23e . . .blamelessly when our Lord Jesus Christ arrives.

Ethical analysis

Twice in this letter, Paul prayed that his hearers would be *amemptos* (inflected as an adjective in 3:13: "blameless") or would behave *amemptôs* (inflected as an adverb in 5:23: "{act} blamelessly"). The word is formed by adding the negating *a* to the verb *memphomai* ("to find fault or complain"). The adjective and adverb mean that nobody would be able to find fault. In the arrival of our Lord Jesus, according to these prayers, nobody would be able to bring any accusation against these followers of Jesus.

This is a very high expectation for ethical behavior. Our contemporary understanding of Christianity is that we are forgiven. If we have been forgiven, there was something for which we were forgiven, and we have admitted to having done things for which we needed forgiveness. Therefore, it would still be possible for others to point out our fault. In this letter Paul called his hearers and us to the standard that we should live in such a way that no one would have any complaint.

Specific changes in behavior

In 2:12 and 4:11-12, Paul commended a strong work ethic.

Paul's words

2:9 Of course you remember, dear ones, our toil and labor;
    working night and day so as not to be a burden on any of you,
    we announced to you the gospel of God.

and

4:11 Be ambitious to live quietly,
     to tend to your own business,
     and to work with your hands,
     just as we commanded you,
12   in order that you should walk worthily of respect from outsiders,
     and not depend upon others.

In 4:3-6 he gives some specific guidelines for behavior in marriage.

4:3 For the will of God is this: your sanctification,
    that you abstain from sexual immorality,
4   that each of you know how to acquire his own wife
    in holiness and honor,
5   not in an emotional experience like those who do not know God,
6   and how not to trespass against and cheat each other in this matter;

In 5:12-22 he is quite specific.

12 We make this request of you, dear ones,

to hold your leaders in respect,
those who are standing up in front of you
and admonishing you in the Lord

13   and to think of them so much more in love because of their work.
Be at peace among yourselves.

14   We encourage you, dear ones, to admonish the unruly,
give cheer to the faint of heart,
be patient with the weak,
think the best of everyone.

15   See that no one gives back evil for evil,
but in everything pursue the good towards each other and
towards all.

16   Rejoice always,

17   Pray without ceasing,

18   Give thanks for all things – for this is God's will for you in Christ,

19   Do not quench the spirit,

20   Do not belittle prophecy.

21   Look for the true character of all things: hold tight what is good,

22   and hold apart from every appearance of evil.

Ethical analysis

In these sections Paul has commended an interesting combination of specific behaviors. He has commended an ethic of hard work at one's own business. He has commended keeping a low profile in the city. And he has commended behaviors that will build up the ecclesia, the community of the believers, particularly in terms of those who disrupt the community.

Paul's statement that he worked night and day is part of an offer-acceptance transaction. He and his team offered the gospel; his Thessalonian hearers received it. This statement emphasizes the manner in which he and his team offered the gospel: they worked at a trade to support themselves and not be a burden on their hearers.[32] In fact, this statement asserts that Paul and his team went beyond what would normally be expected of an apostolic team.

Despite the over-the-top character of providing the gospel free of charge, these words set working night and day as an ethical standard. Paul's words

---

32. As Malherbe, *Letters*, 148, points out, the genitive construction is partitive: all day and part of the night.

here follow conventional paraenesis[33] as a way of commending his behavior to the recipients of letters. Paul and his hearers both understood that Paul expected them to adopt this work ethic.

Almost the same words appear in Second Thessalonians, but there they are presented as an example that everyone is to follow. There is no subtlety there, no sense that Paul's work ethic exceeded our expectations for apostles. Everyone is to work night and day.

Similarly, in 4:11, Paul exhorted these Thessalonians to attend to their own affairs and "to work with their hands." Paul had some conviction about the importance of working with one's hands. Not only was it significant to him that he kept busy at a manual trade, but he also expected that members of the ecclesia would do the same. From these verses alone, we might draw the conclusion that this budding religion was for people who were employed and worked for a living.[34] Perhaps we ought to conclude instead that Paul expected aristocrats to take up serious manual labor. For them it would be a change in behavior.

Paul's appeal that they "be ambitious" asked for a change of behavior. Elsewhere, Paul expressed a concern that the ecclesia make a good impression on others when it met for worship (1 Cor 14:21). Here, however, he asked that the members of the ecclesia make a good impression when they were working. The word translated "worthily of respect" is *euschêmonôs* ("respectably," "with a good reputation"). It has the connotations of behavior that would make a good impression on others, that is, of honorable and respectable behavior. Paul was partly reminding his auditors of what he has already taught them and at the same time urging them to complete the change in the

---

33. Malherbe, *Letters*: 157, sees it important that Paul's self-description is paraenetic. He viewed his life as an example for others.

34. Wayne A. Meeks, *The First Urban Christians: The Social World of the Apostle Paul* (New Haven and London; Yale University Press, 1983). One of Meeks' most interesting points is that the ecclesia in Corinth cut across class lines and that no other known association of ancient time did so.

Malherbe, *Letters*, 65, suggests Paul's words about manual labor here show the members of the ecclesia are mostly artisans. That is certainly possible; if true, however, it would leave open the question of how Paul, having founded a one-class ecclesia in Thessalonica, might have happened to have founded a multi-class ecclesia in Corinth. It seems more likely that the ecclesiae would have had similar social structures.

Malherbe, *Letters*, 160-161, notes that Paul's diction and rhetorical skill place him in a higher class than earlier scholars thought. Paul worked with his hands as a hardship that his ministry called him to (1 Cor 4:12).

way they walk.

In 4:11, in the words "be ambitious to live quietly," Paul seems to be ask-ing for something self-contradictory.[35] Being ambitious normally means to strive to be outstanding. People may be ambitious to achieve great things and thereby become important. People may be ambitious to be leaders in their communities. Here, however, Paul urged his auditors to "be ambitious to live quietly." This is almost the opposite of the usual meaning of ambitious. They are to try to live in such a way that they will not be noticed, in such a way as not to gain acclaim for their deeds and accomplishments, in such a way as not to win respect through their prominence.

As the standards in 4:9-12 are responsibility and respectability, the stan-dard in 4:3-8 is holiness. In 4:4-6a, Paul unpacked what he means by *hagias-mos* by enumerating three specific behavioral changes that he expected: (4:3c) "that you abstain from sexual immorality," (4:4) "that each of you know how to acquire a wife in holiness and honor," and (4:6a) and "how not to trespass against and cheat each other in this matter . . ." These three phrases ask for and expect changes in behavior. Paul asked these Thessalonians to change their behavior from some behaviors that he regarded as immoral to other specific behaviors that he regards as consistent with holiness. Paul ended the passage with the summary observation that God has not called these Thes-salonians for uncleanness but in "holiness" or "sanctification."

This passage allows us to define *akatharsia* ("uncleanness"), a little more clearly. It means sexual immorality; sexual immorality is unclean. It means violating the personal boundaries of others; trespassing against others is un-clean. It means being greedy and cheating others; defrauding others is un-clean. God had not called them into such an unwashed, uncleansed state.

Furthermore, in 5:14a, in a section of instructions that leads into the closing of the epistle, Paul urged these Thessalonians "to admonish the *atak-tos* ('unruly' or 'disorderly')." In Second Thessalonians, the same word, *atak-tos,* leads into a discussion of those who do not work, with the result that the word is commonly translated as "idlers." Historically, however, the word meant those who did not obey the general. When an army takes the field, the general tells the soldiers what they are to do; if all the soldiers perform their appointed tasks, the army may be said to be "well-organized;" they are "well-

---

35. Malherbe, *Letters*, 247.

ruled." *Ataktos* means an unruly person, a person who does not behave as the general expected. By metaphorical extension, the word came to mean those who do not conform to the expectations of a community. These norms and expectations of the community are the rules in respect of which the *ataktos* are unruly, who do not cooperate with their leaders' requests, who by their failure to behave according to the "rules" disrupt the community. "Idleness" is one way that members of the community might be unruly, but there are others.

When Paul encouraged these Thessalonians to rebuke the unruly, he expected two changes in behavior. He expected that the unruly would change by conforming to the expectations of the group. If we accept idleness as the meaning of *ataktos*, this includes expecting them to work, just as he himself did. The second change that Paul expected is perhaps more subtle: he expected the rest of the Thessalonians to admonish them. They would have to say something. For many kind and humble people, that too would be a change of behavior.

First Thessalonians, then, is remarkable in expecting a change of behavior to a high standard of morality and holiness. Again and again, Paul's words refer to this change. His hearers' conversion to the service of a true and living God demanded a clear demarcation of their behavior. In addition to the specifics of hard work, a low profile in the city, and a smooth, cooperative relationship in the ecclesia, they were expected to follow a code of moral behavior. We have every reason to believe that this represented a change for them.

CHAPTER 3

THEOLOGICAL AGREEMENTS

IN First Thessalonians, Paul made many theological statements. Most of them are not issues for direct discussion; they are made as asides. This characteristic indicates that Paul did not expect disagreement on these issues. Because he expected their consent on these topics, we may conclude that they were part of the gospel that Paul preached during the founding of the ecclesia. They are an archeological layer below and older than the surface of the letter.

It is convenient to take up the theological statements in the order of the creed, using the Old Roman Symbol.[36] Paul's comments are reflected in some of the clauses of the creed, and not in others. In each case, I have continued the quotation of the creed until it reached a topic Paul addressed. After discussing Paul's statements that are consistent with the creed, we also need to discuss some that are not.

1. I believe in God the Father Almighty;

Paul's words

1:1 ... God the Father ...

1:3 ... God our Father

1:9 ... a living and true God

3:11 God ... our Father ...

4:08 ... God who is giving you his own holy spirit.

5:23 ... God, the very God of peace ...

---

36. J.N.D.Kelly, "Chapter iv: The Old Roman Symbol," *Early Christian Creeds* (London: Continuum, 2008), 101-130. The Old Roman Symbol can be traced to the mid-second century. I have used Kelly's translation of a Latin creed, from page 102.

Theological analysis

God is referred to as Father in this the oldest extant writing of the Jesus movement. If based on other evidence, we think that calling God "Father" dates back to the very early years of the Jesus movement, this usage confirms that conclusion. Paul's reference to God as Father feels very familiar to us, yet we ought to find it remarkable that this appellation is so ancient.

Most people believe that the Gospels, although they were finalized and put into writing later, incorporate information that had been passed faithfully from speaker to speaker. Nevertheless, First Thessalonians is the first written evidence that even in early days the Jesus movement referred to God as Father.[37]

Since Paul does not elaborate in First Thessalonians on what it means to refer to God as Father, our interpretation is limited. Paul's and his Thessalonian hearers' calling God Father, however, hints that they thought of themselves as being equal one to another.

Paul's reference to God as a living and true God implies a distinction. Paul thought that other gods, by way of contrast, were not actually alive and did not really exist. Greeks and Romans did not make this kind of distinction. Greek religion involved ceremonies and dedications to the local gods; being religious meant taking part in those ceremonies in a serious and respectful manner. The ceremonies that were offered to other gods in other places were, for the most part, of no concern to either Greeks or Romans. In fact there was a tendency to identify, in a theoretical manner, the Athena of one place with the Athena of another place, and so forth. However, there was no tendency to deny the existence of the gods of other places, or, because one's own city was dedicated to Aphrodite, to deny the existence of Artemis of the Ephesians. The assertion that God the Father was a true God, in contrast to other gods, is not a feature of Hellenistic culture.

In fact, it had been a part of Hebraic culture since the Babylonian Exile (586 - 526 B.C.E.). Prior to the Babylonian Exile, the religion of the Hebrews was an ethical monotheism; they had been given a commandment to worship no other gods, but that commandment did not raise theoretical issues

---

37. In referring to God as Father, the followers of Jesus continued a usage that is attested in Judaism although it may not have been common. At any rate, it does not represent a departure from Jewish practice. Amy-Jill Levine, *The Misunderstood Jew: The Church and the Scandal of the Jewish Jesus* (San Francisco: HarperOne, 2006), 43-45.

about whether those other gods existed. During the Babylonian Exile, the words of the prophets Isaiah and Jeremiah declared that the other gods, and particularly the gods represented by idols in Babylon, did not really exist and were not alive. The words of the prophet portrayed the other "gods" as mere statues, unable to hear, unable to see, unable to speak, and unable to step across the room to feed themselves (for example, from early in the Babylonian Exile, Jeremiah 10:2-10; from late in the Exile, Isaiah 44:9-20; 45:20; 46:6-7). These prophetic words set forth for the first time the idea that there was only one God, a Hebraic idea, not a Hellenistic idea, and an idea not generally accepted throughout Hellenism at the time of Paul's ministry.

For Paul to speak of their turning, their conversion, as from idols to serve a living and true God, meant not only that Paul believed that there was only one God, but also that his hearers had come to believe it too. In their conversion, they had already accepted the non-reality of their local gods and goddesses.

In addition, Paul recognized God as the one who was giving his own holy spirit to the members of the ecclesia. Paul used a present tense participle: he was speaking of a gift that was continuing in the present rather than of a gift that had been given in the past. It is not that God had given holy spirit to these Thessalonians; it is that God was giving and was continuing to give holy spirit. In addition, the phrase has an unusual word order. Of course, it is possible to read the whole phrase as a single phrase, a single thought, here represented by "his own holy spirit." The literal sequence of the words, however, is "the spirit, his, the holy."[38] Thinking of the sequence in which Paul's hearers would have heard the words, we might say, God was giving the spirit, it was **his** spirit which God was giving, and the spirit God gave was holy.

Paul referred to God, in the closing prayer of this letter, as the "very God of peace." This is one of the most contentious statements of the letters, because the Roman Empire promoted its role as the creator of peace, as part of its self-image. During the century before Octavian Caesar was hailed as the Emperor Augustus in 27 B.C.E., the noble houses of Rome engaged each other in civil war, in a time of brutal strife. Octavian, however, brought peace to Rome by conquering them all, and in the same victory brought peace to the Mediterranean world. Octavian was a master of publicity, and he spun

---

38. I added the commas; they are not in the Greek

himself as the great benefactor of the Empire by his inaugurating a reign of
peace, the *Pax Romana*. The Roman Empire brought peace to Rome, Italy,
Greece, Macedonia, and to the Near East. Therefore, Paul's naming God as
the "very God of peace" bordered on sedition.

2. And in Christ Jesus His only Son, our Lord,

Paul's words

Paul referred to Jesus as Christ twice in First Thessalonians.

1:1 ... the Lord Jesus Christ ...
1:3 ... our Lord Jesus Christ ...

Paul describes Jesus as God's son only once in First Thessalonians.

1:10 and to await his son from heaven,
whom he raised from corpses,[39]
Jesus ...

Paul used the word *kyrios* ("Lord" or "master") to refer to Jesus five times
in First Thessalonians (see Table 2). In some of these cases, Paul also refers to
Jesus as Christ.

1:1 ... the Lord Jesus Christ ...
1:3 ... our Lord Jesus Christ ...
3:11 ... our Lord Jesus ...
4:1 ... the Lord Jesus ...
4:2 ... the Lord Jesus ...

Theological analysis

Christos is the Greek word for "anointed." However, Greek has no context
for us to understand what it meant. It translates a Hebrew word, moshiaḥ,
which described the kings of Israel. This connotation had originated a thousand years earlier when the prophet Samuel anointed Saul and then David to

---

39. This phrase is usually translated "whom he raised from the dead," but actually the word
"dead" is "corpses."

be kings over Israel and Judah. The messianic hope running through the Old Testament is that God would send another king like David, one who would be anointed. How people in the First Century c.e. understood moshiaḥ and *christos* is the subject of a great deal of scholarly discussion.[40]

To Greek-speakers in Thessalonica, the word *christos* would originally have had no meaning other than the literal sense, "anointed," unless they had learned a new sense for it from the synagogue. If they had, it was the sense of one who is anointed to be king. Many scholars have observed that Paul used the word *christos* as if it were part of Jesus' name, that is, as if it had no meaning other than being a personal name. If, however, it carried meaning, he probably meant and they probably understood that Jesus had been anointed to be an earthly king.

If, near the end of Jesus' ministry, any of his followers expected him to lead an uprising against the Roman Legions and become a king, they might have applied the word *christos* to him. If they used this word about Jesus during his lifetime, it meant "king" or "king-to-be."

They must have been disappointed when he was crucified. Once he had died, he could not become a king; his followers might have abandoned the word *christos*. In historical fact, they chose to imbue the word *christos* with new meaning. However, we do not know how that transition to new meaning was made or when. It is quite possible that when Paul used the word with the Thessalonians, they understood that Jesus would return to reign as an earthly king.

Another possibility is that Jesus' followers might have given him the nickname "Anointed" for some other reason.[41] Other New Testament figures had nicknames: Simon was "Rock," James and John were "Thunderson," Thomas was "Twin," and perhaps Saul was "Stop." Paul seems to have used *christos* with Jesus as if it were a name, so the suggestion that it was originally given

---

40. A previous generation of scholars thought and taught that before the time of Jesus, there was a strong expectation of the coming of the messiah. Recent scholarship has shown that there was not any single doctrine of the Messiah either in the Old Testament or in the literature of the Jewish people after the close of the OT. Rather, the concept of the Messiah as a single figure of expectation is the creation of the New Testament; in the process of that creation, the NT writers brought together several strands of royal, prophetic and priestly expectation. The issue here is what stage that process had reached when First Thessalonians was written.

41. Merill P. Miller, "The Problem of the Origins of A Messianic Conception of Jesus," and Barry S. Crawford: "Christos as Nickname," in Ron Cameron and Merrill P. Miller, eds., *Resdescribing Christian Origins* (Atlanta: Society of Biblical Literature, 2011), 301-336 and 337-348.

to Jesus as a nickname makes sense.

Paul used the word *huios*[42] ("son") to refer to Jesus as God's son. The expression "son of God" had a political association. Octavian Caesar, who served as the first Emperor of the Roman Empire from 27 B.C.E until his death in 14 C.E., used the divine status of his father-by-adoption, Julius Caesar, to portray himself as *divi filius* ("divine son"), or in Greek, *theou huios* ("son of god"). His claim, on the basis of his relationship to the divine Julius, to be *divi filius* helped promote his accession to power and would have been entirely familiar to the Greek-speaking residents of Thessalonica.

In First Thessalonians, Paul did not directly use the expression *theou huios,* but he implied it. He said "you turned toward God (*theon*), away from idols to serve a living and true God (*theôi*) and to await his son (*huion*[43]) from the heavens, whom he raised from corpses, who is rescuing us from the coming wrath" (1:9b-10). Even though the phrase "his son" is not exactly the same as *huios theou,* it is entirely possible that Thessalonians, in the forties and fifties, would have understood that Paul was giving Jesus the Emperor's title.

Neither the divinity of the Emperor nor the divine sonship of the Emperor was a new concept with Octavian; kings had been styling themselves as gods as far back as there is any historical record; three hundred years previously, Alexander the Great had styled himself divine. Antiochus IV, his second century B.C.E. successor in the East, styled himself Epiphanes ("God-manifest"). After Augustus, the Roman Emperors Caligula and Claudius appropriated similar titles of divinity. So unless significant energy had already gone into defining it differently, Paul's hearers would most naturally have assumed that referring to Jesus as God's son meant that Jesus posed a political alternative to the Emperor.

Another important word, *kyrios* ("lord") has the same effect. Paul used the word *kyrios* to refer to Jesus (see Table 2). In ordinary usage, however, *kyrios* was the term a slave might use to address his master, or a student to speak to

42. In First Thessalonians, Paul used the word *huios* as a reference to Jesus in 1:10. He also uses the expression *huioi phôtos* in 5:5 to say that the members of the ecclesia are "sons of light." In that latter context, the expression is a Semitic expression meaning that the Thessalonians are a type of persons characterized by light. This Semitic pattern of thought, expressing similarity as if it were a metaphor of biological descent, may or may not imply anything about his use of the word for Jesus' relationship to God.

43. Note that the word here is *huios* not *pais.* The latter word has occasioned another discussion of Christology.

his teacher. It was also the term used to refer to the emperor.[44] Paul's Greek-speaking hearers would probably have understood it in a political sense. Paul and they may well have understood, in that original preaching, that when Jesus returned, he would establish a political, this-worldly kingdom.

In connection with his *parousia,* he is named *kyrios* or *christos.*

However, the concept of lordship had already been modified away from, and in contrast to, the Emperor's manner of lordship. Two phrases in this epistle point to this modification. First, Jesus is rescuing us from the coming wrath (1 Thess 1:10). Roman social relations were based upon exchange: patrons performed services for their clients in exchange for services that the clients performed for their patrons. While a **lord** expected work from his slaves, he also protected, housed and fed them. In the work that Jesus is said to be doing, rescuing us from the coming wrath, however, there is no explicit exchange. It appears that Jesus' rescuing work is being done *gratis,* without charge. Gratuitous service was not generally associated with lordship.

Second, Jesus had died.[45] Not only had Jesus died (see next section), which no *kyrios* could do and still be a *kyrios*; he had died for us (5:9). His death on our behalf hints at self-sacrifice. Self-sacrifice is not a concept typically associated with *kyrios.* Therefore, by the time this epistle was written, the meaning of *kyrios* as applied to Jesus had already been modified to include self-sacrifice and a rescue that was being offered *gratis.* These modifications, however, do not eliminate the possibility that *kyrios* was heard as a political title. Jesus was Lord, just a different kind of Lord than other *kyrioi.*

---

44. John Dominic Crossan and Jonathan L. Reed, *In Search of Paul: How Jesus' Apostle Opposed Rome's Empire with God's Kingdom* (San Francisco: HarperSanFrancisco, 2004), 166. When Paul used *kyrios* for Jesus, he either initiated or participated in a direct challenge to the emperor. In making this point, Crossan and Reed say it was first raised by Gustav Adolf Deissman, a nineteenth century scholar of New Testament times.
Karl Paul Donfried, "The Cults of Thessalonica and the Thessalonian Correspondence," *New Testament Studies* 31 (1985), 336-56: page 344.

45. 1 Thess 4:14. This passages says, "For since we believe that Jesus died and rose, so also God will through Jesus lead with him those who have fallen asleep." The "since" clause is written as something so certain, that the result clause, the second half of the sentence, is rendered probable. Therefore, we can take it as a statement that Jesus' death is a simple fact. Paul and his hearers believed it actually happened.
Paul also refers to Jesus' death in this epistle in 1:10b.

Ἰησοῦς
1.10 τὸν υἱὸν . . . ὃν ἤγειρεν . . . Ἰησοῦν τὸν ῥυόμενον ἡμᾶς
4.14 ὅτι Ἰησοῦς ἀπέθανεν καὶ ἀνέστη,

Κύριος Ἰησοῦς
2.15 καὶ τὸν κύριον ἀποκτεινάντων Ἰησοῦν
2.19 ἔμπροσθεν τοῦ κυρίου ἡμῶν Ἰησοῦ
3.11 ὁ κύριος ἡμῶν Ἰησοῦς κατευθύναι τὴν ὁδὸν
3.13 ἐν τῇ παρουσίᾳ τοῦ κυρίου ἡμῶν Ἰησοῦ
4.1 παρακαλοῦμεν ἐν κυρίῳ Ἰησοῦ
4.2 ἐδώκαμεν ὑμῖν διὰ τοῦ κυρίου Ἰησοῦ

Χριστός
2.7 Χριστοῦ ἀπόστολοι
3.2 ἐν τῷ εὐαγγελίῳ τοῦ Χριστοῦ
4.16 οἱ νεκροὶ ἐν Χριστῷ

Κύριος Ἰησοῦς Χριστός
1.1 τῇ ἐκκλησίᾳ . . . ἐν . . . κυρίῳ Ἰησοῦ Χριστῷ
1.3 τοῦ κυρίου ἡμῶν Ἰησοῦ Χριστοῦ
5.9 διὰ τοῦ κυρίου ἡμῶν Ἰησοῦ Χριστοῦ 10 τοῦ ἀποθανόντος ὑπὲρ ἡμῶν,
5.23 ἐν τῇ παρουσίᾳ τοῦ κυρίου ἡμῶν Ἰησοῦ Χριστοῦ
5.28 ἡ χάρις τοῦ κυρίου ἡμῶν Ἰησοῦ Χριστοῦ μεθ᾽ ὑμῶν.

κύριος
1.6 μιμηταὶ . . . ἐγενήθητε καὶ τοῦ κυρίου
1.8 ἐξήχηται ὁ λόγος τοῦ κυρίου
3.8 ὑμεῖς στήκετε ἐν κυρίῳ.
4.6 διότι ἔκδικος κύριος περὶ πάντων τούτων,
4.15 οἱ περιλειπόμενοι εἰς τὴν παρουσίαν τοῦ κυρίου
4.16 ὅτι αὐτὸς ὁ κύριος
4.17 εἰς ἀπάντησιν τοῦ κυρίου
4.17 καὶ οὕτως πάντοτε σὺν κυρίῳ ἐσόμεθα.
5.2 ὅτι ἡμέρα κυρίου ὡς κλέπτης ἐν νυκτὶ οὕτως ἔρχεται.

Table 2: Lord Jesus Christ

3. Who was born from the Holy Spirit and the Virgin Mary, Who under Pontius Pilate was crucified and buried,

Paul did not refer to Jesus' birth in this letter. However, he referred to Jesus' death four times.

Paul's words

^{1:10} . . . whom he raised from corpses . . .

^{2:15} who killed the Lord Jesus . . .

^{4:14} . . . we believe that Jesus died . . .

^{5:10} who died for us . . .

Theological analysis

These four references are quite different from one another. However, the first, third and fourth of these expressions use words that have already become traditional.

The first of these is part of a description of the faith to which they have turned. In this new faith they worship God and wait for Jesus, whom (as Paul said almost incidentally) God "raised from the corpses." If God raised Jesus from the corpses, then Jesus had been dead; and if he was dead, then he had died. Therefore, it is a statement of Paul's faith that Jesus had died.

Paul's choice of the words *apo tôn nekrôn* ("from the corpses") is peculiar. However, beyond noting that this usage seems peculiar, we do not know any more about what it means or why Paul chose this particular wording. It may be that he is quoting a formula that has already become traditional in the church.

In this expression, God is active; God did the raising. Jesus did not do anything himself; he did not rise of his own will or power. According to Charles Buck, this expression connotes a relatively low Christology: Jesus was not thought of in this verse as one powerful enough to raise himself.

The statement in 2:15 that the "Jews" killed Jesus, even if it is a huge overstatement, nevertheless indicates Paul's conviction that Jesus was killed and therefore that he died.

The statement in 4:14, ". . . we believe Jesus died . . ." appears already to be a traditional statement. The word "believe" is the word used in a creed: "I believe . . ." This statement may reflect a liturgical usage, perhaps as part of the way the early church performed baptisms. It is a clear statement that the death of Jesus was an early part of the church's theological formation.

The first four words of verse 5:10, *tou apothanontes hyper hêmôn* ("who died for us"), are unique in early Christian literature.[46] It is a statement that

---

46. The implication that Christ's death is beneficial is found in the pastoral epistles (First and

in some way, our Lord Jesus Christ's death benefited Paul and his hearers. The two words *hyper hêmôn* ("for us") are very significant because they imply that Jesus' death was for "our" benefit—"our" clearly meaning Paul and his Thessalonian hearers. The words that immediately preceded this statement, "the acquisition of salvation," describe that benefit. However, it is not clear what "salvation" means in this context. If we read "salvation" as creating forgiveness of sins, as conquering death, or as predestining his followers to a heavenly afterlife, we are reading later doctrine back into it. Paul did not elaborate on it in this letter, and we need to avoid anachronism. Therefore, we must interpret this verse as meaning that Jesus' death benefits his followers in some yet-to-be-elaborated way.

There is a good possibility that the benefit was still vague in Paul's mind and in the mind of the church. After all, it would be another thousand years before Anselm would write his description of that benefit, even though Anselm's description has become commonplace for us. Likewise, it would be fifteen hundred years before John Calvin would elaborate the doctrine of predestination, even though it is difficult for us to think of election other than in Calvin's terms. For Paul, we may conclude that Jesus' death was beneficial to his followers, but we do not know what Paul meant beyond that very simple positive thought. Nevertheless, it is clear from this statement that Paul knew Jesus had died.

4. on the third day rose again from the dead

Paul referred to the resurrection of Jesus twice in First Thessalonians. Both references accompany references to his death.

Paul's words

1:10 . . . whom he raised from corpses . . .
4:14 . . . we believe that Jesus died and rose, . . .

Theological analysis

In the first of these, Paul said that God raised Jesus from the dead, an event in which Jesus was passive. In the second of these, Paul said that Jesus rose, implying that Jesus himself was the agent of his resurrection. Either way,

---

Second Timothy and Titus), but those documents were composed later than Paul's authentic letters. They are not "early" Christian literature.

Paul and his hearers believed in the resurrection.

Exactly how Paul understood that resurrection, however, is beyond us. We do not know whether Paul meant that Jesus was seen in a vision or present in a body that could be touched. These two expressions in First Thessalonians give us too little to go on.

5. ascended to heaven, sits at the right hand of the Father, whence He will come to judge the living and the dead;

Paul's words

The passage on hope for the deceased (4:13-18) refers to Jesus' future arrival three times.

> 4:14 . . . so also God will through Jesus
> lead with him those who have fallen asleep.
> 4:15 . . . for the Lord's arrival;
> 4:17 . . . for the meeting with the Lord in the air; . . .

Two more statements say that we shall be with him.

> 4:17 . . . in this way we shall always be with the Lord.
> 5:10 . . . so that
> whether we keep watch or sleep
> we both might live with him.

The two prayers casually mention Jesus' arrival.

> 3:13 in order to steady your hearts
> to be blameless in holiness
> before God our Father
> in the arrival of our Lord Jesus with all his saints.
> 5:23 May God, the very God of peace,
> make you entirely holy,
> and may your entire spirit—and your life and your body—
> be kept protected,
> blamelessly in the arrival of our Lord Jesus Christ.

Two more associate salvation and wrath with his arrival.

> 1:10 and to await his son from the heavens,
>   whom he raised from corpses,
>   Jesus, who is rescuing us
>   from the coming wrath.
> 5:9 God has not set us up for wrath
>   but for the acquisition of salvation
>   through our Lord Jesus Christ.

Furthermore, the statement of 5:3 reflects the coming wrathful judgment.

> 3   Whenever they say, "Peace and Security,"
>   their destruction comes on them suddenly,
>   just like labor-pains surprise a pregnant woman,
>   and no way will they escape.

Theological analysis

Perhaps the most important thing to say about Paul's expectation for Jesus' return is that Paul and his hearers expected it to happen during their lifetimes. We also need to note, however, that while the creed expects Jesus to return as judge, Paul expected him to return as king, although Paul may have included judgment in his concept of the return of the king.

In the very early years, the ecclesia expected all believers to continue alive until the Lord came. Paul's use of the word "we" in 4:17a indicates that he himself expected to be alive at the Lord's arrival. Regardless of our interpretation of the rest of the passage, this "we" indicates that participation in the *parousia* ("arrival") originally included the living.

In fact, the rest of the passage 4:13-18 reflects a concern about whether deceased members of the community would be able to participate. That concern had to have arisen out an expectation that the *parousia* would come during the lifetime of the members. Paul's response to this concern stressed the hope that both those still alive and those already deceased would be with him. The statement of hope for those who had died is a new hope; but that newness only reinforces the perception that the original expectation was a *parousia* for the living.

The prayer in the middle of the letter (3:11-13) also mentions the *parousia* almost incidentally. The third clause of the prayer, that God "steady your hearts to be blameless in holiness before God our Father in the *parousia* of our Lord Jesus" is not an open ended "keep you today and always" but a closed time period: "keep you in the *parousia*," implies that the *parousia* will come while they are still alive.

The final blessing of the letter (5:23) may also indicate that Paul expected the *parousia* to happen in the lifetime of the believers. After a first clause asking that the God of peace (the Greek word for peace is *eirênê*) sanctify his hearers completely, the second clause prays, "and may your entire spirit—and your life and your body—be kept protected, blamelessly in the arrival of our Lord Jesus Christ." The word "preserved" is *têreô* ("to keep under guard"). The phrase *en têi parousiai* ("in the *parousia*") may mean "under the control of" or "under the jurisdiction of" or "in connection with" the arrival, but the *en* may also serve as a temporal marker. It is a stretch to translate the *en* as "until," but the combination of *têreô* and *en* suggest that "you . . .be kept protected . . . in the arrival . . ." Keeping spirit and soul and body together suggests that they be kept alive. The implication, again, appears to be that the *parousia* will be for the living, that Paul and the very early church expected the *parousia* to happen during their lifetimes.

Combining the evidence of the two prayers with the exegesis of 4:13-18 makes it probable that Paul believed and preached that the *parousia* would come in the lifetime of the first generation of believers.

We tend to think of the judgment of the world as something that will take place at the end of time, and nations from all of human history will be judged (meaning, categorized as good people or bad people). Paul, however, may have expected that Jesus would arrive to establish an earthly kingdom, to overthrow the Roman Empire and establish God's kingdom in at least some corner of the world. Around 200 years previously, the family of Judas Maccabeas led a successful rebellion against the Seleucid Empire and established the Hasmonean dynasty in Jerusalem. Perhaps the memory of that successful rebellion formed a part of Paul's thinking and of his expectation for what Jesus would do upon his return. Such a hope would be a subversive kerygma.

a. *Parousia* was politically subversive

We have already seen three counter-claims against the Emperor: Paul's reference to God as the very God of Peace countered the Empire's slogan of "Peace and Security." Paul's naming Jesus as God's son countered the Emperor's deification. Paul's frequent reference to Jesus as *kyrios* disputed the Emperor's lordship. Each of these was contentious and contradicted the Emperor's self-promotion.

We have also already seen that *kyrios* had been modified, first, through the concept of his being a dead *kyrios* and, second, through the statement of his rescuing us from the coming wrath as a non-obligating gift. This is a radical contrast between the Emperor and Christ. Paul did not spell out the contrast, but we can extrapolate the terms: the Emperor established his power through violence. The Empire's method was Peace-through-Conquest, controlling people by military might. In opposition to the method of the Empire, Paul appears to have envisioned peace coming through some different channel.[47] Paul's expectation of a future kingdom became the hope for Jesus' return as expressed in the creed.

There are four pieces of evidence in First Thessalonians that suggest Paul was expecting an earthly kingdom. First is the number of times Paul referred to Jesus' arrival. Second is the connection between Paul's imagery of Jesus' arrival and Daniel 7. Third is the number of terms that could be either spiritual or political. Fourth is his treatment of the slogan "Peace and Security."

Paul referred to the *parousia* of Jesus six times in First Thessalonians, which has only five chapters. The longer, authentic letters—Romans, First and Second Corinthians, Philippians, and Galatians—do not mention the *parousia* with anywhere near this frequency.[48] In First Thessalonians, this topic is spread out evenly throughout the epistle; the concept appears at least once in each of the first three chapters and twice in the last two; it was never far from Paul's thought. Christ's future arrival was always close to the top of his mind when he wrote this letter. Paul had this image in his mind when he began composing and kept it in his mind throughout the composition.

---

47. Paul's presentation of the gospel as subversive did not endure; it was soon replaced by theology that was more sustainable within the Empire. However, there appears to have been an early stage when Christianity was politically subversive.

48. Six times in five chapters compares with eight references to the *parousia* in First Corinthians, a letter more than four times as long. There are 5 chapters in First Thessalonians, which occupies 7 pages in the Nestle-Aland edition, compared with 16 chapters in both Romans and First Corinthians, which occupy 33 pages and 31 pages respectively. First Corinthians would need to refer to the *parousia* 28 times in order to have a comparable frequency.

Parousia has become a technical word in New Testament studies, associated with Jesus' return from heaven. It is here translated "arrival" so as to avoid anachronism. It is the word that Greeks used, and continue to use, to indicate that they are present; just as English speakers answer a roll call by saying, "present," Greek speakers use a form of this word. However, the word also had a political connotation: when the Roman Empire conquered a region, the conquering general made a parade into the major city to show off his mighty army. Such a parade was known by the word *parousia*.[49] It denoted the arrival of the general and his army. Therefore, Paul's frequent use of this term has a connotation of military occupation.

The reference to Jesus' arrival in the fourth chapter is the most developed. In this passage, Paul presented the arrival as a future event. Christ will come and we, deceased first and living second, will be gathered together to welcome him, and then we will be with him.

Paul illustrated Christ's arrival with military sound effects (see the discussion in Part III, chapter 2), which have given us the contemporary meaning of apocalypse. The word "apocalypse" has come to refer to the military campaign. It is no wonder that contemporary movies of apocalypse are war movies.

The sounds are all consistent with a victory parade. What Paul has given us in verse 16 is the noise of a victory parade with its provenance translated from the ground to the sky. Paul might have intended these military sounds to appeal to veterans or their descendants among Paul's hearers.

However, it is not eschatology. Speaking etymologically, the *eschaton* is what comes last. Paul's words do not necessarily imply the end of the world. They refer instead to a beginning, the beginning of Christ's reign. Although we read each of Paul's sayings about Jesus' arrival as referring to the end of time, there is nothing in Paul's words to suggest that he meant it as the *eschaton*.

In our own time, we think of the resurrection as going to heaven. Resurrection, however, could be a resurrection back to life in the world. Paul's teaching that the dead will be raised could mean that he thought of them as ascending to heaven; but it could also mean that they were being raised from

---

49. Malherbe, *Letters*, 272, observes that *parousia* derived from pagan Greek usage for the entrance of a king or god.
Donfried, "Thessalonian Cults," 344.

the dead to share in ruling an earthly kingdom. They had been promised the kingdom. They had every right to enjoy it. If the *parousia* was to be the establishment of a holy kingdom, they should be raised to take part in Christ's reign. Their participation would be consistent with that reign's being a historical, this-world kingdom.

Two of Paul's other references to the *parousia* seem more casual, referring to it almost incidentally. In 2:19 Paul said how important the Thessalonians are to him; he said that they were the prize he can boast about having won. Then, apparently, he thought that the one person to whom he might make that boast is Jesus, in his *parousia*. The important thought is Paul's pride and pleasure in the Thessalonian ecclesia. Nevertheless, this repetition of the word shows how prominent *parousia* was in his thinking as he was composing this epistle.

In 1:10 Paul referred to the *parousia* without using the word: Paul said that his addressees were waiting for God's son from heaven; although Paul did not use the word "return," the word "to wait" implies it. The important fact of their conversion to a true God involved waiting for the return of his son.

The church has grown accustomed to delay in Jesus' return, as nearly two thousand years have passed; we no longer expect his return to be soon. Perhaps Christianity has developed in an appropriate way, with less emphasis on the waiting. That, however, is not an accurate picture of the religion practiced by Paul and the Thessalonians. For them, waiting for Jesus' return was a major part of this embryonic religion.

Finally, the whole pericope 5:1-10 is about the *parousia*, although once more Paul did not use the word. The point of this passage is Paul's encouragement of his hearers to be sober and vigilant, for the day of the Lord is surely coming.

The position which this pericope occupies, and the length of the pericope in comparison with the rest of the epistle, coming just before instructions that are part of the closing of the epistle, underscores how important the *parousia* is to this letter. Adding the significance of this passage to the other five uses of the word *parousia* shows Jesus' return to be a primary theme of the epistle.

Furthermore, the specific references to Jesus' return in this epistle can all be understood in a this-worldly sense. They refer to Jesus' return to establish a kingdom and displace the Roman Empire.

In addition to *kyrios, huios, christos, eirênê* and *parousia*, which have already been discussed, there are four more words that we today hear as spiritual but which could have been heard as political by Paul's Greek listeners: *euangelion* ("good news" or "gospel"), *apantêsis, ekklêsia* ("church," but "assembly" is better), and *basileia* ("kingdom").

As the Roman Empire extended its reign in the last decades of the century before the Common Era, it gave people the good news that they were conquered as *euangelion*.[50] The good news was, "We have conquered you. You are liberated from the tyranny of your former rulers and their infighting." When Paul and others first used the word *euangelion*, his Greek-speaking hearers would probably have thought he meant another conquering general. We today think of Christ's conquering the world in a spiritual sense. Paul's hearers probably understood the word *euangelion* in an original military-political sense.

When the general arrived, his *parousia*, it was good politics for the people of the city to go out to meet the arriving army. The word for the people's going out was *apantêsis*.[51] After all, if their territory has been conquered, they would be well advised to welcome and be ready to work with the new authorities. The conquerors might favor those who made an effort to welcome them, while any who held back might find their situations aggrieved.

Thus, *parousia* referred to the arrival of the general with his army, *euangelion* referred to the spin put on his arrival, and *apantêsis* referred to the welcome given to the "liberating" army. Paul was taking over loaded words when he used *parousia* to refer to Christ's return and *apantêsis* to refer to his fol-

---

50. In First Thessalonians, Paul used the word *euangelion* in 1:5; 2:2, 4, 8, 9, 14; 3:2.
Helmut Koester, *Ancient Christian Gospels* (Philadelphia: Trinity, 1990), 3-4, indicates that *euangelion* was used in a new way in the time of Augustus, and taken over by early Christian missionaries.
Helmut Koester, "The Memory of Jesus' Death and the Worship of the Risen Lord," (HTR 91, 1998: 335-350).
Koester, "Memory and Worship," 349, notes that "gospel" was issued for the emperor's proclamation of the new age.

51. In First Thessalonians, Paul used the word *apantêsis* in 4:17.
Donfried, "Thessalonian Cults," 344.
Malherbe, *Letters*, 277, objects that the political use of *apantêsis* referred to people's voluntarily going out to escort the new governors into the city, whereas in 4:17, the living are "snatched" up, and nothing suggests that they will return to the city.
Earl J. Richard, *First and Second Thessalonians*, (Collegeville, Minnesota: The Liturgical Press, 1995), 246, simply notes the civic welcome given important visitors.
Crossan and Reed, *Search*, 167-68, describe the use of *apantêsis* in Josephus' *Jewish Antiquities* 11:327-28.

lowers' being gathered to him, and *euangelion* to refer to the gospel of God. Unless Paul had redefined these words, it would be most likely that Greek-speaking people would hear them in this political sense.

The word *ekklêsia* ("ecclesia," "church," but "assembly" is better) that Paul used for the assembly of Christians has the same ambiguity:[52] In the Greek version of the Jewish scriptures, *ekklêsia* and *synagogê* are used interchangeably to describe the gathering of people for worship.[53] The choice was made, away from the eyes of historians, that those who became modern Jews would use the word "synagogue" and those who became Christians would used the word "ecclesia." In Greek contexts, however, *ekklêsia* has a somewhat different connotation. It refers to the more or less democratic legislature of a city. The *ekklêsia* was a gathering where citizens had the right to speak and to vote. For Paul to have chosen *ekklêsia* as the word to use for the Christian group, when he might easily have chosen the word *synagogê*, suggests that the followers of Jesus had autonomy to govern themselves. They had freedom of self-government, very different from what most people experienced under the Roman Empire.[54]

When Paul used the word *basileia*[55] ("kingdom"), we today understand that he meant a spiritual reality or an aspect of the afterlife. However, when Paul used that expression in First Thessalonians, it probably had not yet taken on that meaning. To the Greek-speaking residents of Thessalonica, it would have had a clear and simple political meaning. A kingdom was a politically organized region, a constituent member-kingdom of the Roman Empire. *Basileia* could conceivably refer to a competing kingdom that would replace the Roman Empire altogether. Unless Paul had previously defined it differently, his hearers probably understood that he meant a kingdom of this world and time.

Paul's Thessalonian hearers, then, probably understood these ambiguous

---

52. In First Thessalonians, Paul used the word "ecclesia" in 1:1; 2:14.

53. Richard, *Thessalonians,* 38, observes that *ekklesia* and *synagogê* were both used for the gathered worshipping community.
Malherbe, *Letters,* 98-99, notes that as also representing the "people of God," Paul likely used it to refer to his converts as the new people of God. It is less clear how the native Greek speakers understood it.

54. Crossan and Reed, *Search,* 47, interpret the word "ecclesia" as the somewhat deliberative body of a Greek city.

55. In First Thessalonians, Paul used the word *basileia* in 2:12.

words politically. Together they meant that Jesus would return victorious, as a conquering general. The members of the ecclesia would go out to meet him, and he would establish a peaceful kingdom for them.

If one or two words were ambiguous, perhaps we could discount the ambiguity. When, however, so many words have the same ambiguity, it becomes harder for us to dismiss the this-worldly aspect of the kerygma Paul preached at first.

The connection between 4:13-18 and Daniel 7 also indicates a political interpretation. This description of the *parousia* uses two parallel expressions: "in the clouds"[56] and "in the air." This redundancy suggests that Paul was not expressing a solitary thought, but, at the least, he was thinking of two different things. One of these is the Lord's *parousia*, and the best guess about the other is that he is thinking of the vision in Daniel 7.[57] This connection in turn suggests that the Lord's *parousia* will inaugurate his dominion, just as Daniel's vision predicts the dominion of the "son of man." The Daniel passage predicts a change to a genuinely humane form of government by the people themselves.

The apocalyptic vision of Daniel 7 illustrates the contrast between oppressive foreign governments, and a genuinely humane government by the people. The vision begins with a succession of four monsters. The first monster is a lion with eagles' wings (7:4). The second is a bear with three tusks in its mouth (7:5). The third is a leopard with four bird wings on its back and four heads (7:6). The fourth beast has great iron teeth and ten horns (7:7). Then Daniel describes the appearance of an eleventh horn.

> Suddenly another horn grew up among them, small in comparison, and three of the horns were displaced because of it. There were eyes just like human eyes on this horn and a mouth speaking extravagant things. And it made war against the holy ones (Daniel 7:8b).

56. Louis F. Hartman, C.SS.R and Alexander A. Di Lella, O.F.M., *The Book of Daniel: A New Translation with Notes and Commentary* (The Anchor Bible, vol. 23; Garden City, New York, 1978), 101-102, states that clouds are often associated with Hebrew theophanies and refers to Exod 13:21; 19:16; 20:21; Deut 5:22; and I Kings 8:10; Sir 45:5.

57. John Dominic Crossan, *The Historical Jesus: The Life of a Mediterranian Jewish Peasant*, (HarperSanFrancisco, 1991), 239-44.

While the little horn is speaking arrogantly, the Ancient of Days suddenly appears and sits upon His throne. Then a "son of man" comes **in the clouds** and is presented before the Ancient of Days, and to him is given an everlasting kingdom.

> To him was given dominion, and all the peoples of the earth according to their kind, and all glory and worship: and his dominion was an everlasting dominion, which shall not be taken away, and his kingdom, which shall not be destroyed (Daniel 7:14).

After the son of man has received the everlasting kingdom and the vision is over, the seer asks one of the attendants to explain the vision. The attendant explains that the four monsters represent the succession of ancient empires and that the son of man represents the "holy ones" or "pious ones" of Israel.

The descriptions of the deeds of the eleventh horn and its counterparts in this and other chapters have led scholars to identify this monster as Antiochus IV Epiphanes, who ruled the Syrian Empire, including Judaea, from 175 to 163 B.C.E. This king attempted to unify his kingdom by encouraging and forcing his subjects to adopt Hellenistic culture. His program so deeply offended the Jews that Mattathias and his five sons led a successful revolution. After the death of Mattathias, the revolutionary effort was led in turn by three of his sons. One of them, named Judas, was such a successful general that he was called "the Hammer." This family is known as the Maccabees, from the Aramaic word for "hammer."[58]

Although the Book of Daniel was composed during the time when Antiochus was pressuring the Jews to adapt to Greek culture, it presents itself as the visions and stories of a prophet who lived some four hundred years earlier, in Babylon, in the late sixth century reign of Belshazzar. When the visions and stories are read in that perspective, they are predictions of persecutions *in the future* and a revelation of *God's secret plan*, which is the original meaning of apocalyptic: it is a prediction that has been hidden and is now appearing.

The vision in Daniel 7 does not imply the end of the world. Instead, it presents an everlasting dominion and a kingship that shall never be destroyed,

---

58. Jonathan A. Goldstein, *I Maccabees*, AB 41 (Garden City, New York: Doubleday & Company, Inc., 1976), *passim*.

given to the son of man. It is not necessary, however, to interpret the expressions "everlasting" and "never" as absolute terms. They are exaggerations. It is entirely faithful to the text to interpret the kingdom given to the son of man as a kingdom that will last an exceptionally long time.

The best guess, based on the duplication in 1 Thess 4:13-18 of "in the clouds" and "in the air" is that Paul was thinking of Daniel 7 when he wrote this passage. This similar use of the words is evidence that Paul's kerygma was a change of reign in this world.

The phrase "in the clouds" also appears in the Gospels, in two contexts, both of which recall the inauguration of the dominion of the "son of man" in Daniel's vision. One set of these sayings predicts the apocalyptic coming of the Son of Man **in the clouds**:

> They will see the Son of Man coming in the clouds with great power and glory. At that time he will send his messengers and gather his chosen people together from the four winds from the depth of the earth to the height of heaven" (Mark 13:26-27 and parallels Matthew 24:30-31 and Luke 21:27).

The use of the future *opsontai* ("they will see") implies that this is a future event. This verse implies an event of shattering consequences: a cataclysmic, world-changing event. The express reference to power and glory confirms that, though future and though cataclysmic, it is a political event: a change of reign.

Paul's use of the same "in the clouds" phrase as Mark's Gospel implies that they both may have been thinking of Daniel 7. Mark's Gospel also suggests a remembrance of Daniel 7 by the mention of the four winds. In Daniel's vision, the four winds were what stirred up the sea to produce the four monsters (Dan 7:2).

The other context of a saying with this phrase is Jesus' trial. When Jesus is asked whether he was a king, He answered,

> I am, and you will see the Son of Man sitting at the right hand of power and coming with the clouds of heaven" (Mark 14:62b and parallel Matthew 26:64b; the parallel in Luke 22:69 does not mention the clouds).

This answer implies a correlation between Jesus' kingship and his future arrival as the Son of Man. That correlation makes it quite explicit that the saying envisions a political event.

The use of "in the clouds" in First Thessalonians and the two uses in the Gospels all give the appearance of a cataclysmic change; but none of these passages make it clear that they predict the end of the world. The cataclysmic event could simply be a transition to a new and different kind of reign. Given that the Gospels perceived the Roman Empire as an oppressive foreign government,[59] these passages also stand for a change to a genuinely humane form of government by the people themselves.

In Daniel, the expression "son of man" is a Semitic expression for a generic human being. It is not a title. "One in human likeness" over-translates it but has the right idea: the "son of man" is one who looks like a human being, who is a human being. In the Gospels, however, Son of Man became a title for Jesus. The concept that Jesus would return and would be given an everlasting dominion, like the son of man of Daniel 7, was part of Christianity from a very early time, perhaps soon after the crucifixion. Probably it was the similarity of Jesus' expected dominion to the dominion of the "son of man" in Daniel that led the followers of Jesus to call him the Son of Man. Since Paul did not use the title "Son of Man" in First Thessalonians, we may provisionally conclude, Son of Man became a title for Jesus after Paul wrote that letter.

The message of Daniel 7 is the gift of dominion. It is also the message of 1 Thess 4:13-18. In Daniel 7, the gift of dominion to the holy ones or pious ones of Israel took it away from the eleventh horn, symbolizing Antiochus IV Epiphanes. By the time Paul wrote, Antiochus and his dynasty had been replaced by a much larger, much more powerful monster, the Roman Empire. Paul's reference to the prophecy of Daniel is a key to his meaning that when Christ will step down in the clouds, dominion will be taken from the Roman Empire and given to the ecclesia.

The fourth piece of evidence of the political meaning of this letter is Paul's decisive treatment of the slogan "Peace and Security." Just as the nine Greek words previously discussed are ambiguous, so also this slogan is ambiguous. It

---

59. Crossan *Historical Jesus*, 313-20, discusses demonic possession as a psychosocial reaction to foreign oppressive governments.

might take its meaning from a religious context; some commentators believe the slogan circulated among Christian prophets, who were members of Paul's ecclesia.[60] If these commentators are correct, "Peace and Security" was a false prophecy that set to one side the hope that Jesus Christ would return soon and begin his reign. Christ is not coming back, they say; relax and enjoy the life in Christ.

There are references to false prophets in the Old Testament. The genuine prophets, Jeremiah, Ezekiel, and Micah each were opposed by false prophets. In each case, the genuine prophets had announced calamity to the people of Judah. The false prophets announced peace. To a false prophet who said, "No calamity will come upon you," Jeremiah said he hoped the other prophet was right; but then he said to wait and see who was correct (Jeremiah 23: 16-17).[61]

Ezekiel prophesied that the hand of the Lord would be against the false prophets who promised peace when there was no peace. Ezekiel said that God's wrath would be against them. This is a much stronger response than Jeremiah's wait-and-see attitude (Ezekiel 13:1, 9,15).

Micah, on the other hand, saw that the false prophets spoke in a way that benefited themselves.

This is what the LORD says to those prophets who mislead my people,
who proclaim peace when they are chewing with their teeth,
but pronounce war against those who do not feed them (Micah 3:5).

So there is background in the Old Testament for false prophets and particularly for ones who prophesy peace and security. Thus, it is possible that there were false prophets in the ecclesia and that Paul's words are directed

---

60. Abraham Malherbe has concluded that there were false prophets in the Thessalonian ecclesia, similar to the ones of whom Jeremiah, Ezekiel, and Micah complained.
Malherbe, *Letters*, 292, says that the expression *eirênê* and *asphaleia* is less likely to represent a political slogan of the Roman Empire than a message of false prophets in the ecclesia of the Thessalonians.
Malherbe, *Letters*, 302, identifies the "inescapable ruin" as Paul's sharpest language in this letter.
Malherbe, *Letters*, 303, says that identifying the slogan as political has no basis in exegesis.

61. In Jeremiah 28, the prophet Hananiah prophesied the end of the kingdom of Babylon, that in two years God would bring back to Jerusalem all the vessels of the Lord's house which King Nebuchadnezzar of Babylon carried away to Babylon. Jeremiah affirmed the prophecy in the exorbitant hope that it might be true.

against their reassuring, calming predictions.

Other commentators recognize these words, "Peace and Security," as a political slogan of the Roman Empire. The Roman Empire did in fact establish peace and provide security, so that people were able to prosper. If these commentators are correct, then Paul's decisive treatment of this slogan is consistent with his proclamation of the reign of Christ.

Paul's response is stronger than that of any of the ancient prophets. The curse in 5:3 is a simple and final statement, a pronouncement of certain doom. Destruction will come upon them inexorably, and they will in no way elude it. Paul's mind was made up, but he appears to be unemotional. In comparison with other passages where Paul cursed his opponents, this one is bloodless. Paul was not hot with anger, as he is reflected in swearwords in Philippians[62] or the curse in Galatians.[63] Here, the curse is very simply stated: their destruction will be abrupt. If those who said "Peace and Security" had been members of his own Christian community, Paul's typical behavior would have been to denounce them more violently and at greater length.

The bloodless simplicity of this curse implies that it is directed against the Roman Empire and its slogan. It was the Roman Empire that crucified the Lord Jesus. It is the Roman Empire that will be displaced by his triumphal return. It is the Roman Empire whose displacement is being prophesied throughout the letter.

Paul's treatment of the slogan "Peace and Security," then, is the fourth piece of evidence that the message Paul originally preached in Thessalonica was the replacement of the Roman Empire. It points to the same conclusion as the evidence of the connection with Daniel 7, the prevalence of the word *parousia* and the hope to which it refers, and the nine words which all might have been understood politically. Together with the evidence that Paul and his Thessalonian hearers expect Christ Jesus to return during their lifetime, these several pieces of evidence add up together to show that not only did they expect his return immanently but they expected that he would arrive as a political force, to establish God's kingdom here on earth, as a replacement at least in part for the oppressive Roman Empire.

---

62. Philippians 3:2 "Beware of the dogs, beware of the evil workers, beware of those who mutilate the flesh."

63. Galatians 5:12 "I wish those who unsettle you would castrate themselves!" Castration is an exaggeration of circumcision, so it is an à propos curse to those who insist on circumcision.

On the whole, Paul has portrayed Jesus' return as king, in comparison with the creed's statement of his return as judge. This passage, which announces the swift destruction that comes on those who are saying "Peace and Security," appears substantially to be pronouncing judgment on the Empire, and participates in what appears to be anger against oppression. This anger may well also connect with the anger expressed in 1:10, which speaks of Jesus rescuing us from the coming wrath," and with the implied contrast of what he says in 5:9: if "God has not set us up for wrath," perhaps his hearers would understand whom God had set up for wrath. Therefore, it is possible that Paul understood that in addition to being a return as king, Jesus' return would also be in the role of judge.

b. Resurrection was subordinate to *parousia*

As we have sketched out the words of the creed, Jesus' return comes after his resurrection. The creed follows a logical sequence: Jesus died, he was raised from the dead, and he will return to judge the living and the dead. Our belief pattern today follows the same logic. We celebrate the resurrection of Christ as the primary event of our religious faith. However, curiously, it does not appear to have been so for Paul, at least not in terms of what he wrote in First Thessalonians.

In First Thessalonians, the resurrection of Jesus is subordinate to the *parousia*. The *parousia* was of ultimate importance to Paul when he wrote this letter: it was even more important to him than the resurrection.

In verse 1:9 Paul mentions that God raised Jesus from the corpses, but the emphasis is that Paul's converts are waiting for his return. The primary emphasis of the statement is on their expecting his return. In the sentence structure and presumably in Paul's thinking, the resurrection is subordinate to the *parousia*.

In 4:14 and what follows, the subordination is more complex. There are three events in play: Jesus' death, his resurrection, and his return. In the first half of verse 14, Paul referred to two of these events: Jesus' death and resurrection. In the second half of the verse, he said that God will, through Jesus or because of Jesus, lead with him those who have fallen asleep. The expression "lead with him" refers to the return. In verse 14, then, Paul was thinking of all three events.

However, the statement "we believe that Jesus died and rose," in 4:14, is a premise in the reasoning that follows. Paul's words indicate that he and his hearers already believed that Jesus died and rose. Paul used the word "believe" as part of his presentation of the new thing that he was telling them, that they should have hope for deceased members of the ecclesia to meet the Lord in his *parousia*. Belief in the resurrection of Jesus was a premise for hope for their participation in the Lord's kingdom.

In 4:16, Paul said that the dead will rise. This statement stands independently, by itself. Then in 4:17, Paul said that the rest of us (meaning those who are still alive when the Lord returns) will be snatched up, together with those who have already died, to meet the Lord together. Verse 4:18 finishes the thought: "And in this way we shall always be with the Lord." "Be[ing] with the Lord" comes last in the sequence of thoughts and is the most important thought. The sequence of these statements reinforces the idea that the resurrection is not the most important thought in this passage; the most important thought in this passage is the *parousia*. The resurrection can be viewed merely as the means by which the deceased are able to participate and to have equal status in the *parousia*.

It is consistent with the wording of First Thessalonians to understand the resurrection as a preliminary to the future return of Christ. In order for the Lord to step down from heaven to begin his reign, Jesus must have been raised from the dead and taken up into heaven. As preliminary, however, the resurrection was a less important part of the religion than the promise of the *parousia*. It was Christ's *parousia* they were waiting for; it was in the *parousia* that the dead and the still-living would be gathered up to meet the Lord in the air; and it was in the *parousia* that they would all be alive with him.

At the end of the instruction not to grieve (4:13-18), Paul explained that by means of our being gathered together into Christ's *parousia*, the living and the dead will be together with Christ. At the end of the instruction to be alert (5:1-10), he repeated the same assertion, this time identifying those who are still alive when Christ arrives with guards on sentinel duty, and with this reference tied the two instructions, 5:1-10 for the living and 4:13-18 for the dead, together. In this second version, however, Paul added the key thought that we will be alive together in the *parousia*.

Paul did, however, give us another clue to interpret: verse 5:10 continues that Jesus died for us that we might live with him. It is natural for us today to interpret this inclusion as heavenly: We will be with him in heaven. That, however, adds later doctrinal development to Paul's thought; if we infer the meaning "in heaven," we interpret the phrase beyond what Paul said. It is probably more accurate to understand that we will be "with him" in the *parousia*. If we are correct in thinking of the *parousia* as the inauguration of an earthly kingdom, where our Lord Jesus Christ will reign, then it would be better to interpret the "with him" as being with him **in his reign**: we will reign with him.

However, Paul said that we will **live** with him. Paul's use of the verb *zêsô- men* ("{so that} we might live") appears to turn the meaning of the verse away from this "reign with him" interpretation. If Paul meant that our Lord Jesus Christ "died for us so that, whether we keep watch or sleep, we both might live with him," he puts an emphasis on **live**, which would seem to point in the direction of living rather than in the direction of reigning.

Paul has used the expression, "so that . . . we both might live with him," to tie together these last two passages. The first passage (4:13-18) primarily expressed the hope that those who have died might participate in the *parousia* of Christ; the second (5:1-10) focused on the need that those who are still alive might be alert and vigilant when that day comes. Paul's use of the word **live** hints at the life in the kingdom.

Our contemporary perspective thinks of Jesus' resurrection as all-important. The fact that Paul was at all able to subordinate Jesus' resurrection to his return suggests that he may have had a different understanding: that the resurrection of Jesus was important only as the necessary basis for him to be able to return from heaven. In this formulation, the return becomes the primary focus; in order for Jesus to return from heaven, he would have to have been raised from the dead and carried up to heaven. The resurrection, then, is a logical step along the way toward belief in his return.

6. and in the Holy Spirit, the Holy Church, the remission of sins, and the resurrection of the flesh.

Paul's words

1:5 . . . holy spirit . . .
4:8 . . . who is giving you his own holy spirit

Theological analysis

Paul's two uses of the words "holy spirit" reflect two quite different realities. The words "holy spirit" in 1:5 refer to the character of the Thessalonians' response to the gospel. Their response was energetic in a holy way.

Likewise, the words in 4:8 refer to a gift that God has already given them. Therefore, we have energy on the one hand and a gift on the other. It is not difficult to join these concepts: the gift that God has given them is the energy of their response to the gospel.

While it is not possible to say that Paul intended to combine these two thoughts in exactly this way, nevertheless this combination is a very good beginning toward the recognition of the third person of the Trinity. Today we understand the Holy Spirit as the holiness that is in us. It would be centuries, however, before that theology would be worked out in detail.

We find, then, that the indirect statements in First Thessalonians add up to belief in several of the items of the creed, but that the orientation of theological material seems to have focused on the *parousia* as a political military event. It subordinates the resurrection of Christ Jesus to the anticipation of his return.

The epistle, then, exhibits the kerygma as expecting a change in behavior and changes to loving each other, to sincerity and openness, to sobriety and vigilance, to rejoicing and praying, and to faith, love, and hope.

The Thessalonians are to change their behavior because they have been called to the new, higher standard, because that is how they will overflow with grace, because that is how they will be steadied and become blameless in their hearts unto the *parousia*. Paul encourages them to belong to the light. They belong to the day, so it is fitting for them to live as persons of the daylight.

The new standard of behavior that will please God is actually a standard for the heart. Paul said that his behavior with them was without trickery or deceit, manipulation, insincere flattery, or any intention to make an impression on others; just so Paul commended such honesty-of-self to them. Paul set the standard of caring for them as a nursing woman cares for her own children; that standard is an illustration of the love for each other that is the new morality of this early form of Christianity.

7. Inconsistencies

There are things Paul said that seem to be inconsistent with the creed and with the religion of the heart expressed in this letter.

Paul's words

2:18 . . . but the satan hindered us.

3:5 . . . lest the tempter had tempted you . . .

1:10 . . . from the coming wrath.

2:16 . . . The wrath of the end-time has already begun for them.

5:9 God has not set us up for wrath

Theological analysis

First, Paul referred to Satan. In 2:18 Paul said emphatically that he had many times wanted to come to visit them. Then he adds, "but the satan prevented us." It is hard to know what to do with this noun, "the satan." It is even a question whether to capitalize it, as a proper noun meaning the Devil, or leave it in lower-case, as referring vaguely to an opposing force. In the Hebrew language the word being transliterated means "the accuser." The Old Testament frequently uses an image of a courtroom where God is the judge and there is a prosecuting attorney, for which the word is "satan." Here Paul used the term as a transfer word, without translating it into a meaningful Greek expression. It is a very uncharacteristic expression for Paul to use. He does not often speak this way. That makes it even more difficult to interpret.[64]

In the most ancient passages of the Old Testament, God stands alone, as the only God whom the covenant people are to worship. In passages from the period between the Testaments, the Devil takes a place opposite God as the source of evil. In some later streams of Christianity, the Devil as the source of evil is as real as God. It is difficult to know for certain where Paul stood in this range of theological options. Was he a dualist, believing in God as the source of good and in the devil as the source of evil? Did he speak in a dualistic way without meaning to imply a dualism? Or is there another explanation for this comment?

A possible explanation for why Paul had not returned to Thessalonica and why he expressed himself this way is that there was the Roman equivalent of a warrant out for his arrest. The Book of Acts suggests in Chapter 17 that he left Thessalonica because there was an investigation that sought to detain and question him. This is a possible explanation of his departure. We do

---

64. Paul actually referred to satan several times: 1 Cor 5:5, Romans 16:20, and 2 Cor 11:14. The reference in 2 Cor 12: 7 is translated "thorn in the flesh." 2 Thess 2:9 is generally thought not to be Paul's writing.

have a reference, in his own words (2 Corinthians 11:32-33), to an occasion early in his ministry when he escaped rather than face arrest and questioning. Therefore, it appears that during an early stage of his ministry, Paul chose to avoid arrest. When he wrote First Thessssalonians, it was still an early stage of his ministry; he might still have been choosing to avoid arrest. Perhaps he knew authorities in the province of Macedonia were still looking for him, and for that reason was not willing to return.

This possibility is consistent with a political interpretation of the gospel. If the *parousia* of Jesus Christ had a political dimension, then it would be consistent for Paul to think of the Roman Empire as the opposing force. If, therefore, his return to Thessalonica was inhibited by the Roman government, he might speak of it as the satan.

Throughout history, others have spoken this way, naming the despised governmental authority as the satan. If Paul was speaking this way, he means "the government prevented me." It was actually his decision to avoid questioning and detainment, but people often project that sort of decision onto a hated government.

Second is the reference to the tester in 3:5. Paul sent his ambassador to find out if the tester had destroyed his ecclesia. It is certainly possible to interpret these words as referring to a theologically explicit devil. As they stand, in their unique appearance in this passage, they are vague. Paul's question was how they were bearing up under their difficulties. The "tester" personifies those difficulties.

These two references to the dark side seem out of synch with the attitude of love for each other, of rejoicing, praying, and giving thanks for all things. They are a different attitude, one that blames. While they may be consistent with a political reading of the gospel, they are inconsistent with the faithful, loving, hopeful attitude that is central to the gospel.

The phrases "from the coming wrath" in 1:10 and "God has not set us up for wrath" in 5:9 are jarring. They are spiritually inconsistent with the gospel. Furthermore, the idea is that Jesus is saving us from wrath is quite different from the way we usually conceive salvation. We today might read "wrath" as a response to our sins. However, Paul may have been thinking of something else. Both passages set up a distinction between them and us, between those who will suffer wrath and those who will be saved from it.

This passage does not actually say who will experience the coming wrath.

In saying that Jesus is rescuing us from it, the passage appears to say that the wrath will fall on everyone else. Jesus functions as a lightning rod diverting the power away from those of us who huddle around him.

To the extent that Jesus' *parousia* was expected to initiate a reign in the historical world, the coming wrath would be the flip side of the good news about Jesus Christ. The oppressive foreign regime would be replaced when Jesus came, and for the oppressors, it would not be pretty.

Such a reading in effect integrates Paul's expression of the coming wrath into the foremost message of the gospel. If Paul originally proclaimed that Jesus would replace the current kingdom, then wrath against the current kingdom would make sense.

Likewise, Paul's expression of the wrath-for-the-end-time that has already fallen upon Judaea seems contrary to the gospel, just as does Paul's accusation against the Jews. The accusation is neither true nor honorable. It is a spiritual low point in the epistle.

However, these verses are integral to the development of the structure of the epistle as Paul moved from faith and its consequences to love as made specific in Paul's love for this congregation. Properly understood, they fit perfectly with the flow of the argument. They also contribute a passion that is not seen elsewhere in this epistle.

The three verses (2:14-16) express his anguish over the consequences that his congregation must pay. Indeed, they point to a potential growth area for Paul. From the viewpoint of the attitudinal standard that he himself preached, he needed to work through what may have been a resentment. Still, in giving evidence to the pain, which he felt at being persecuted and opposed, these words also give evidence to the pain he felt on behalf of these Thessalonians, and they also help to explain his concern for them.

Paul's apparent dualism and his references to wrath indicate that he has not consistently thought through his inner religion. They suggest that he himself has not yet grown into its maturity.

CHAPTER 4

THE ALLUSIONS TO HISTORICAL EVENTS

The five groups of passages.

PAUL alluded to historical events in five groups of passages in this letter. These allusions are all stated in a way that indicates Paul did not expect disagreement about them. Therefore, they are first of all matters on which he and his hearers were agreed.

In 2:1-2 he described how he found courage to preach in Thessalonica (Group 1). In 1:4-10 and 2:13 he described how they responded to his preaching (Group 2). In 2:14-16 he talked about several events, beginning with some recent difficulties (Group 3). In 2:17-3:6 Paul discussed sending Timothy to investigate and Timothy's report (Group 4). In several passages, there are indications that some time has passed: in 1:7-8, 4:13, and 2:17-18, he indicated that some time had passed since the founding of the ecclesia; the instructions he gave in 4:11-12 and 5:12-15 pertain to a mature community; and the tone of his rehearsal of their shared history in 1:4-10 and 2:1-12 is consistent with their being reminders of old history (Group 5).

In addition to those allusions, verses 2:14-16 contain several references to historical events. Since we have accepted 2:14-16 as an authentic part of the letter, it is possible for us to explicate the historical events that lie behind Paul's comments and construct a timeline of events.

Group 1: He found courage to preach in Thessalonica.

Paul gave us a wealth of autobiographical material in 2:1-2.

Paul's words

> 2:1 For you yourselves recall, dear ones,
>   our entrance on your scene,
>   that it did not happen in vain,
>   but having previously been badly treated
>   and insulted in Philippi,
>   as you know,
>   we found courage in our God
>   to speak to you
>   the gospel of God, in a great contest.

Historical analysis

In the first phrase of these two verses, Paul speaks of his *eisodos* ("arrival," or "entrance").[65] Paul's next words, "that it did not happen in vain" suggest that his arrival had import. His arrival ultimately meant that he preached and they responded, so in some sense the word *eisodos* suggests a dramatic moment in a play when an important actor comes on the stage who will do something to move the drama of the play along. The drama of his preaching and their conversion might have happened differently. It might have been in vain; but it was not. The tight connection of the two verses suggests that they knew, recalled, and remembered the circumstances that he describes next. They remembered, and he knew they remembered, his entrance onto their stage.

In the second verse, he said that he had been badly treated and insulted in Philippi. Paul used two striking words: *propathontes* ("having been badly treated") and *hybristhentes* ("having been insulted"). The prefix *pro-* means previously or beforehand. The root word *pathontes* means being on the receiving end of an experience, and it usually means something bad happened. The root word combined with the prefix means that he had endured something *previously*, that is, before his entrance on their scene. The word *hybristhentes*

---

65. Liddell and Scott, *A Lexicon Abridged from Liddell and Scotts Greek-English Lexicon*, (Oxford: At the Clarendon Press, 1891). The Greek word includes a range of meaning from "arrival" to "entrance on stage."

is actually stronger than the English "being insulted," because of the Greek sensitivity to insults and their need to maintain dignity. Therefore, what Paul described here is behavior, in Philippi, that went beyond reasonable bounds.[66]

Paul himself said in another letter that he had preached in Syria and Cilicia, that is, in Asia Minor (Gal 1:21). Since he speaks of having needed to escape from Damascus (2 Cor 11:32-33), we think that Paul had preached in Damascus. There is no reason to think that crowds in the Near East were better behaved than the people in Philippi. So therefore, Paul already had experience with hecklers. It is reasonable to expect that he had developed some thickness of his skin. Therefore, it does not seem that the bad treatment or the insult in Philippi could have been ordinary heckling.

Long after the events of First Thessalonians, Paul wrote a very warm letter to an ecclesia in Philippi, acknowledging their generous support (Phil 4:16). Whether Paul founded that ecclesia or someone else did, and whether it had been founded during the visit before Paul came to Thessalonica, First Thessalonians does not say. From the two words, *propathontes* and *hybristhentes*, however, it hardly seems likely that he left an ecclesia behind during his sojourn there before coming to Thessalonica.

After that bad experience, he had to get up his courage to speak the gospel in Thessalonica. The word he used to express finding his courage, *eparresiasametha* (" we found courage"), suggests that it was no little matter.[67] This word implies that he found the bad treatment highly stressful, as if Paul had been so profoundly discouraged that it was a major accomplishment for him to speak in public again. If Paul did not mean to portray a real struggle, he could have chosen a simpler and shorter word.

We are going to take a guess a little later on regarding what this mistreatment might have been. For the moment, however, there is no indication of what the bad treatment and the insult were. Paul did not elaborate. What he said implies that it was such an assault that it profoundly distressed him. He was disturbed to the extent that when he got to Thessalonica he had to reach

---

66. Some scholars have an interesting interpretation of the two words, *propathontes* and *hybristhentes*, that describe Paul's distress. Earl Richard, *Thessalonians*, 91, thinks Paul meant a rude crowd heckling the speaker. Malherbe, *Letters*, 136, agrees, noting that while in the contexts of crowds' admonishing philosophers, the word *paschein* connotes suffering in general. *hybrizein* refers to insults.

67. Malherbe, *Letters*, 136-7 connects *eparessiasametha* with the philosophical tradition, which is consistent with his reading of Paul as a participant in that tradition.

deep down inside himself to find his courage.

He did not elaborate on how he found that courage, but his connecting the foul treatment to his finding his courage suggests that there was not anything in between. He was in Philippi first, and then he journeyed to Thessalonica, without stopping elsewhere.

We have accepted a little help from Philippians, Galatians, and Second Corinthians to give us perspective on his bad experience in Philippi. We have two steps in the drama: Paul had a bad experience in Philippi. Then he came to Thessalonica. In Thessalonica, he found courage to preach the gospel of God.

Group 2: They responded to his preaching.

Paul described, not his preaching, but their response to it, in two passages. In 1:4-10 he said:

Paul's words

^{1:4} knowing, dear ones, that you are loved by God who chose you,

⁵ because our preaching the gospel did not come to you
as mere words
but in power and in holy spirit and in great conviction,
as you know what we became among you, because of you.

⁶ And you have become imitators of us and of the Lord,
receiving the word, in much conflict,
with the grace of holy spirit,

⁷ with the result that you have become an example to all the
believers in Macedonia and as far as Achaia.

⁸ From you the word of the Lord has gone out
not only in Macedonia and in Achaia,
but in every place, your faith in God has been announced
so much that there is no need for us to tell others about you.

⁹ For others announce what sort of entrance we had among you
and how you turned towards God away from idols
to serve a living and true God,

¹⁰ and to await his son from the heavens,
whom he raised from corpses,
Jesus, who is rescuing us

from the coming wrath.

Paul described their response in much the same way in 2:13.

> ^{2:13} And for this reason it is especially important for us in particular[68]
> to give thanks to God that,
> taking possession of our preaching about God,
> you received it not as a human word
> but as what it really is,
> the word of God,
> who is at work in you, the believers.

Historical analysis

The second event alluded to in First Thessalonians is that after he preached, they responded. As a result, Paul founded an ecclesia. Paul lists four different things: that the gospel came to them (1) in power (2) and holy spirit and (3) in great conviction. This much could be Paul's description of his contribution to the event, namely that his preaching was powerful, that it was filled with holy spirit, and that he preached with great conviction. He also said, however, (4) that they received his preaching for what it really was, the word of God, and that saying indicates that Paul was really talking about their response: they responded powerfully, they responded in holy spirit, and they responded with great conviction, receiving Paul's kerygma as the word of God.

Paul made a strong contrast between the power of their actual response and the possibility that his work might have been in vain. His language in 2:1 contrasts their actual response to him with the possibility that his work might have been worthless. Again, in 3:5 he mentioned the possibility that the tempter had tempted them and his work could have been in vain. In chapter 3, the contrast is fairly clear: for Paul's work to have been in vain would mean that the ecclesia had ceased to exist. Here, however, where Paul's work had not been in vain, their powerful response means that an ecclesia

---

68. My translation is particularly indebted to Paul Schubert's interpretation of this passage as a resumption of the Thanksgiving Period. See Paul Schubert, *Form and Function of the Pauline Thanksgivings* (Berlin: Verlag Von Alfred Töpelmann, 1939), 18. "For us in particular" translates *kai hēmeis.*

had been planted.

The gospel came to them *en dynamei* ("in power"). Since Paul did not elaborate on what he meant, we can only guess. Perhaps he meant that they responded to his preaching with excitement. The word "power," however, usually implies some kind of movement or change. Since physical objects tend to stay at rest or to continue moving in the same direction, it takes power to change their movement. Getting a group of people to slow down or speed up or change direction likewise requires the application of some power. Human beings do not make any change in their lives without expending some kind of energy. For these Thessalonians to change from being pagans to being followers of Jesus Christ required energy. It would be difficult to become a member of Paul's ecclesia, not because Paul put up barriers to make it difficult, but because their relatives, friends, and neighbors resisted their leaving their previous practice. It would take some power to give up their other connections and social contacts to live into this new "artificial family." They responded to Paul and joined together in forming the ecclesia, a new social entity; perhaps this is what Paul meant by the power of their response.

Perhaps also, this phrase "in power" belongs with the next phrase, "in holy spirit," so that the power with which these Thessalonians responded to the gospel was God's power manifested in them.[69] They became alive with the power of God. It is not hard to imagine them energized and full of excitement about the good news Paul brought them. Perhaps he was speaking of their enthusiasm.

We also commonly use the name Holy Spirit to refer to the Spirit of God within; perhaps by "holy spirit" Paul meant the presence of God in them. So, therefore, in describing the response of these Thessalonians as "with holy spirit," Paul may have meant that God was in them and present with them in their response.

He may, instead, have meant a quality of their response, that is, his words describe the spirit with which they responded. If so, the words "with holy spirit" refer to a spirit of faith, love, and hope. That is indeed an exact descrip-

---

69. In Greek, the *pneuma* ("spirit") is literally the breath, the life energy marking the difference between life and death. Paul said they responded with holy spirit. The manuscript tradition does not let us distinguish between a holy spirit and the Holy Spirit. This style of making the distinction between common nouns and specific names by using capital letters came later. Although it is possible that Paul meant the Holy Spirit, the third person of the Trinity as defined by later Christian theology, nevertheless it is necessary to avoid anachronism.

tion of the spirit that is holy, both in terms of being a characteristic behavior and attitude of persons who are holy and in terms of being a spirit that belongs to and comes from God. It is a description of the character or spirit of their response.

Was their response ecstatic? References in two other documents suggest that it was. The Book of Acts associates the arrival of the holy spirit with wind, tongues of fire, and speaking in tongues (2:1-36). In that passage, pilgrims from distant places heard the good news being proclaimed in their own languages. Similarly, in the discussion of tongue-speaking in 1 Cor 12-14, tongue-speaking clearly emerges as an important ecstatic experience; in that context, Paul said tongues needed to be interpreted, but he did speak of glossolalia as a worthwhile gift in itself. Regardless, the experience of speaking in a language which others might understand but which the speaker does not understand is ecstatic.

The Book of Acts treated an ecstatic response of the spirit as evidence that people were qualified to be members of the ecclesia. The spirit fell upon the gentile household of Cornelius while Peter was preaching, and Peter took it as evidence that they should be baptized (Acts 10). It may be that the members of the Corinthian ecclesia considered speaking in tongues as an important a qualification for their life together; Paul's somewhat negative appraisal of speaking in tongues in that letter may indicate they overvalued it. Nevertheless, we have to consider the possibility that speaking in tongues was considered a manifest qualification for membership in the ecclesia during the early years of Paul's preaching in Europe.

Therefore, it may be that when holy spirit came upon these Thessalonians, they also spoke in tongues. Then this out-pouring of the spirit would be evidence for including them in the society of Jesus' followers, proof that they were to be joined together with other true followers of Jesus. It may therefore represent what Paul meant by saying that the people to whom he was writing this letter had responded to his preaching with power and holy spirit.

There are only three references to holy spirit in First Thessalonians: the one in 1:5 we are currently discussing, one in 1:6 where it is "in the grace of holy spirit," and one in 4:8 where Paul referred to God as the one "who is giving you his holy spirit." This last reference states that the "holy spirit" is a gift; and the implication of 1:6 is that these Thessalonians have already received this gift. It is not something expected in the future, but some observable phenomenon already demonstrated. This sounds like an ecstatic experience of some sort.

Paul also said that they responded *en plerophoria pollei* ("in great conviction"). Theirs was not a lukewarm response. They responded with a whole-hearted affirmation of the good news. They did not join the ecclesia with doubts or with a backup plan in case it did not work out. Their embrace of the new belief was whole-hearted. The statement is both evidence that Paul thought their response was whole-hearted and also a reminder to them of the strength of their original response to the gospel.

The result of Paul's preaching and their response was the formation of an ecclesia. Although First Thessalonians tells us virtually nothing more about what constitutes an ecclesia,[70] it was an organization of a society of some kind, similar to synagogues and to the "ecclesiae" already existing in Judaea and Syria.

The Thessalonian ecclesia, however, was made up entirely of non-Jews. Paul said in 1:9 "you turned to God from idols." As mentioned, he does not say, "Some of you turned to God from idols," so he is referring to all of the members of the ecclesia. They had all been idol-worshippers before their conversion. They were an all-gentile congregation.

In addition to this statement in 1:9, there is a more subtle indication in 2:14-16 that all the members of this ecclesia were non-Jews. Paul said the Christian ecclesiae in Judaea were badly treated by the Jews. Then Paul continued that the Jews killed Jesus and the prophets. This statement of blame would be offensive to any Jews who were members of Paul's ecclesia of the Thessalonians. If Paul had been thinking of Jews who were members of that ecclesia, he might have tempered his remarks. The fact that he let his anger show in verses 2:14-16 strongly suggests that his intended audience was made up entirely of non-Jews. Since this epistle in particular exhibits a very close warm relationship between Paul and this ecclesia, it seems probable that there

---

70. There is very extensive bibliography on the sociology of the early ecclesia. One could start with Meeks, *Urban Christians*. Abraham J. Malherbe, *Social Aspects of Early Christianity* (Philadelphia: Fortress Press 1977, 2nd ed. 1983), Gerd Theissen, *Social Reality and the Early Christians: Theology, Ethics, and the World of the New Testament* trans. by Margaret Kohl (Minneapolis: Fortress Press, 1992).
There are some clues in 1 Thess 5:12-15, but they are controversial and add nothing to our discussion here.

were no persons in it who might be offended by this excessive statement, and that means there were no Jewish members. Except for Paul himself, this congregation was entirely gentile.

This subtle reading, that Paul would not have written so offensively if any other members of the ecclesia of the Thessalonians had been Jews, seems probable but is somewhat less than certain. However, in combination with the first point, where Paul implied that they **all** turned to God from idols, it seems highly likely that this was an all-gentile congregation.

The only indication that there were difficulties at the time when Paul founded the ecclesia (and it is difficult to interpret) is three words in verse 1:6. Paul said, "you have become imitators of us and of the Lord, receiving the word **in much conflict** and with the grace of holy spirit." The words, *en thlipsei pollei* ("in much conflict"), have sometimes been understood as a reference to persecution of the ecclesia at the time of its founding.[71] The word *thlipsis* often refers to persecutions, but it need not mean that here.

Paul's converts, however, were exposed to criticism when they turned to God. Individuals who converted by themselves would have been criticized by their families. Families who converted as entire families would have been criticized by their neighbors; some families might have left members behind when they converted, who would then be critical. People who worked together in a shop and might have converted as a group would still be vulnerable to criticism from their customers and suppliers. Their critics might have said that the Roman system functioned well because the gods of Rome smiled on the exercise of Roman piety; and the service of the local gods provided for local prosperity. To abandon the worship of the local gods and the gods of Rome imperiled the entire society. Therefore, the new converts received a share of criticism. That criticism may lie behind Paul's reference here to "much conflict."

Conversion, therefore, was a troubling experience for these early followers of Paul and Jesus. Their turning to a living and true God was a change that affected every aspect of their lives.[72] The "conflict" pertained to the fact that they accepted the gospel. The act of turning, as Paul said, toward God and away from idols occasioned both stress and joy. The turmoil of conversion is

---

71. Malherbe, *Letters*, 127-28, attests this reading in others but argues against it.

72. Richard, *Thessalonians*, 149, says conversion meant a thorough change in cultural values.

enough to explain it.[73] However, Paul's use of the word *thlipsis* here alerted his hearers to the role this word would play later in the letter.

In 1:4-10, then, Paul described how they responded to his preaching: they became an ecclesia of followers of Jesus and Paul. They became the first known ecclesia in Europe and the first known all-gentile ecclesia.

In this same passage, Paul also said that these members of the ecclesia in Thessalonica had "become an example to believers in Macedonia and Achaia" and that the report of their coming to faith had spread, not only throughout Macedonia and Achaia, but also had spread beyond those borders. These two statements establish how remarkable it was that Paul had planted an ecclesia in Thessalonica: people were talking about that accomplishment. It also establishes two other very important points.

First, it establishes that there was a network of communication between the ecclesiae in the very early years of the Christian movement. Ecclesiae in Achaia knew about ecclesiae in Macedonia. The ecclesiae in Macedonia and Achaia knew about ecclesiae in Judea; and that makes it likely that the ecclesiae in Judaea knew about the ecclesiae in Macedonia and Achaia. Paul said that the report went beyond Achaia to every place, which could refer to Illyricum in the Northwest of the Balkan peninsula (Romans 15:19), but could also refer to Judaea. Followers of Jesus were interested in news about other followers of Jesus and passed information around.

Second, it also means, as we shall discuss later, that there was a stretch of time between the founding of the ecclesia in Thessalonica and the writing of the letter. There had to have been enough time for Paul to have traveled beyond Achaia. There had to have been enough time for reports about the ecclesia of the Thessalonians to have traveled that far. What Paul said about their being examples for believers and about the reports about them indicates that some significant time had passed.

This passage, 1:4-10, has an emotional tone that is consistent with a significant passage of time. These words may sound like the rehearsal of a fresh memory to some people and like the recollection of an older memory to others. These statements, however, are a historically precise reminder. They cull out the exact nature of what is historically significant. If they were recent memories, there might be more of an indication of enjoyment in them. Paul

---

73. Malherbe, *Letters*, 127.

and his hearers would still be in the original flush of emotion. On the contrary, these words describe the historical event of the planting of the ecclesia in the concise manner that comes from years of perspective. Therefore, it seems more likely from the manner of expression that Paul was reminding them of events several years in the past.

We have referred to the Book of Acts and to First Corinthians to shed light on what may have been an ecstatic component of conversion; but the basic fact of their conversion is established without those references. We have a third step in the drama: The basic historical fact attested by these passages is that some of the Thessalonians responded to Paul's preaching and became the first known all-gentile ecclesia.

Group 3: Recently there had been some difficulties.

In 2:14-16, Paul spoke first of their recent difficulties and then was carried away with expressions of other frustrations.

Paul's words

> 2:14 For you have become imitators, beloved,
>   of the ecclesiae of God which are in Judea in Christ Jesus,
>   for the same thing was done to you that was done to them,
>   you at the hands of your own countrymen,
>   just as they from the Jews,
> 15 who killed the Lord Jesus and the prophets,
>   and chased us out, not pleasing God,
>   and opposing themselves to all people,
> 16 preventing us from preaching to save gentiles,
>   as a way of filling up their sins.
>   The wrath of the end-time has already begun for them.

Historical analysis

The verb *epathete* ("experienced") that Paul used when he said "you have endured the same thing" is equally able to mean something bad or something good. It means simply that something has happened to its subject. Some other party has acted in an unspecified way upon the ecclesia of the Thessalonians; the ecclesia received the action. This word could be used to refer to a neutral event; however, it was used more often to refer to a negative experience.[74] This word does have a tendency to sound negative. If something happened, it probably was something bad. The most general word we could use is "difficulty." The ecclesia has endured some difficulty. To say "were mistreated" or "suffered" or "were persecuted" would be an over-statement. It would be more balanced to translate this phrase, "the same thing was done to you that was done to the ecclesiae in Judaea."

We know this much, that the ecclesia endured some difficulty. That does not tell us what happened. At the most it gives us a flavor of the event. It was something bad that happened to them.

The members of the ecclesia of the Thessalonians experienced these difficulties at the hands of their own countrymen. Whatever happened, its agent was other Thessalonians. The words Paul used, *hypo tôn idiôn symphyletôn* ("by" or "from your own countrymen"), mean specifically other Thessalonians. A *symphyletos* is a member of the same tribe or *phylê*. The Greeks used *phylê* as voting blocks. Members of the same *phylê* voted together and elected their representatives to council. Membership in a *phylê* was hereditary and usually reflected where members' ancestors lived when the *phylai* were created. The use of the word *symphyletôn* strongly implies that the troublers of the ecclesia were voting citizens of Thessalonica.

The modifier *idiôn* stresses the connection between the members of the ecclesia and their troublemakers. Not only did their troublemakers belong to the same *phylê*. They were *their own (idiôn)* countrymen.

At any rate, the troublemakers in Thessalonica were not Italians, nor were they Romans, nor were they Jews. None of those people could belong to the same voting block as the citizens of Thessalonica. The troublemakers had to be other Thessalonians.

It may well be that the exact form of the trouble was pressure to return to the customary Thessalonian worship. After all, it was the worship offered to the local gods that guaranteed local prosperity. These followers of Jesus jeopardized the prosperity of the entire community by withholding their worship. The community could put a great deal of pressure on them. Paul had good reason to fear for the existence of his community.

Whatever difficulty the ecclesia in Thessalonica experienced, it was similar to what had been previously experienced by the ecclesiae in Judaea. When

---

74. Liddell & Scott, *Greek-English Lexicon*, 536a.

Paul said that the ecclesia of the Thessalonians had suffered the same thing that the ecclesiae in Judaea had suffered, he incidentally told us that in Judaea, Jews made difficulties for the congregations of the followers of Jesus. That is not a lot of information. It does tell us, however, that the troubling of the Judaean followers of Jesus was already going on, before Paul wrote this letter.

Paul gives us the impression that such trouble in Judaea had been going on for awhile. If it had been going on for years, it was some kind of campaign or movement. The difficulties the Judaean congregations suffered from the Jews may have begun even before Paul first arrived in Thessalonica. This movement began before these recent difficulties in Thessalonica, or Paul could not have said in this letter that the Thessalonians had become imitators of the Judaean congregations.

He brought it up casually that the ecclesiae of the Jesus movement in Judaea had suffered at the hands of Jews. This casual statement would not be possible if the Thessalonians did not already know about the troubles between the followers of Jesus in Judaea and other Jews. Therefore, the casualness of this statement implies that the followers of Jesus in Thessalonica already knew about an on-going pattern of troubles in Judaea. Their knowledge reinforces the conclusion, based on 1:8, that there was an information network between the ecclesiae of Jesus, even if they were on different continents.

It is no surprise that Paul knew what was going on in Judaea; he kept moving from place to place. He associated with other people who shared information regarding ecclesiae in other places; as he said in 1:8, he had heard reports about this congregation everywhere, specifically farther away than Achaia.

Perhaps Paul's history as one who persecuted the ecclesia offers a clue to the persecution that others continued after Paul's conversion. Paul admitted, in First Corinthians 15:8-9 and in Galatians 1:13,[75] that he had persecuted

---

75. We have been following an epistemological decision to read the earliest letter first and not interpret it based on material from later letters. It seems to be acceptable, however, to add a reference to an event which is earlier in time but referred to only later. This needs to be done with care, because memory does modify the event. Paul's statements that he persecuted the church, still, are relatively straightforward.

It is not acceptable, however, to interpret theological statements in an epistle using references to the same or more developed theology in later epistles. The latter process would obscure the development of his thought.

the ecclesia. Although he wrote both of those letters after he wrote First Thessalonians, his persecution of the ecclesia was before his conversion. Therefore
it was before his first preaching in Thessalonica.

Surely he was not the only Jew to have persecuted the ecclesia. Perhaps
other Jews persecuted the ecclesia in the same way that Paul had. Perhaps
what he meant by the thing that was done to the ecclesiae in Judaea was
the exactly same thing that he himself had done to the ecclesiae there. Such
persecution, in that case, was a movement of some duration, having begun
before Paul's conversion.

The casualness of the reference, again, implies that Paul's hearers would
not argue the point with him. We would expect that they not only knew of
the troubles but would agree with Paul that it was "Jews" in Judaea who were
responsible. From our contemporary point of view, it was **some Jews** who
troubled the ecclesiae of Jesus; it was not **all** Jews;[76] Paul's words are ambiguous. The expression can be understood to refer to those particular individuals
who troubled the ecclesiae of Jesus. Those particular individuals were Jews,
as the statement says. The statement, however, is global, and as a global statement it is not only an exaggeration but also is an expression of prejudice.

Paul said that they killed Jesus and the prophets. This expression is just as
ambiguous as the previous statement about who troubled the congregations
of Jesus in Judaea. It could refer to all Jews, or it could refer to some of them.
If Paul meant a particular faction among the Jews, then there is a question
whether he thought there was some continuity between the Jews who killed
Jesus and the ones who later troubled the congregations of Jesus' followers.

It is a straightforward simple statement, without any of the Greek par-
ticles that might indicate subtlety, to the effect that the Jews killed Jesus. It is
a false statement, because it was the Roman Empire that executed Jesus; the
Roman Empire held power, and it considered crucifixion to be its proprietary
method for executing criminals. It did not permit authorities other than itself
to use crucifixion as a means of execution.[77] Even if members of the Jewish
community conspired and even if they brought pressure on the local representatives of the Roman Empire, nevertheless, it was the Empire and its sol-

76. Malherbe *Letters*, 169, notes that a comma makes a difference, and that Paul meant "some
Jews," not all.

77. Richard J. Cassidy, *Paul in Chains: Roman Imprisonment and the Letters of St. Paul*, New York,
Crossroad Publishing Company, 2001), 180-81.

diers who carried out the execution. For Paul to have forthrightly made this historically untrue statement gives it a strong emotional tone. It continues to sound like an emotional outburst.

Since he made this false statement as if it were a simple fact, Paul appears to have been carried away by his emotions. It is fair to say that he believed this statement. He thought and felt, at this time in his career, as indicated by the simplicity of these words, that the Jews were responsible for killing Christ Jesus. His emotions clouded his judgment.

Since he expressed this false statement simply, it also appears that he did not expect disagreement from his hearers. If his hearers disagreed with this part of the statement, it would weaken Paul's objective in writing the letter. Even if he was emotionally carried away, Paul was a skilled rhetorician. A skilled rhetorician would use such a global exaggeration as this only if he were confident that it would not hurt his argument.

Therefore, the members of the ecclesia of the Thessalonians shared the same prejudice. They agreed with Paul that the Jews killed Jesus.

The killing of Jesus had happened some fifteen to twenty years before the writing of this epistle. The killing of the prophets had happened a long time before that. Perhaps Paul had in mind a succession of executions spread over the previous six hundred years. Not only did Paul think that the Jews killed Jesus; he also thought that their killing Jesus was a part of a pattern of rejecting the messengers that God sent to them. Not only did Paul think so; the members of his ecclesia thought so too. Prejudice against Jews had an early beginning in the ecclesia.

With the expression "chased us out," Paul has shifted attention away from Jesus and the prophets to himself. The reference has become personal. Paul spoke here of how he personally had been opposed. It is an expression of his personal feeling of being rejected. His expression here is an emotional response; his emotion led him to speak as if all Jews were at fault. Perhaps this sense of being personally opposed is a key to why he globalized the agent.

The verb *ekdiôkô* ("chased out") could refer to any of several events. Perhaps Paul was thinking of having been chased out of Damascus;[78] perhaps Paul crossed the Bosphorus into Europe because he was being chased out of

---

78. In 2 Cor 11:32-33 Paul tells of having been let down outside the wall of Damascus in order to avoid being seized by the governor. A very similar story is told in Acts 9:23-25, where it says that Jews were responsible.

Asia. [79]Perhaps when he wrote "chased out" he was thinking of his departure from Philippi. Any of these is a possible interpretation; we have no basis for judging among them. In any case, when he was chased out, it was prior to his writing this letter.

Both of the verbs, that they "killed" Jesus and the prophets and "chased us out" are in the aorist tense, a tense that indicates that something happened in the past, but does not indicate when it happened or over what duration. This past tense is strikingly different from the present tense of the next three participles: "not pleasing," "opposing," and "preventing."

The phrases "not pleasing God" and "opposing themselves to all people" modify and expand upon "chased us out." By chasing Paul away, they acted in a manner that was not pleasing to God. This is Paul's point of view; even if we agree that opposition to Paul was not pleasing to God, nevertheless it was not the viewpoint of those who opposed him. In fact, they probably thought they were protecting their true and pure religion by opposing a dangerous radical. Therefore, it is Paul's opinion that their opposition was not pleasing to God. This observation helps identify this statement of Paul's as an emotional outburst.

"Opposing themselves to all people" anticipates Paul's expression in the next verse. In the next verse, Paul said that he could benefit the non-Jews by preaching to them, giving them the great benefit of saving them. By chasing Paul out, his "chasers" denied them salvation. This verse, however, says that the denial of the benefit affected **all** men, not just the few in any location from which Paul had been chased out. As already noted, Paul was generalizing in the previous verse, as if **all** Jews were responsible for killing Jesus; perhaps this thought shows the same tendency to globalize.

"As a way of filling up their sins" also expands upon "who killed" and "chased out" and "preventing." Paul considered each of these to be a sin. We do not know, however, what Paul meant by saying that their sins became full.

The participle *kôluontôn* ("preventing") is also present tense. We do not know when Paul began to see that some people were preventing him. This tense means that the activity was continuing when he wrote. Paul continued, at least as late as the writing of First Thessalonians, to meet opposition to his

---

79. Paul said nothing himself about how he happened to cross the Bosphorus to evangelize Europe; however Acts 16:6-10 reported that after being forbidden by the Holy Spirit to preach in Asia, Paul had a vision of a man of Macedonia inviting him.

preaching.

Paul said that the Jews were preventing him from preaching to non-Jews. Paul has told us about his personal experience of being opposed. It is an exaggeration for him to suggest that all Jews were preventing him from preaching. It is another exaggeration to think that they actually kept him from preaching; perhaps a better word would be "hindering." Paul, however, actually said that they were preventing him. We have to sort out what happened from Paul's internal experience of it. Some Jews were attempting to prevent Paul from preaching. The focus here is not on what "they" have done to others, but on Paul's experience of what they have done and are doing. This distinction validates the interpretation that these words were emotional.

The last sentence of this passage has proved to be most difficult. It is not only difficult to think about because we do not know the context; Paul was talking about some historical event, but we do not know what event that was. The verse is also difficult because of its syntax. We need to consider how to translate this sentence one word at a time. This sentence begins with a verb, *ephthasen*,[80] which might mean "has come." Paul used this verb in another place in this letter (4:15), and there it means "will anticipate" or "arrive before" or "precede." When Paul used the word *ephthasen* to mean "precede," he was using the word in an antique sense. If Paul used the word in an antique sense in 4:15, perhaps he was also thinking in this antique way in 2:16. Perhaps what he meant was "has come in anticipation." For the moment, we have to supply the word "something." Tentatively, our translation so far is "Something has come (in anticipation)."

The next words are "upon them." Our translation now is "Something has come upon them (in anticipation)." By "them" Paul must have been referring to the Jews who were the subject of "killed," "chased," "not pleasing," "opposing" and "preventing." He must mean the Jews in Judaea, and therefore the sentence means that something has happened to the Jews in Judaea.

Then comes the subject of the sentence, the word *orgê* ("wrath"). Our translation now is "wrath has come upon them (in anticipation)." Paul has already used the same word, "wrath," in 1:10, where he associates the "coming wrath" or "the approaching wrath" with the awaited return of Jesus. In that context, "wrath" is eschatological, meaning that it is to be associated with

---

80. See the discussion of *phthasomen* on page 179.

Jesus' *parousia.*

The final two words of the sentence, *eis telos* ("for the end") could mean "finally" or "at last." Either of these translations would negate the anticipatory sense of *ephthasen,* and would be rendered "Wrath has finally come upon them." If, however, *eis telos* means "for the end," the phrase *orgê eis telos* fits together easily as "wrath of the end time." Taking *eis telos* this way and picking up the antique sense of *ephtasen,* the sentence becomes "wrath of the end time has come upon them (in anticipation)," or "wrath has come upon them in anticipation of the end time." Thus we are left with three alternatives: "Wrath has finally come upon them," or "wrath of the end time has come upon them (in anticipation)," or "wrath has come upon them in anticipation of the end time."

At any rate, the event referred to here is some catastrophe. Probably, however, Paul was thinking of an event in Judaea. He has been speaking about the Jews of Judaea throughout this passage. Furthermore his reference is to a recent event. It would make sense for it to have been an event only a short time before Paul wrote the letter. There would be no reason for Paul to mention an event in the distant past. There had been some event, which might have been an earthquake or a fire or a famine, in Judaea which Paul interpreted as an act of wrath in anticipation of the end.

We have mentioned First Corinthians and Galatians to give us a perspective on the persecution of the Christian congregations. However, based on the conclusion that 2:14-16 is authentic to the letter as Paul originally wrote it, this verse is a sufficient statement that the ecclesia in Thessalonica had recently experienced some difficulty from other citizens of Thessalonica; that similar difficulties had been experienced by the congregations of Jesus in Judaea; it is also exposes Paul's prejudicial attitude about Jews and indicates that he did not consider that his prejudicial statement would harm the argument of his letter; and it also states that there had recently been a catastrophe in Judaea such as would be typical of the end-time.

Group 4: Paul sent Timothy to investigate.

Paul gave his hearers quite a full description of how he came to send Timothy to them and what Timothy reported back to him, in 2:17-3:6.

Paul's words

²:¹⁷ We, then, dear ones, being separated from you

for a long enough time,
physically, not emotionally,
became exceedingly eager to see you in person,
with a great desire.

18 So that we wanted to come to you,
I, myself, Paul, not once or twice,
but the satan hindered us.

19 For who is our hope or grace or wreath to boast of—
except you—before our Lord Jesus in his arrival?

20 You are our glory and grace.

3:1 When we could bear it no longer, we chose
to be left alone in Athens

2 and we sent Timothy, our dear brother
and God's co-worker in the gospel of Christ,
to steady you and to encourage you in your faith

3 that you not be shaken in these current difficulties,
for you know that we can expect troubles;

4 I kept on telling you so ahead of time, when I was with you,
that we were going to have difficulties,
just as has happened and as you know.

5 Because of this, being no longer able to bear it,
I sent Timothy to learn of your faith,
lest the tempter had tempted you
and our work had been in vain.

6 Just now Timothy has returned from you to us
and has announced to us your faith and your love
and that you always have a good memory of us,
wanting to see us just as we want to see you.

Historical analysis

As discussed in the previous section, there was some new development in Thessalonica, something that the members of the ecclesia endured at the hands of their fellow-citizens. We also know about this event because of what Paul wrote in 3:3-4. In 3:3-4, Paul refers to this recent event as a *thlipsis* in referring to "**these current difficulties**" which had just happened.

Paul's comment represented by "we were going to have difficulties" is hard to translate. The Greek expression literally speaks of where "we lie;" an English proverb says that when a person has made his bed he has to lie in it, meaning that people have to deal with the situations they create. This Greek expression is similar; *keimetha* ("we lie") describes the situation of followers of Jesus. Paul meant that followers of Jesus should expect troubles. His expression "we were going to have difficulties" uses a verb *mellomen* ("we are going to"), which implies that the future is a natural result of the present. Difficulties and troubles are a natural result of the decision to follow Christ.

Paul went on to say that he had already told them, back in the time when he was present with them, that such *thlipses* were part of a predictable future. In fact, he not only had already told them; he had "kept on telling them." The verb *proelegomen*, ("we kept on telling") uses the imperfect tense, which indicates continuing activity; Paul told them, continually, to expect troubles.

Paul's expression, "as you know," reinforces the claim that Paul had already alerted them to expect troubles. By saying "as you know," he said that he had told them and added "ahead of time," and then doubled the time stamp by saying "when I was with you." He said, "as you know" to remind them that he had told them and that they already knew it! Paul called upon them to remember what he told them, suggesting that they might have forgotten it. Paul apparently hoped that by reminding them of what he had told them before and by saying that troubles and difficulties are part of the natural expectation of Christians, they would be steadied in their faith. Nevertheless, Paul was so frightened for them that he feared his work had been in vain— that the ecclesia had ceased to exist.

Upon hearing of their troubles and becoming afraid, and wishing that he could see them face to face, Paul sent Timothy on a mission to find out the truth. According to what he says in 3:1-2, Paul was in Athens at that moment. Curiously, he says "we decided to be left alone in Athens," but he was not all by himself when Timothy departed, judging by his use of the plurals in the next phrase, "we decided to be left alone in Athens." Even the word *monoi* ("alone") is plural. Nevertheless being left "alone" in Athens was some sort of sacrifice that Paul was willing to make in order to gain news of these Thessalonians. Sending Timothy on a fact-finding mission was a dramatic act.

We do not know precisely when this was, except that we know that it was shortly before he wrote this letter to the Thessalonians. It is quite possible that this sojourn in Athens was a way-stop on a larger journey that included

Corinth, but there is no indication in First Thessalonians regarding where he had been just prior to writing the letter or where he was going next.

While it is commonly understood that this visit to Athens followed immediately after Paul's departure from Thessalonica,[81] there is nothing in these verses in First Thessalonians to indicate that this happened during Paul's first visit to Athens. The news of recent events in Thessalonica and Paul's sending Timothy to investigate could have happened during a later visit to Athens. Since we are led to believe, both by Acts and by Paul's own letters, that Paul made multiple visits to Corinth,[82] it is not improbable that Paul also made multiple visits to Athens as well. It was quite possible to travel non-stop to Corinth by ship, since Corinth was a major port on the shipping routes of the Roman Empire. The well-worn land route to Corinth, however, lay through Athens.

Paul was in Athens when he sent Timothy. He may have moved on from Athens before Timothy returned and may already have been somewhere else when he wrote First Thessalonians. However, placing him in Corinth when he wrote the letter based on identifying Timothy's return from Thessalonica (1 Thess 3:6) with Timothy's rejoining Paul in Corinth (Acts 18:5) is not justified. We do not know for sure where Paul was when Timothy returned. Nevertheless, 1 Thess 3:6 reads quite naturally that Timothy rejoined Paul in the same place from which he had been sent out.

When Timothy returned with the news that the ecclesia of the Thessalonians continued to be faithful to Christ and that they remembered and loved Paul, then Paul wrote them this letter. The joy of knowing that they were faithful is part of what informs this letter.

The sequence of events is:

---

81. This understanding is based on reading Acts 17:10-18:5, in which Paul leaves Thessalonica, stays briefly in Athens, and then goes on to Corinth, where Timothy rejoins him, as if it describes the same events as 1 Thess 3:2-6. The problem is, of course, that in this passage in Acts, Timothy remained in Beroea and did not accompany Paul to Athens and could not have been sent by Paul from Athens to Thessalonica.

82. Acts 18:1-18 and 20:2 refer to two different visits to Corinth; 1 Cor 3:6 and 2 Cor 10:14 both refer to the founding visit; 1 Cor 16:5-5 refers to a plan to visit and spend the winter in Corinth; what 2 Cor 2:1 says about "another painful visit" implies that there was a painful visit; and 2 Cor 13:1 says "This is the third time I am coming to you" and the mention of Cenchreae in Rom 16:1 and of Prisca and Aquila in Rom 16:3 hint that Romans was written in Corinth. Both sources, then, appear to agree that Paul made multiple visits to Corinth.

a. Some recent event made Paul fear for his ecclesia.

b. Paul sent Timothy from Athens to inquire for their existence and status.

c. Timothy returned with news of their well-being and continuing love.

d. Paul wrote First Thessalonians, partly out of joy at this news.

Group 5: Some time had passed.

Several passages suggest that there was a stretch of time between the founding of the ecclesia and the writing of this letter.[83]

Paul's words

1:7 with the result that you have become an example to believers in Macedonia and as far as Achaia.

8 The word of the Lord has gone out from you
not only in Macedonia and in Achaia,
but in every place, your faith in God has been announced
so much that there is no need for us to tell others about you.

Historical analysis

Paul did not say where he went when he left Thessalonica. It is reasonable that he continued along the route south to Athens and from there on to Corinth, where he spent more time and eventually planted an ecclesia. Corinth functioned as the capitol of the Roman province of Achaia, which consists of the Peloponnesus and part of the Balkan peninsula northwest of Athens. In due time, Paul went beyond Achaia. Perhaps after leaving Corinth

---

83. The Book of Acts gives us the impression that he was in Thessalonica only for a short time before he was chased out.

Malherbe, *Letters*, makes much of the impression he gets from the letter that it was written soon, perhaps six months, after Paul left Thessalonica. The letter is indeed warm. Others of us get the same impression of warmth without thinking that it had been such a short time. Is it not possible for warm feelings to persist over a period of as long as seven years? Some of us have the experience of warm feelings towards a congregation lasting more than thirty years. A time span of seven years would not lessen the warmth.

Malherbe, *Letters*, also seems to argue, although he is not quite as explicit, that the autobiographical events Paul described in this letter would not have taken more than six months. There is, however, no indication that Paul intended his autobiographical notes to be exhaustive. He did not say everything that happened since he left Thessalonica. In fact, he merely touched the surface.

Part of the impression of earliness may be related to the letter's focus on their response of faith.

he went as far as Illyricum. At any rate, he journeyed "beyond Achaia."

In 1 Thess 1:7-8 Paul says that these Thessalonians have become a "type" for all believers in Macedonia and Achaia and that the report of their faith has gone out, not only in Macedonia and Achaia, but in **every place**. This statement suggests either that Paul had heard reports of these Thessalonians while he was in some place **beyond Achaia**, or that a traveler from beyond Achaia had met him and had given a positive witness of the faith of these Thessalonians.

This evidence suggests that there was a long enough time for Paul to have planted the ecclesia in Corinth, and then for him to have traveled beyond Achaia, for word to spread, and for Paul to have heard reports of the success and work of the ecclesia in Thessalonica. This evidence suggests a period of years rather than of months.

Paul's words

4:13 I do not want you not to know, brothers,
   about those who are sleeping,
   so that you do not grieve like others who do not have hope.

Historical analysis

The death of some of the members of the ecclesia is a second indication of the passage of time. Paul said in 4:13 that he did not want them to be ignorant about those who sleep ("sleep" here is a euphemism for death). Based on just these few words, Paul might have been referring to friends or relatives or even parents of these Thessalonians. Later in the same passage, however, Paul said that when Christ steps down from the clouds in the sky, the dead will be raised first, and then, second, we the living will also be snatched up to join the Lord in the air. In this way Paul asserted that both the dead and the living will participate in the *parousia* of the Lord. The general public, however, the friends, co-workers, relatives and even parents, were not expected to participate in the *parousia*; only the members of the ecclesia expected to do that. Therefore, when he spoke of "those who have fallen asleep," Paul meant members of the ecclesia who had died. Therefore, enough time had passed for some members of the ecclesia to have died.[84]

---

84. Luedemann, *Apostle*, 238, makes quite a point of the difference in timing between 1 Thess 4:13 and 1 Cor 15:51. We do not have a sense in First Thessalonians how many members had died; it might have been only a few. But the sense of "We shall not all die" (1 Cor 15:51) may

If only a few members had died, that would have been enough for the community to grieve, and—perhaps more to the point—that would have been enough for the community to become concerned about how those deceased members would be able to participate in the *parousia*. If Paul originally preached the kerygma that Christ's *parousia* would happen in the lifetime of his converts, that only the living would participate in the *parousia*, this concern that some had died was legitimate.

How long would it take for some to have died? It might help if we had some guesses about the age and health of the group. Paul might have been a teenage student when Jesus was crucified; that would put him in his mid- to late-twenties when he planted the ecclesia of the Thessalonians. If he attracted converts his own age, as clergy often do, they might have been in good health. If the original members of the ecclesia were young and healthy, it is possible for a good number of years to pass before some members died. Of course in a small group of healthy people, "some," being a small number, might die at any time.

If mortality rates can be found for Thessalonica in the mid-First Century, then a mathematician could give us some statistics. Statistics, however, do not always reflect the situation of a given population. Even with good general data, science still could not predict the mortality of individuals or of a specific population.

It is easy to imagine that within eighteen months, some might have died. It is even possible that some might have died within an even shorter period. Likewise, at the other end of the scale, it becomes hard to imagine that the ecclesia would not have experienced any deaths after seven years. It is possible for a small, healthy group to survive a period of seven or more years without any deaths; but it seems less likely and harder to imagine. Some time had elapsed. The length of time could be anywhere from eighteen months to seven years.

Paul's words

2:17 We, then, dear ones, being separated from you
        for a long enough time,
        physically, not emotionally,

---

suggest that a majority of the original members had died; thus the letter to Corinthians may come from a time eight to ten years later than First Thessalonians.

became exceedingly eager to see you in person,
with a great desire.

¹⁸ So that we wanted to come to you,
I, myself, Paul, not once or twice,
but the satan hindered us.

¹⁹ For who is our hope or grace or wreath to boast of–
except you–before our Lord Jesus when he arrives?

²⁰ You are our glory and grace.

Historical analysis

Paul said that he had wanted to come to them several times but had been prevented. His manner of expression suggests a significant period of time. Further, he expressed himself as yearning to see them. That kind of lonely yearning seems more likely if it had been a protracted absence. It was more likely a period counted in years rather than months. If it had been years, then Paul's expression that he had wanted to return to Thessalonica several times and been prevented makes sense. Both the expression of his yearning to see them and his expression of frustration at being prevented seem more appropriate if it had been a period of several years.

Of course, there is no accounting for the strange ways people express themselves. Paul might have said exactly this even if it had only been a few months. The shorter period of time, however, seems less likely.

Paul said, in 2:17, that he has felt separated from them *pros kairon hôras* ("long enough").[85] The words I am translating "long enough" do not translate easily. *Kairos*, however, has the sense of a "right" time or a "fullness" of time, as in things that happen when it is the right time for them to happen. *Kairos* is the opportune moment. For Paul to say that he has not seen these Thessalonians for an opportune moment seems to suggest that he feels it is high time for him to see them again. I, for one, would feel this way about wanting to see a congregation after a year or more.

We have to take this expression, *pros kairon hôras*, in the context of what Paul is saying: he said that he wanted to see them but that he had been pre-

---

85. Distorted by the attempt to conform to the chronology of Acts, and affected by *oligon kairon* of Rev. 12:12, this phrase has been understood as a short time. But the context argues for a long time, since Paul is speaking of his yearning to see them. A short time neither accounts for the expression nor for the context.

vented from coming to see them, more than two times. This has the sound of
a period of eighteen months or more and quite possibly up to seven years or
longer. In this context it certainly does not make sense to translate *pros kairon
hôras* as referring to a short period of time.

Paul's final words in this segment, his statement that these Thessalonians
are the success that he will boast of when the Lord Jesus arrives, can be made
to make sense in any time frame; Paul could be saying how much these Thessalonians mean to him even if he had seen them only a few months ago.
There could even be some indication that, because of his departure and absence from them, they were uncertain of how he felt about them. However,
these words fit better into the context of a longer absence. If it has been a
relatively long time, then it makes sense for Paul to express what they mean
to him. They responded to his preaching and recognized it as what it is, the
word of God; they are thus his great success, perhaps his first success in Europe. His expression of pride in them makes the most sense if it has been a
fair length of time since he has seen them.

In 3:3-4, which we have already discussed, Paul said that he had already
told them that they were likely to experience difficulties, as already discussed.
He told them, during the original visit, that enduring difficulties was an even-
tuality Christians ought to expect. Both the "how we lie" expression and the
verb *mellomen*, ("we are going to"), suggest a long term perspective.

Paul's words

9   Now concerning brotherly love,
     you do not need us to write you,
     for you are God-taught to love one another,
10   For you are doing this towards all the dear ones
     in all of Macedonia. We encourage you, dear ones,
     to excel even more.
11   Be ambitious to live quietly,
     to tend to your own business,
     and to work with your hands,
     just as we commanded you,
12   in order that you should walk worthily of respect from outsiders,
     and not depend upon others.

Historical analysis

When in 4:11-12 Paul advised his hearers to try to live quietly, not attract attention, and mind their own business, the reason for such behavior, he said, was to make a good impression on outsiders. *Euschêmonôs* ("with a good reputation") has the connotations of honorable and respectable behavior, which would make a good impression on others. The concern for making a good impression on others is a concern of a mature community.

This point is difficult to evaluate, for Paul could have been giving such advice to a community that was only a few months old. If, however, he had been giving such advice to a young community, such advice would have come out of his experience with other communities. In that case, the communication would have been something that Paul knew, but which they, caught up in the excitement of their recent conversion, did not know. This expression, instead, functions as a reminder of what they both know. It is a mutual conversation, rather than a directional communication. It is consistent with a mutual conversation that Paul said they were *theodidaktoi* ("God-taught"). He further said that there was no need to write them on this subject, suggesting that this admonition was something already familiar to them. So therefore Paul's words about living in a way that will make a good impression on outsiders were a familiar expression.

Furthermore, it seems that the concern for the good opinion of outsiders does not pertain to a very young organization as much as to a mature community. A young organization is more likely to be caught up in its own events than concerned about the opinion of outsiders. This argues for there having been several years between the establishment of the community and the writing of this letter.

Paul's words

> ^{5:12} We make this request of you, dear ones,
>> to hold your leaders in respect,
>> those who are standing up in front of you
>> and admonishing you in the lord
> ¹³ and to think of them so much more in love because of their work.
>> Be at peace among yourselves.
> ¹⁴ We encourage you, beloved, to admonish the unruly,
>> give cheer to the faint of heart,

> be patient with the weak,
>
> think the best of everyone.
>
> [15] See that no one gives back evil for evil,
>
> but in everything pursue the good towards each other and
> towards all.

Historical analysis

Likewise, Paul's closing words seem to be addressed to a mature community. The instructions that he gave are well balanced and mature. They
sound like reminders of what his hearers already know and practice. They do
not deal with the issues of imbalance that are typical of young and adolescent
communities.

When Paul spoke of their conversion in 1:4-10 and 2:13, his manner of
speaking, as already observed, has the flavor that he was speaking of an event
more than a year prior. Paul's description of their conversion is concise, rather
than highly emotional. Therefore, its style is consistent with the lapse of a
relatively long period of time between the founding of the ecclesia and the
writing of the letter.

Paul's concern expressed in 4:10-12 that they work with their hands and
behave in a manner that will win them respect is consistent with their being a mature community. His admonitions expressed in 5:12-15 pertain to
a mature community in the same manner. His rehearsal of their conversion
in 1:3-10 and 2:13 is likewise consistent with a lapse of time since it happened. Combining these observations with the time required for Paul to have
traveled beyond Achaia and for word of the faith of this ecclesia to have
spread beyond Achaia, with Paul's frustrated expression that it has been long
enough, and with the time needed for some of the members of the ecclesia
to have died makes a strong case for an expanse of time. The weight of all
of these factors together gives us an impression that it had been some years
rather than a few months. If there were some factors indicating a long period
and some indicating a short period, the evidence would be less clear. But
when this many factors point in the same direction, for a longer period of
time, the evidence is much more clear.

The sequence of historical events.

Having looked at these five groups of passages, we can now set the events alluded to in First Thessalonians into the sequence in which they occurred.

1. Paul may have been driven out of Asia by religious critics.
2. Speaking in tongues may have been experienced as a gift of the holy spirit and evidence that the receivers were qualified to be members of the ecclesia.
3. There was a network of communication between congregations, across provincial and continental boundaries.
4. From an undetermined beginning, some Jews—including Paul—abused the ecclesiae in Judaea.
5. From an undetermined beginning, some Jews hindered Paul from preaching to non-Jews.
6. Paul was abused and treated outrageously in Philippi.
7. Paul preached in Thessalonica
   a. Some Thessalonians responded with power, holy spirit, and much conviction.
   b. He established an all-gentile congregation.
   c. At this time, Paul resented those Jews in Judea who opposed him.
   d. This prejudice was intelligible and shared.
8. Paul went on to Achaia and beyond Achaia.
9. Some event in Judaea anticipated the wrath of the end time.
10. Some members of the ecclesia of the Thessalonians died.
11. Immediately before Paul wrote First Thessalonians, new trouble in Thessalonica gave Paul anxiety about the existence of the ecclesia.
12. Paul was in Athens when he learned of this trouble in Thessalonica.
13. Paul sent Timothy on an investigatory mission.
14. Upon Timothy's return, Paul wrote to them to rejoice. He wrote to express his joy, but he also wrote for some other reasons, which are not yet apparent.
15. Some indefinite time after the writing of the letter, Jesus' followers began to refer to him as "Son of Man."

In order to bring out the other reasons, those which are not yet apparent, for Paul to have written this letter, we turn now to the detailed analysis of how the segments of the letter function together.

PART III

NEW ISSUES

CHAPTER 1

THE FUNCTIONS
OF THE SEGMENTS

PART II explored topics that were mentioned as asides rather than as direct presentations. Part III looks at topics that are presented more directly, the topics which Paul wrote the letter in order to say. On which of those topics was it Paul's objective to convince his hearers, and on which topics did he prepare for resistance or opposition? In order to draw this conclusion, it will be necessary to look at each of the segments of the letter and draw conclusions as to how they fit together. The way the parts fit together will also shed some light on whether the message was urgent. Part III, chapter 1, then, explores the relationships of the segments, and chapter 2 will give detailed discussion of the points on which Paul needed to be convincing.

First Thessalonians is a letter. As a letter that was part of ancient culture, it is one side of a conversation, in this case a conversation between friends who were very dear to one another. Immediately, the character of this letter is distinct from Paul's letter to the Romans, because Paul and the members of the ecclesia in Rome had never met, and from Paul's first letter to the Corinthians, because that letter appears to some readers to be in the middle of a disagreement. As a letter that was part of a culture very different from ours, First Thessalonians has a context of societal events and personal events that both the writer and the recipients knew, but at which we can only guess.

Some letters, however, have more of an agenda behind them than others. Therefore, our question is, did Paul have an agenda for writing First Thessalonians? If he did, what was it? Was it his agenda to commend certain behaviors and answer some questions? Or was there something of which he needed to convince them?

First Thessalonians has three levels of organization. The most obvious and least controversial is that there is an Introduction (in which six coherent segments, including the salutation, form a section, from 1:1 to 3:13), the Ethical Instruction (in which four coherent segments form a section, from 4:1 to 5:11), and a closing from 5:12 to 5:28.[86] The second level of organization is that the letter takes up topics of faith and its consequences in 1:3 to 2:16, then topics concerning love in 2:17 to 4:12, and then topics concerning hope in 4:13 to 5:11[87] (See the discussion in Part II, chapter 1). The third level of organization is that the Introduction prepares for the points that are to be made in the Ethical Instruction and that in the Ethical Instruction, Paul presents two potentially controversial arguments and uses two other statements to distract his hearers from the potentials for controversy, so that the letter skillfully presents the two potentially controversial points.[88]

We will consider the six coherent segments in the first part of the letter individually and then the section as a whole. Then we will examine the four coherent segments in the second part of the letter and then that section as a whole. Next we will look at the letter's closing. Finally, we will be able to reflect on the letter as a whole. This will lead us to a conclusion regarding the two controversial points, and how the rest of the letter presents them.

The six parts of the Introduction

The six coherent pieces in the Introduction are: the salutation, the Thanksgiving, the recapitulation, the statement of the background and the digression, the continuation of the background, and a transitional prayer.

1. The salutation

---

86. Hurd, *Earlier Letters*, Chapter III, "Concerning the Structure of 1 Thessalonians," especially 50-52.

87. Hurd's comment in "Concerning the Structure of 1 Thessalonians," 82-83, on the organization of First Thessalonians around love, faith, and hope was a suggestive starting point for my analysis of the three-fold structure of the letter. My analysis of how the constituent segments fit this three-fold structure differs respectfully from his.

88. Although Malherbe, *Letters, passim,* recognizes that chapters 1-3 are preparation for 4:1 to 5:11, he treats the four segments of the latter section as all of equal importance.
Robert Jewett's analysis in *The Thessalonian Correspondence: Pauline Rhetoric and Millenarian Piety* (Philadelphia: Fortress Press, 1986), is quite different, as he sees the first half as a letter of praise and the second half as five "proofs" or examples, all of which are of equal value.

The salutation is 1:1.

Paul's words

1   Paul and Silvanus and Timothy:
      to the Thessalonians' ecclesia
      in God the Father and in the Lord Jesus Christ:
      grace to you and peace.

Rhetorical analysis

On the surface, this salutation identifies the persons who are sending the letter and the persons to whom the letter is addressed, as is typical of personal letters written during the centuries closest to the time of Christ. Paul's salutations often vary the standard form by adding descriptive words, such as identifying Paul as an apostle or as a servant of Christ Jesus; this salutation does not add any description of Paul or his team. Likewise, it does not include any description of its intended recipients.

2. The Thanksgiving

The coherent piece in 1:2-10 is usually referred to as the Thanksgiving.

Paul's words

2   We give thanks to God always, concerning you all,
      remembering you in our prayers without fail,
3   remembering your work of faith
      and your labor of love
      and your steadfastness of hope
      before our Lord Jesus Christ in the presence of God our Father,
4   knowing, dear ones, that you are loved by God who chose you,
5   because our preaching the gospel did not come to you as
      mere words
      but in power and in holy spirit, and in great conviction,
      as you know what happened among you because of us.
6   And you have become imitators of us and of the Lord,
      receiving the word in much conflict
      with the grace of holy spirit,
7   with the result that you have become an example to all the believers
      in Macedonia and as far as Achaia.

⁸   The word of the Lord has gone out from you
        not only in Macedonia and in Achaia,
        but in every place, your faith in God has been announced
        so much that there is no need for us to tell others about you.
⁹   For others announce what sort of entrance we had among you
        and how you turned towards God away from idols
        to serve a living and true God,
¹⁰   and to await his son from the heavens,
        whom he raised from corpses,
        Jesus, who is rescuing us
        from the coming wrath.

Rhetorical analysis

This section of First Thessalonians is fairly typical of the passages that immediately follow the salutations in Paul's letters. The first sentence begins with a main verb *eucharistoumen* ("we give thanks"), develops the thought with several participial phrases, and concludes with a result clause. The main verb *eucharistoumen* is the exact word Paul used in most of his authentic letters and is the reason why this passage has been classified as the "Thanksgiving."[89] The participles "remembering,"[90] "remembering" and "knowing" introduce the three phrases of this first sentence.

In association with the first "remembering," Paul said, "without fail." He had just previously said "always" in conjunction with the "we give thanks." So "always" and "without fail" seem redundant, but the effect probably was emphatic. This statement emphasizes Paul's commitment to the members of this ecclesia.

The second "remembering" moves directly to the subject of the letter. The phrase referring to their work of faith, their labor of love, and their steadfastness of hope announces the subject matter of the letter. The naming of these three virtues, faith, love, and hope is repeated near the end of the letter, in 5:8, forming a bracket around the substance of the letter. This use of the same words to begin and end a passage is known as an *inclusio*, because this

---

89. Paul Schubert, *Pauline Thanksgivings, passim*.

90. Paul used words that literally translate as "making a remembrance" for the first phrase, where the meaning is carried by the noun and the participle is a relatively neutral expression. The literal translation is awkward in English.

rhetorical device functions so as to include the material it brackets. From this *inclusio*, we know that the material between the brackets is the substance of the letter and that what precedes it and what follows it are an opening and a closing that do not contribute materially. The substance of the letter, then, lies between 1:2 and 5:8.[91]

The third participial phrase, beginning with "knowing," brings up the topic of Paul's preaching and their response. There is actually a succession of three points in this statement. (1) He offered them the gospel. (2) They responded by accepting the gospel and becoming an ecclesia. (3) There is something amazing and wonderful about this sequence of events. The Thanksgiving (1:2-10) makes these three points, the first two explicitly and the third by implication.

Paul remembered and knew these characters of their response. Although clearly he was talking about things that were as much their experience as his, here he stated it as something that he remembered. As the objects of the participles "remembering" and "knowing," these are things **he** knew and remembered.

By reminding the Thessalonians of their original response to the gospel, Paul here subtly encouraged them to continue to live in the same way. He has reminded them of their work of faith, their labor of love, and their steadfastness of hope. He has reminded them of the dynamism of their response, of the holiness of their spirit, and of their great conviction. He has reminded them of how they caused reports of their faith to spread throughout Macedonia and Achaia. He has recalled them to their turning to serve the living and true God, and he has recalled them to their patient awaiting the arrival of our Lord Jesus from heaven.[92] By reminding them of how they received the gospel, Paul commended to them that they continue to act in the same way, with the same spirit and power.

The essential statement of the Thanksgiving is that the ecclesia came into being, powerfully, in response to the preaching of the gospel. Therefore the

---

91. The three verses immediately following 5:8 are included because 5:10 wraps the previous two passages together, and 5:11 offers a final instruction to encourage and build one another up.

92. Malherbe, *Letters*, 81-86: Malherbe's important insight that the entire letter is paraenesis is based on the identification of conventional expressions in Paul's letter with the conventions of paraenesis. However, the fact that the behaviors Paul discusses in the Thanksgiving are commendable does not exhaust their function in this letter.

ecclesia is a community of faith. Faith, then, is the response of becoming an ecclesia. Paul began the letter with a discussion of faith.

It is very difficult to distinguish whether Paul meant that faith was their response or whether he saw it as God's choice of them. The phrase translated "that you are loved by God who chose you" is ambiguous. The participle *eidotes* ("knowing") takes the object, *eklogê* ("election," "choice," "being picked out"), so that the phrase, as usually translated, says that Paul and his team knew their "election." Their "election" could, in theory, mean either that God had chosen them, or it could refer to a choice that they had made. The word *eklogê* comes immediately after the words "by God," so that people would tend to hear it as "by God chosen." Also, Paul used the word *eklogê* five other times; all of those uses refer to God's election of Israel, the chosen people.[93]

However, the context of *eklogê* points in the other direction. Here, it could also mean their choice of turning to God, their response of faith. In verse 5, he said the gospel did not come to them as mere words but in power and in holy spirit and in great conviction. In verses 6-8 he noted that they became imitators of Paul and of Jesus Christ, receiving his preaching in both conflict and grace, with the result that people in other places had heard of their story. Then in verses 9-10 Paul summarized this segment by saying that they turned from idols to serve a living and true God and to await his son from heaven.

Perhaps Paul did not clearly distinguish their choice and God's choice. Both readings amount to the same thing: their having become an ecclesia of Jesus, a community of faith, and God's choice of them amount to the same reality viewed from different perspectives.

3. The recapitulation

The section, 2:1-13, is often thought of as an Apology, by which the ancients meant the sort of speech people might make to defend themselves in a court trial. However, in its most general statement, it is a recapitulation

---

93. Richard, *Thessalonians*, 63, says that Paul's four other uses of *eklogê* are all in Romans 9-11, where they mean God's choice of Israel.

The phrase is *eklogên autôn*. To my knowledge, commentators take the genitive of *autôn* as an objective genitive, so that the "election of them" means that God chose them, rather than as a subjective genitive, which would mean their choice of the gospel from among the competing alternative religions. This latter reading would fit well with the rest of Paul's sentence.

of the Thanksgiving.

Paul's words

1   For you yourselves recall, dear ones,
      our entrance on your scene,
      that it did not happen in vain,
2   but having previously been badly treated
      and insulted in Philippi
      as you know,
      we found courage in our God
      to speak to you the gospel of God,
      in a great contest.
3   For our proclamation came
      neither to deceive or trick or manipulate,
4   but just as we have been entrusted
      by God to preach,
      just so we speak,[94] not pleasing humans
      but God who discerns our hearts.
5   We never spoke in flattering words, as you know,
      nor as a pretext for greed, God is my witness,
6   and we were not seeking to impress people,
      neither you nor others.
7   Although we were entitled to use our authority
      as apostles of Christ,
      we were gentle among you
      as a nursing woman nourishes her own children.
8   Yearning, we choose[95] to give you not only God's good news
      but our own selves, so dear had you become to us.
9   Of course you remember, dear ones, our toil and labor;

---

94. The verb is present tense in Greek, so I have translated it as a present tense, even though the present tense of "we speak" is strange in English. The phrase "we have been entrusted," being perfect passive indicative, gives a temporal context to this phrase, suggesting that we have been entrusted, beginning some time in the past, because we spoke in a way that pleased God then, and we speak in the same fashion now.

95. Likewise, the present tense of "we choose" is surprising. We might expect that when he was with them originally Paul chose to give them himself as well as the gospel, but what he actually says this that he is continuing to give himself in the present.

working night and day so as not to be a burden on any of you
we announced to you the Gospel of God.

¹⁰   You and God are witnesses
how blameless, righteous, and pleasing to God we were
with you the believers,

¹¹   just as you know, we were to each one of you
like a father to his own children,

¹²   encouraging you and cajoling you and giving you an example
how to walk worthily of God
who is calling you to his kingdom and glory.

¹³   And for this reason it is especially important for us in particular
to give thanks to God
that, taking possession of our preaching about God,
you received it not as a human word
but as what it really is, the word of God,
who is at work in you, the believers.

Rhetorical analysis

This passage recapitulates the Thanksgiving, in that it makes, in its essence, the same three statements: Paul preached; they responded; there is something surprising and awe-inspiring about that sequence of events.

The recapitulation has a different emphasis than the Thanksgiving has: in the previous passage, Paul fleshed out the description of their response. In this section, he fleshed out the description of how he preached.[96] The two sections also have different points of view. In the Thanksgiving, he remembered their response, as the three participles "remembering," "remembering" and "knowing" in 1:2, 1:3 and 1:4 attest. In the recapitulation they knew the character of his ministry, as the phrases "you yourselves recall" in 2:1, "as you know" in 2:2 and 2:5, "of course you remember" in 2:9, "you and God are witnesses" in 2:10, and "just as you know" in 2:11 indicate. Between these two coherent pieces, Paul remembered their response and they knew the character of his ministry.

This shift of perspective makes an interesting chiastic structure, saying that he remembered something about them and that they knew something

---

96. Malherbe, *Letters*, 134, notes that the perspective changes from the letter's recipients to the writer, and says this change is frequently overlooked.

about him. Such chiasmus is typical of Paul's writing, but it also underscores the parallel and continuity of the two sections.

In this passage, Paul explicated the character of his ministry with them. First, in verse 2 he told the story of his escape from Philippi and contrasted that experience with his finding the courage to preach the gospel in Thessalonica. Second, in verse 3 he said that he offered the gospel without trickery or deceit or manipulation. Third, in verse 4 he put God's trusting him to preach in the context that God looks on the heart, where one knows whether or not one is lying. Paul said he had spoken in a manner solely intended to please God. This context means that Paul must have been speaking without duplicity; he must have been telling the truth as he knew it. This is an emotional truth telling, which has a different character of truth than intellectual truth, meaning statements that can be proved intellectually. Nor is it "speaking from the heart" as speaking with an emotional energy; it is a speaking out of his self-knowledge. This third point, then, is similar to the second point: speaking from the heart, as God knows his inner, personal truth, he spoke without deceit, in the manner that pleases God. Fourth, in verse 5 he said that he spoke in words that told the truth, not in the hope of flattering people or gaining their approval or their financial support. Fifth, in verses 7-9 he set his preaching in the context of the support that he was entitled to as an apostle; he could have relied on their support and been a "heavy" burden to them, but instead he was gentle as a nursing mother would be to her own children.

In Roman society women who served as wet-nurses for infants were known for their tenderness. It was a sufficiently commendable thing for them to be gentle and loving in their care of the children placed in their charge. However, Paul extended the metaphor by adding in verse 7 that he was "gentle with them as a nursing mother nourishes her own children." Identifying the children as her own makes the gentleness of the care go beyond what would be the wet-nurse's professional standard. Here Paul has claimed not only that his ministry went beyond the professional standard, but that they knew it did.

Just as in verse 7 Paul said that his care for them went beyond the standard for wet-nurses, in verse 8 he indicated that he went beyond the professional standard for evangelists. It would have satisfied those standards for Paul only to have proclaimed the gospel, baptized them, and helped them organize themselves into an ecclesia. It would have satisfied those standards if he had been supported by their gifts (just as teachers were paid out of tuition). Far from being a burden to them, he labored night and day in order to provide the gospel to them, free of charge. Not only did he give them the gospel; he also gave them himself. While the lack of duplicity in the first through the fourth points of this passage amounts to a gift of himself, Paul's clear statement that he gave freely of himself recapitulates the same point: he and the apostolic team chose to give them their own selves in an expression of affection and love. Paul went beyond the standard by giving them his heart. Nor was the giving of his heart something that just happened. Paul chose to give them his heart, and that is the act that went beyond professional standards. Not only did Paul give them his heart; they knew he did. The choice to give them his heart is something of which they were fully aware.[97]

Sixth, in verse 10 making the claim to having been blameless, righteous, and pleasing to God in his encounter with them, Paul brought the passage to a climax in a triplet of participles: encouraging them, cajoling them, and giving them an example of how to walk worthily of God. *Parakalountes* ("encouraging") and *paramythoumenoi* ("encouraging" or "cajoling") are very close in meaning. They both could be rendered in English as "encouraging." It could be that Paul used the second word to underscore the meaning of the first word; there is just enough difference in meaning between the two words to suggest that Paul meant to broaden the sense as well as to underscore it. The third word in the parallel series, *martyromenoi* ("witnessing" or "giving an example"), however, is a different thought. The Greek word *martyr* meant a witness at a trial; it was close in meaning to "telling the truth." Here the word suggests that "we gave you ourselves as a witness."

Then, in a statement that is remarkably parallel to the main verb of the Thanksgiving, Paul stated the amazing result of his preaching: They received his preaching about God as what it really was, the word of God. The passage as a whole, then, says Paul preached, they responded, and that is remarkable. This passage 2:1-13 says the same thing as 1:3-10, with the emphasis shifted from the character of their response to the character of the apostolic team's preaching.

---

97. Richard, Thessalonians, 101. Although Richard is aware of the way in which Paul strengthened these two statements, he does not mention that they were fully aware that Paul's ministry went beyond professional standards. Their knowledge constitutes the claim on them that Paul is making in preparation for the later parts of the letter.

Verse 2:13 is the final verse of this passage.[98] There are several subtleties about this verse. Verse 2:13 begins *kai dia touto kai hêmeis eucharistoumen*. The first *kai* is a simple conjunction, usually translated "and." The words *dia touto* mean "for this reason" and refer back to the entire preceding passage, 2:1-12. The second *kai* intensifies the following word, *hêmeis,* which is the "we" pronoun. Since the verb *eucharistoumen* has a first person plural inflection, the pronoun is not necessary. What the intensive *kai* and the pronoun do is to make the phrase very emphatic: "And for this reason it is especially important for us in particular to give thanks . . ." Being emphatic in this way, this clause appears to resume the Thanksgiving and intensify it.[99]

Verse 13 repeats the *eucharistoumen* of the Thanksgiving. This repetition could be heard as the beginning of a Thanksgiving for a separate letter, but it is not. It is rather an *inclusio*, indicating that the Thanksgiving and the recapitulation are a single section, expressing the same subject from two different points of view.

The two passages develop the *eucharistoumen* in different ways. The Thanksgiving describes the manner of their response, but the essential element is their response to the gospel. The recapitulation expresses the manner in which the apostolic team presented the gospel, but the essential element is their response to the gospel.

Faith is illuminated by the single and open-heartedness of the apostolic team. This coherent segment, then, has continued the discussion of faith.

The marvelousness of their response would make more sense if Paul had done a poor job of presenting the gospel. We would understand the miracle if Paul had said, I preached but I did a terrible and inadequate job; nevertheless, you responded and recognized the gospel for what it really is, the word

---

98. There is scholarly disagreement: most scholars assign 2:13 to a new subsection. For a survey, see Hurd, *Earlier Letters*, Chapter 3, *passim*. Also, see Jewett, *Thessalonian Correspondence*, 72-76 for another analysis.

99. Verse 2:13 has been challenged as an interpolation because it so precisely repeats verse 1:2. With that repetition, First Thessalonians has two statements of Paul's Thanksgiving. The only other New Testament letter with two Thanksgivings is Second Thessalonians, which (1) is usually thought not to be authentic and (2) there is a different reason why Second Thessalonians has two such sentences. What stands out in 2:13, however, is the additional *kai*. When *kai* does not function as a coordinating conjunction, it marks the following word as unusually important. In this case, it marks the "we" and is here rendered as "for us in particular." This emphasis is the key that the verse has a unique function within the structure of the Thanksgiving and the recapitulation: it identifies 2:1-13 as a section that recapitulates the Thanksgiving.

of God. In that case, their response of faith would be a recognizable miracle. Instead, Paul appears to say how perfectly he ministered to them.

Scholars have proposed four reasons why Paul wrote this section. The first proposal is that Paul's statement is a conventional form of paraenesis.[100] While Paul's discussion in 2:1-12 of his behavior may seem self-centered and self-laudatory, it was customary for ancient letter writers to point to their own behavior as a way of commending it to their addressees.

However, if this passage is paraenesis, the advice he offers is extremely elementary. If the nascent religion of Paul's kerygma was a religion of the heart (see Part II, chapter 1), then all of the promotion of sincerity in 2:3-8, where he said he did not preach using tricks or flattery, or out of greed, or out of any desire to please people rather than God, is the matter for the first round of preaching. Surely they would already have heard it! If love for one another already abounded between them (1 Thess 4:9-10), they did not need this elementary lecture. If he had said instead that they were such slow learners that he could only give them milk and not meat and that he had to be as gentle with them as a nurse, then such elementary instruction might be appropriate. Indeed, he does say that he was gentle with them as a nursing mother, but without the put-down. Lacking the put-down, why was he so elementary? We need to find some other reason for Paul to have rehearsed such elementary material as this.

A second explanation is that he had been accused of doing exactly the opposite of what he claims here.[101] If Paul were defending himself against an accusation of being a greedy charlatan, this passage would be an *apologia*. Something in the tone of this passage has led commentators to think of it as a defense, as if Paul here defended himself against specific accusations that had been made against him. However, there is nothing else in this letter that indicates that Paul was being accused of being self-serving in his preaching.

A third explanation is that Paul's claim to have taught without deceit or manipulation was a claim frequently stated by teachers. Teachers of philosophy found it good marketing to distinguish themselves from mountebanks.

---

100. Malherbe, *Letters*, 155, 157, but see also 163; While this material is paraenetic, it has a genuine root in the gospel.

101. Richard, *Thessalonians*, 87-90.
Donfried, "Thessalonian Cults," goes further, suggesting that during the difficulties *(thlipseis)* which the ecclesia experienced, they felt that Paul had mistreated and abandoned them.

They displayed their ability to argue impressively and eloquently in order to attract paying students. In these verses, Paul presented himself as an "ideal philosopher."[102] In Paul's time, philosophy was the study of how to live, so that Paul's presentation of the gospel was a competitor in the same market place as contemporary philosophies. Paul's saying in verse 2 that he spoke *en pollôi agôni* ("in a great contest") may indicate that he thought of his presentation of the gospel as a contest, with other "philosophies," for the hearts and minds of his hearers;[103] they had choices between the gospel and other philosophies, and it mattered greatly which they chose. Therefore it is quite credible that Paul, in some degree, thought of the gospel as a philosophy and spoke of his efforts in terms that would draw on philosophical traditions. Thus, for Paul to distinguish himself from his competitors makes sense.[104]

It was appropriate for Paul to make the argument that he was not a charlatan when he originally preached the gospel. It is quite believable that he marketed himself and the fellowship of Jesus in the same manner as other teachers of philosophy. Paul wrote this letter, however, some years after his first preaching in Thessalonica, and that presentation of himself and his material no longer has the same appropriateness. In order for us to conclude that the nature of this material is the marketing of a philosopher-teacher we would need to find a reason why Paul would talk about those marketing concerns at the time he wrote the letter. Therefore, this third explanation is not satisfactory either.

The fourth explanation is that Paul was explicating his role as founder of the ecclesia as part of a preparation for what he would ask of them later in the letter. The suggestion here is that in order to buttress what he will ask later, Paul chose to remind them of his relationship to them, stressing the endearing character of the role he played in presenting the gospel to them. What Paul says in this section, however, goes beyond reminding them of their relationship. What Paul asserts about the nature of his ministry is related precisely to his being their founder.

---

102. Malherbe, *Letters*, 80, compares the antitheses in 2:1-12 with descriptions of the ideal philosopher; 143, other teachers of philosophy distanced themselves from avaricious preachers, and Paul used the same contrasts here.

103. Richard, *Thessalonians*, 79, suggests that *en pollôi agôni* is the contest for the hearts and minds of the city folk.

104. Malherbe, *Letters*, 154, refers to Dibelius, who suggested that Paul needed to distinguish himself and his contribution from charlatans and theirs; the need to make this distinction places Paul solidly in the tradition of the philosophers.

When Paul said that he wanted to give them not only the gospel but himself, that is a statement that encapsulates the whole of the gospel. Just as an onomatopoetic word makes the sound that it names, this phrase does what it describes. The gospel frees us to love one another; this phrase expresses the love that the gospel makes possible. The statements of 2:3-12 express the essential character of the Jesus movement as a spiritual relationship that enables the followers of Jesus to live together without deceit, trickery or manipulation, etc. His actions, as he described them in this passage, matched his words and therefore contributed as a validation of his message and their response.

Paul made a point that they remembered and knew the manner of his presentation. He said "you yourselves recall" in verse 1, and "of course you remember" in verse 9. He called them to be witnesses in verse 10, and again said "just as you know" in verse 11. Not only did Paul make a statement of the manner of his proclamation; beyond making the claim, he stated that they knew this character. Indeed the fact that they responded to his preaching is probably evidence of their knowledge of this character. If they had evaluated Paul's ministry differently, they would probably not have become an ecclesia.

At the time when he wrote the letter, this passage functioned as a reminder of his sincere character and strengthened their relationship. This reminder that he was their founder set them up to respond positively to what he will ask. Thus it appears that in this passage Paul was preparing to make some request of them. The strength of this passage, its rather extreme statement, is an extraordinary preparation. We shall find that it is a preparation for an extraordinary request.

4. The statement of the background of the letter and a digression

Paul stated the background[105] to the letter in 2:14, but he interrupted himself in 2:15-16.

Paul's words

¹⁴   For you have become imitators, dear ones,

---

105. By "background" I mean Paul's discussion of the precipitating events. It would be confusing to use the rhetorical term *narratio* because the *narratio* pertains more to courtroom speeches than to deliberative rhetoric. Paul has discussed events in the past in 1:2-10 and in 2:1-13, but those have the purpose of predisposing his audience to his message; the "background" in 2:14 and 3:1-10 states the events that precipitated the writing of the letter.

of the ecclesiae of God which are in Judea in Christ Jesus
in that you have endured the same thing as they,
you at the hands of your own countrymen,
just as they from the Jews,
15 who killed the Lord Jesus and the prophets,
and chased us out, not pleasing God,
and opposing themselves to all people,
16 preventing us from preaching to save the gentiles,
as a way of filling up their sins.
The wrath of the end-time has already begun for them.

Rhetorical analysis

This brief section begins a discussion of recent events that precipitated the writing of this letter. Something had happened to the ecclesia of the Thessalonians. The word *epathete* ("experienced" or "endured") suggests something unpleasant. The most general word we could use is "difficulty." The ecclesia had **endured some difficulty**. Whatever the difficulty might be, it is the same difficulty that the ecclesiae in Judaea endured at the hands of Jews. Paul probably meant that the Judaean ecclesiae endured some opposition from some of their Jewish neighbors. Paul's words do not suggest any detail or nuance of this difficulty. We have to keep our concept as general as possible.

Whatever the ecclesia of the Thessalonians endured, it was at the hand of their *symphyletoi* ("fellow citizens," "countrymen"). As discussed above, *symphyletoi* are people with whom one votes; they are fellow-citizens.[106]

This segment has moved on from the discussion of faith to a discussion of the consequences of faith. In responding to the gospel and becoming an ecclesia, Paul's hearers have come to suffer some difficulties, difficulties that they have in common with other ecclesiae of Jesus. Because they share these difficulties with other ecclesiae, Paul was still discussing faith.

In these first three segments of the Introduction, Paul has devoted the first two segments to emotionally positive treatments of faith. Only then did he come to the emotionally less positive aspect of faith. He handled the easier approaches to the topic first; then he handled the more difficult aspect of the topic. He set up a positive context so that the treatment of the less appealing subject is made more palatable and acceptable.

---

106. See discussion on page 90f.

In introducing the consequences of faith, Paul not only brought up the subject of their difficulties; he also has set them in a context of being predictable troubles shared by others. The unusual use of *mimêtai* ("imitators") serves Paul in two ways. It introduces the major event that has prompted the letter, that is, whatever difficulty the ecclesia of the Thessalonians recently endured at the hands of their fellow citizens. Paul has used this word to begin the rehearsal of the facts of the case. Here the word *mimêtai* introduces the topic of the recent difficulty.

Second, Paul's use of the word suggests that their experience is the same as the experience of others. In effect he has told them that they have not suffered any worse than others have. In effect he has told them that the difficulty they have experienced is an ordinary consequence of their faith. He developed this thought in 3:3, saying that such difficulties are in the very nature of the Jesus movement, and in 3:4 saying that he had told them in advance that there would be difficulties of this sort. So for Paul to refer to these difficulties as an **imitation** of the ecclesiae of Jesus in Judaea links the experience of the Thessalonians to that of others. In other words, Paul has provided an answer to the problem in the same words he used to bring up the problem. Verse 14's use of the word *mimêtai* is an integral part of the letter.

In verses 15 and 16, Paul went off on a digression about those who caused difficulty for the ecclesia of Jesus and for him. They are both an emotional outburst and the spiritual low point of the letter (see Part I, chapter 2).

5. The continuation of the background

The statement of the background continues in 2:17-3:10.

Paul's words

¹⁷ We, then, dear ones, being separated from you
for a long enough time,
physically, not emotionally,
became exceedingly eager to see you in person,
with a great desire.
¹⁸ So that we wanted to come to you,
I, myself, Paul, not once or twice,
but the satan hindered us.
¹⁹ For who is our hope or grace or wreath to boast of—

except you—before our Lord Jesus in his arrival?

20   You are our glory and grace.

3:1   When we could bear it no longer, we chose
      to be left alone in Athens

2   and we sent Timothy, our dear brother
     and God's co-worker in the good news of Christ,
     to steady you and to encourage you in your faith

3   that you not be shaken in these current difficulties,
     for you know that we can expect troubles;

4   we kept on telling you so ahead of time, when we were with you,
     that we were going to have difficulties,
     just as has happened and as you know.

5   Because of this, being no longer able to bear it,
     I sent Timothy to learn of your faith,
     lest the tempter had tempted you
     and our work had been in vain.

6   Just now Timothy has returned from you to us
     and has announced to us your faith and your love
     and that you always have a good memory of us,
     wanting to see us just as we want to see you.

7   Because of this we are encouraged, dear ones,
     because of every effort and difficulty of ours on your behalf,
     to create your faith,[107]

8   that now we live, since you are steadfast in the faith.

9   What thanksgiving we are able to return to God concerning you!
     We rejoice before God because of you,

10   night and day praying exceedingly to see you in person
     and make up what is lacking in your faith.

---

107. Paul spoke of his *kopos* and *mochthos* which he performed in order to preach to them—and the corollary of their response of faith, in 2:9. Here *dia tês hymôn pisteôs* has the same meaning: the desired result of creating their faith. The *anangkê* and *thlipsis* are what he endured to create their faith. It echoes verse 3:4. His work has not been in vain. Reading *anangkê* and *thlipsis* as a reference to current suffering by Paul, reports of which might cause them concern, misconstrues *dia tês hymôn pisteôs* and reads a later passage back into this one.

Rhetorical analysis

In the previous segment, Paul began his statement of the events leading to this letter by saying that the ecclesia of the Thessalonians had endured some difficulty. He picked up the sequence of events in 3:5, saying that he sent Timothy to learn the status of their *pistis* ("belief," "faith," or "trust"), meaning whether or not the ecclesia still existed as a community. Paul's work would have been in vain if the ecclesia had ceased to exist.

In 3:3 he said he sent Timothy in order to steady them, so that they not be shaken *en thlipsesin tautais* ("in these difficulties," "in these troubles"). He managed both to express his extreme concern for the negative effect these troubles might have had on them and at the same time to dismiss those troubles, in 3b-4, as the ordinary experience of the followers of Jesus. It is a remarkable piece of writing. It parallels his use of *mimêtai* in 2:14 to connect their difficulties with the difficulties experienced by others.

When Timothy returned, he gave Paul a report of their continued existence, of their faith and love, of their good memory of him, and of their yearning to see him again. The ecclesia continued to exist, and it continued to exist properly, in its essence as a community of response to the gospel. This was a great relief to him. He said in verse 3:8 that, having received this good news of their well-being, he could live!

After his digression, Paul picked up the statement of the background in 2:17 with a statement of what it meant to him to be separated from them. Paul described his longing to see them (verse 17), using the word *aporphanisthentes* ("being separated"). Next he said he was frustrated in his attempts to come to them (verse 18). Then he said they were his source of pride, his *doxa* ("glory," "reputation") and *chara* ("grace," "joy") (verse 20). These statements describe his love for them.

Paul reiterated this theme of separation and longing by saying that he chose to be left alone in Athens. The sense of "being left alone" must refer to his sense of separation. He had just said that he had come to the point that he could stand it no longer. What he could stand no longer was the separation and worry about the Thessalonians. The decision in 3:1 to send Timothy echoes the expression in 2:17 of being *aporphanisthentes*. Verses 2:17 through 3:5 are one passage, and it is a very tight passage.

Timothy, when he returned, told Paul of their faith and love (3:6). Faith, here, refers both to the comprehensive meaning of their faith—their response to the gospel—and to that response's being one of the triad of virtues. In the rest of 3:6, Timothy's report continued to tell about their love: that they always had a good memory of Paul and longed to see him too. Paul's expression in verses 7-9 restates his love and pride in them.

Oddly, Timothy's report of their faith and love omits the third and last virtue: hope. Furthermore, in 3:10 Paul spoke of his prayer to see them in person so that he might supply what was lacking in their response to the gospel. In terms of the three virtues, the one that is missing is hope. It is a jump to suggest that when Paul referred to what was lacking in their faith, he meant the one virtue which was omitted from Timothy's report, but this juxtaposition, however, ought to make us alert to any message of hope which Paul presents as important to the fullness of their faith.

This background passage, then, has stated the events, that led Paul to write this letter. Some difficulty in Thessalonica caused him great concern and anxiety for the continued existence of his ecclesia, so he sent Timothy to investigate. When Timothy returned with the announcement that they were well and that they longed to see Paul as much as he longed to see them, Paul wrote this letter.

This coherent segment expresses Paul's love for his Thessalonian hearers and details the steps he took. In 2:17 Paul declared how much he wanted to see them. In 3:1-6 he told them how his sending Timothy was an act of love. Then in 3:7-10 he expressed how much Timothy's news meant to him. Therefore, it appears that he has begun his treatment of the second of the three virtues.

6. The Transitional Prayer

The verses in 3:11-13 are a prayer.

Paul's words

¹¹ God himself, our Father, and our Lord Jesus,
    guide our path towards you;
¹² the Lord fill and make you overflow
    with love for one another and for everyone,
    just as we love you,
¹³ in order to steady your hearts
    to be blameless in holiness

before God our Father

in the arrival of our Lord Jesus with all his saints.

Rhetorical analysis

Although the words of verses 11-13 are addressed to his Thessalonian hearers, the verbs *kateuthunai* ("guide"), *pleonasai* ("fill") and *perisseusai* ("make to overflow") are infinitives and identify this as a prayer of blessing. The three verse length, for a total of sixty-five words not counting the "amen" found in some ancient manuscripts, makes it a substantial blessing.

The prayer of blessing in 5:23, at the end of the letter, is very similar. They both have the words "blameless . . . in the arrival of our Lord Jesus." This one lacks the word "Christ," but it adds "in holiness before God our Father" and "with all his saints" at the end of the verse. This prayer, coming in the middle of the letter is actually the longer of the two.

It was customary for Paul to offer such a prayer as this at the end of his letters. Romans 16:25-27 is a prayer of only slightly longer length but of even greater complexity. The prayer in Romans is the longest and most complex of Paul's closing prayers. As Romans is Paul's longest and most polished work, a polished and complex final blessing seems appropriate. The two prayers in First Thessalonians 3:11-13 and 5:23-24 are the next longest and next most complex. There are similar blessing-prayers, all at the ends of letters, in 1 Cor 16:23, 2 Cor 13:13, Gal 6:18 and Phil 4:23, but they are all quite brief.

Formal analysis identifies this as a closing prayer. The appropriate conclusion from this analysis is that 1 Thess 3:11-13 is a closing **of some kind.** This conclusion could be used to argue that First Thessalonians was originally two letters, the first ending at 3:13. Contemporary scholars in general have not been convinced by arguments to divide First Thessalonians.[108]

This prayer asks specifically that God fill their hearts with love. The prayer also asks that they may be found blameless, without fault in the day of the arrival of the Lord Jesus. That second phrase, however, is a result clause.

---

108. François Vouga, "La première épître aux Thessaloniciens" in *Introduction au Nouveau Testament: son histoire, son écriture, sa théologie*, Édité par Daniel Marguerat, Troisième édition mise à jour, (Paris: Labor et fides, 2004), 247, says that Walter Schmithals divided 1 Thessalonians into two letters.
Earl Richard, *Thessalonians*, 11-19, also suggests a division into an earlier letter and a later letter. Malherbe, *Letters*, 79, refers to both Schmithals' and to Richards' partitioning of the letter and comments, saying that the partitions have not been well received by other scholars.

Their being found without fault will be the result of their overflowing with love. If they are filled with love, they will be blameless. In this coherent segment, Paul has continued the treatment of the second of three virtues.

Analysis of the Introduction as a whole

Now that we have considered the functions of each of the six passages in the Introduction of the letter, we can look at four explanations of this section as a whole. (1) In part it is autobiographical material. (2) All of it, in fact, holds up the right way to live and therefore is paraenesis. (3) It is exceptionally long for a Thanksgiving, yet it is a tightly organized section with a single theme. (4) It is also all preparation for the ethical instruction that Paul will give later on.

In addition, there are four peculiarities that run through chapters 1-3: (a) Why did Paul address them as the "ecclesia of the Thessalonians"? (b) Why did he speak of them as being "in God"? (c) Why did he speak of them as "believers"? and (d) Why does he so often say "as you know" and the like? These peculiarities reveal the function of this section as preparation for the next section.

1. Alternative explanations of this section

First, the string of denials in 2:3-6 has been taken as autobiographical. It has appeared to some scholars as if Paul had been accused of being a charlatan. However, that self-defensive mode characterizes only this small portion of chapters 1-3. It makes more sense to say that the whole section is autobiographical. The Thanksgiving describes Paul's presentation of the gospel along with a description of their response to it. The recapitulation presents Paul's contributions with the focus on Paul's ministry. The background continues the story of what Paul did when he learned of the difficulties that the ecclesia had experienced, namely, that he sent Timothy to investigate and received Timothy's good report. All of the parts of this Introduction include things that Paul did, and so it is appropriate to refer to the whole section as autobiographical.

However, as autobiographical material, it addresses only two periods of Paul's life. It refers to the time when Paul was founding the ecclesia. The text does not indicate how long a period of time that was; it was long enough to

found an ecclesia, but a small portion of Paul's life. It also covers the time
for Timothy's mission to investigate. We might suppose that such a mission
might take a few weeks. Therefore, the total amount of time addressed by
the letter is a rather small portion of Paul's life. Even though the material is
autobiographical, we would not call it a biography.

Second, recent scholars regard chapters 1-3 as paraenesis.[109] By mentioning his hearers' positive response to the gospel in chapter 1, Paul effectively
commended strong faith. By mentioning the sincerity of the apostolic team
in chapter 2, Paul effectively commended sincere living. By discussing his
concern and love for them in the two segments of the *background*, he commended loving concern. Paul further commended accountability by sending
Timothy to discover how they were. All of this section, then, is paraenesis.

Paraenesis typically used expressions which Paul used throughout this
section; using the convention, people might say, "you know," "as you know,"
and "just as you know." Reference to imitation of behavior was a paraenetic
convention. Contrasts, such as "not this, but that" were used as a paraenetic
convention, just as Paul offered several contrasts in 2:4-11. Pointing out that
the letter is a substitute for being there was a paraenetic convention. Paul used
all these features of classical paraenesis generously throughout chapters 1-3.[110]

The relationship between the letter writer and the intended recipient is
one of the important features of paraenesis. In First Thessalonians Paul built
on the warmth of their history with family language. He compared himself to
a nursing mother (2:7) and to a father (2:11), but even more significantly, he
called them *adelphoi* (literally "brothers," but here translated as "dear ones").
He called them *adelphoi* fourteen times in First Thessalonians, and six of
those are in chapters 1-3.[111] This is much more than he used this word in

109. Malherbe, *Letters*, 80, observes that paraenetic features are used throughout the letter and
give it a warm pastoral style.
Malherbe, *Letters*, 216, says that Chapters 4 and 5 are Paul's main purpose in writing. The
paraenetic cast of the autobiography in chapters 1-3 strengthens Paul's relationship with them in
preparation for the later section.

110. O. Larry Yarbrough, *Not Like the Gentiles: Marriage Rules in the Letters of Paul* (SBL
Dissertation Series: Atlanta, Georgia: Scholars Press 1985), 85, gives us a nice summary of
Abraham Malherbe's work on this issue.

111. In chapters 1-3, he calls them *adelphoi* in 1:4, 2:1, 9, 14, 17; and 3:7. In the four topics in
chapters 4-5, he calls them *adelphoi* in 4:1, 10, 13; 5:1, and 4. In the closing section he calls them
adelphoi in 5:12, 14, and 25. That is an approximately even distribution throughout the letter.

any other letter.[112] This focus on relationship was a paraenetic convention. It helps identify that this is a letter of advice. Beyond the conventional use, however, this prominence of *adelphoi* adds to the warmth of First Thessalonians and underscores the importance of Paul's relationship with his hearers. Paul and these Thessalonians belonged to each other as members of a family.

Many commentators present Paul as being dispassionate, as stating theological propositions in their intellectual purity. People today are predisposed to regard Paul's theological statements as true for the simple reason that they are in the Bible. It is a good perspective to realize that Paul had no idea that his words would become scripture. He was writing letters to his dear converts. It is good balance to recognize the level of affection that is being expressed and to realize that truth is not an emotionless proposition. Paul has let his emotions show. That openness is appropriate, considering that the essence of this developing religion is love for one another, not in an emotionless way, but in a way that is open emotionally.

This emotional openness makes chapters 1-3 effective paraenesis. People are likely to take advice, presented so gently through personal example, because it is given with so much love and vulnerability.

Third, in attempting to grapple with the singleness of chapters 1-3, some scholars have seen it as an extremely long Thanksgiving.[113] This reading would be making a Thanksgiving of three chapters; no other Thanksgiving is more than a few verses in length; most scholars consider that chapter 1 ends the Thanksgiving. That opinion gains weight from the reference to wrath at its end, because some of Paul's other Thanksgivings end with a reference to wrath. Nevertheless, as we have seen, the whole section exhibits a remarkable unity.

Words for thanksgiving unify these chapters. Both chapter 1 and chapter 2 include a *eucharistoumen* clause. Then Paul used the word *eucharistia* ("thanksgiving") in the resumed background section, to describe the prayers he was able to give God for their continued well-being and love. This repetition of the root word ties all of chapters 1-3 together.

---

112. Malherbe, *Letters*, 109, observes that Paul used *adelphos* much more frequently in 1 Thessalonians than elsewhere.

113. Schubert, *Pauline Thanksgivings*, 7, 17, 18-19, 22, and 25. On page 18, he says that 1:2—3:13 is a single section, unified by the repetitions of the root *eucharist-*, and that the apparent digressions are disguised elements of the pattern.

The benefits of this interpretation are that it exposes the unity of the section and it fits a historical occasion of the letter. It also highlights the emotional centering of the letter on the ecclesia's existence. Therefore, it is best to interpret chapters 1-3 as an exceptional—and single— section.

Fourth, chapters 1-3 are a most unusual preparation for what he has to say in chapters 4-5. The focus on the relationship between Paul and the ecclesia is not a focus on their relationship in general. In this section, Paul focuses narrowly on their response of faith as the event of their coming into existence as an ecclesia, and in particular on his role as their evangelist and founder.

2. Four peculiarities that focus on the existence of the ecclesia

Paul's address to the "ecclesia of the Thessalonians" contrasts with his other letters. The other authentic letters are addressed to the people **in a place**: "to the beloved of God in Rome" (Rom 1:7); "to the ecclesia of God which is in Corinth" (1 Cor 1:2 and 2 Cor 1:2); and "to the holy ones in Jesus Christ in Philippi" (Phil 1:1); and "to the churches of Galatia" (Gal 1:2). Rome, Corinth, and Philippi are all cities. Galatia is a region rather than a city, but like the cities, a region refers to a political identity in a geographical location. The two Thessalonian letters, distinctively, are addressed to people: the Thessalonians.

At first glance, this difference does not appear to mean anything. I have not seen any commentary on this distinction in any of the standard sources.[114] Being a much busier port city than Thessalonica, Corinth attracted immigrants, and it is probable that many of the members of the ecclesiae in Corinth were not citizens. Ancient Greek cities did not integrate foreigners into their citizenry. Immigrants continued to be guests.[115] The ecclesiae in Corinth may have included both Jews and Greeks; the Jewish members of the ecclesia would not have been citizens unless they were citizens who had previously converted to Judaism, so the ecclesiae in Corinth may have been made up of both citizens and immigrant-guests. If that were so, it would make sense for Paul to address them as the ecclesiae in a city. That manner of

114. Specifically, neither Richard nor Malherbe refer to it.

115. The Greek word *xenos*, which is often translated "stranger" or "foreigner," actually evokes a network of hospitality in which people reciprocally hosted guests from other cities. To be a *xenos* meant to be in a *xenos* relationship in which a household in one city hosted guests from another city and expected reciprocity.

speaking was a way for him to include both citizen and non-citizen members in his address. For Paul, however, to refer in this letter to his recipients as "the ecclesia of the Thessalonians" implies that he was thinking of them as citizens.

Paul's statement in 1:9 confirms this conclusion. He said, "you turned." Since he attributed this conversion to all of them, this statement has the force of indicating that this congregation was entirely made up of non-Jews, consistent with their being citizens.

The word *symphyletoi* in 2:14 is an unusual word for Paul. Paul's use of *symphyletoi* is consistent with his use of the **ecclesia of the Thessalonians** in 1:1 and with "you turned" in 1:9. This consistency strongly suggests that Paul had the same thought on his mind throughout the passage. Perhaps Paul kept coming back to the issue of their citizenship because the problem was caused by their fellow-citizens.

Paul's use of the prepositional phrase "in God the Father and in the Lord Jesus Christ" also contrasts with his words in other letters. In other letters, Paul used the genitive case to say, "of God:" "to all the beloved of God in Rome" (Rom 1:7), and "to the ecclesia of God which is in Corinth" (1 Cor 1:2 and 2 Cor 1:2).[116] So the use of the phrase "in God" in Thessalonians is different from other letters. The preposition *en* has the primary meaning that something is in a location. The prepositional phrase in the Thessalonian letters modifies ecclesia, so that the most straightforward reading would mean that the ecclesia is "in God." The preposition also often means "in accordance with," so that this usage could mean "by the will of God." In addition, *en* has an instrumental sense: the ecclesia exists through the instrumentality of God the Father and the Lord Jesus Christ.[117]

Why did Paul describe this ecclesia as existing because of God's decision and activity? He spoke this way because he was focused on their coming into existence as an ecclesia. The point of the Thanksgiving is that the ecclesia came into being, and the recapitulation makes the same point. It is most unusual for two adjacent segments in Paul's writing to make the same point.

In 2:1 Paul's statement that his entrance on their scene was not in vain refers to the creation of this ecclesia, and in 3:5 he speaks of the possibility

---

116. Galatians does not have an expression that is parallel to this usage. Philippians has an expression similar to that of First Thessalonians, saying "to the holy ones in Christ Jesus who are in Philippi."

117. Liddell and Scott, *Greek-English Lexicon*, 221a.

that the ecclesia had ceased to exist as making his work in vain. Therefore, the creation and continued existence of the ecclesia was a primary concern throughout this section of the letter.

Paul's use of the word "believers" in 1:7 foreshadowed a direction the church has followed. Since First Thessalonians is the oldest extant Christian document, this is the first documented use of this word to refer to the followers of Jesus. In English, the word "believers" normally connotes persons who give intellectual assent to doctrine, such as the propositions that there is a God who is the creator of the world, that Jesus is God's Son and our Lord and Christ. "Belief" is a matter of thinking that those statements are true. *Pisteuô*, however, also means trust. Trust is not simply a matter of what one believes. Trust is a matter of having confidence in another person. The word might be rendered as "those who trust," or "those who have confidence." "Faith" comes close to the meaning of *pistis*, because the English word can be used either for belief or for trust. In English, unfortunately, it generally means one or the other, rather than both at once, which, I suspect, is the way Paul meant it.

In 3:5 Paul said he sent Timothy in order to know their "faith." The word here is the same word, *pistis*. He finishes this verse saying, "lest . . . our work had been in vain." Paul's work would have been in vain if the ecclesia had ceased to exist; so therefore, what Paul wants to know and what he meant by *pistis* is the response of faith that has reality in the creation and continued existence of the ecclesia.

Paul used the same word *pistis* in his discussion of Timothy's report, in 3:6, but here by joining it with *agapê* he indicated that he referred to one of the three virtues. Surely, in 3:5, by *pistis* he meant the entire *gestalt* of the ecclesia's existence; but in 3:6 he not only is working on the theme of the love that dominates this portion of his outline but also is giving them and us a hint of the message of hope that he will get to in 4:13-18.

In 2:4 Paul said, "we have been entrusted by God to preach." The word translated here as "entrusted" has the same root as the word in 2:10 translated "believers." On the basis of that usage, we might think of *pistis* as a gift bestowed by God rather than as an attitude which believers have independently by themselves.

This section of the letter has focused on the ecclesia's coming into existence. The salutation opened this theme by addressing the "ecclesia of the Thessalonians" which was "in God." The Thanksgiving focused on their response of faith. The recapitulation focused on their response to the apostles' sincere preaching. Each segment, then, has revolved around the existence of the ecclesia.

Paul's use of phrases referring to their knowledge points us in another direction. Such phrases were a common feature of paraenesis.[118] Even so, Paul seems to have overused such phrases in this letter. He used *kathôs oidate* ("as you know"), in 1:5, in the Thanksgiving. In the recapitulation, he said *Autoi gar oidate* ("For you yourselves recall") in 2:1. In 2:2 and 2:5, he said *kathôs oidate* ("just as you know"). In 2:9, he said *mnêmoneuete* ("you remember"), in 2:10, he said *hymeis martyres* ("you are witnesses"), and in 2:11 he said *kathaper oidate* ("just as you know"). This is a heavy stress on their knowledge of the events and characters that Paul was describing.

In the continuation of his statement of the precipitating events, Paul does not use the expression "as you know;" however, he does indicate something he expects them to know, saying *proelegomen hymin* ("we were continuing to tell you"). If in fact they did not remember his having told them this ahead of time, this would be a dangerous thing to say, because it might set up a "No, I do not remember that" answer. From this point of view, Paul had to have been confident that they would remember that he had said this. This statement, then, has the same function as the "as you know" statements.

Each time Paul said "you know" or "as you know" or "just as you know" he has gotten a response in his hearers' minds. While we cannot rule out the possibility that they thought, "No, I do not remember that," or "I do not remember it that way," it seems more likely that they said silently in their own minds, "Yes, I do know that." Paul has used a salesman's technique to get his hearers to say "Yes" to a series of questions, so that he can lead up to the important sales question. The extraordinary frequency of this phrase prepares for a special request.

These frequent phrases reminding Paul's hearers of what they knew are clustered in the Introduction. In that sense, they are part of the preparation for the Ethical Instruction.

---

118. Malherbe, *Letters,* 84, includes "the familiar *oidate*" as a paraenetic element.
Donfried, Karl Paul. "Thessalonian Cults," 348, quotes Nils Dahl's reflections made to a Society of Biblical Literature Seminar in 1972 as referring to Paul's frequent use of *oidate* and the like as 'superfluous rehearsals and reminders.' On the contrary, as I show in the text, I find Paul's use of these statements to be quite purposeful.

It is a commonplace of salesmanship that greater preparation needs to be laid before the larger request can be made. If a person is asking only for spare change, the question can be asked immediately. However, if the request is to be for $20.00 or $500.00 or more, groundwork needs to be laid: a story needs to be told that will create points of identification and sympathy. This opening section has become long because it prepares for a big request.

It is also possible that because of the importance or stress of what Paul needs to say, Paul has simply delayed getting to that subject. When people are reluctant to get to the point, they delay. According to this interpretation he has put it off as long as possible because he is reluctant to get to the point. We need to consider that the extraordinary length of this initial section, particularly with its overwhelmingly positive assertions about the ministry of the apostolic team, represents delay.

This opening section has focused on the relationship between Paul and this ecclesia, and in particular on what he did for them in the past. His statement of all that he did for them has set them in a deficit position so that they owe him! They owe him obedience in regard to that which he is about to ask them. He does not say, "Obey me in this because of what I have done for you." He did not need to be so crass. The message is sufficiently transparent without his having to make it explicit. The focus on what Paul has done and given for them is a strong and compelling preparation.

If, then, we view chapters 1-3 as a unified preparation, we have a stronger position. It has not seemed reasonable to others in the past that this entire section was unified as an exceptionally long Thanksgiving. Yet the section has a clear unity. There is a single focus on the ecclesia's coming into existence and on the relationship between the ecclesia and Paul that spans this whole section. The section is unified by that relationship.[119]

The length itself of the preparation, its focus on their relationship and

---

119. Mark Matson has sugggested that this whole section is *êthos*, that is, building on the speaker's character; a speaker presents himself in a very positive light in order to foster positive feelings toward himself, and it is true that in the third segment, 2:1-12, Paul focused on the nobility of his actions. However, that section really focuses on the relationship between Paul and these Thessalonians, which is the same focus as the salutation, the Thanksgiving, the background, and the transitional prayer. That focus on the relationship likewise predisposes the hearers to a favorable hearing, the sort of presentation that is normally part of the *prooemium*, the introduction. From this insight, we might well consider all of chapters 1-3 as introduction, as setting the remembrance of their relationship as the necessary background for the requests that he will make in the next section.

on Paul's role as their founder, and his subtle use of references to what they knew—all point towards some extraordinary importance or difficulty regarding what Paul will ask them. These rhetorical devices follow the salesman's rule of building a preparation for the important closing question; they focus on the relationship and build a positive obligation; they build a series of Yes answers leading up to the important question. In addition they appear to be a delaying tactic, suggesting stress around what is yet to come.

It could be that this is a well-thought-out strategy: he said nice things about his hearers and about their relationship to put them in a positive mood to hear what he has to say next. However, it could be that the stress has led Paul, perhaps on an unconscious level, to enumerate these positives, as a way of reassuring and building himself up before embarking on what he expects will be a stormy conversation. The strategy may not have been conscious.

This hypothesis contends that Paul had one or more messages that he had to deliver which were very important to him or which he was very reluctant to say. It caused him great stress, in this interpretation, to have to say these things, and he put off saying them as long as possible. He not only delayed getting to the point, he also used the tools available to him to prepare for that message or messages.

The hypothesis that Paul experienced some difficulty about the upcoming subjects explains every feature of the Introduction. It explains why he has focused in the salutation on their existence as an ecclesia of citizens. It explains why he focused in the Thanksgiving on their response of faith. It explains why he focused in the recapitulation on the sincerity of the apostolic team and as their role as loving and parental founders of the ecclesia. It explains the concern for their existence in the discussion of the background. It puts the emotional outburst of the digression into an important emotional context. It explains the unusual length and complexity of the transitional prayer. Even more important, it exposes the unity of this entire section, as Paul moved to the potentially controversial topics in the Ethical Instruction.

The four passages of Ethical Instruction

The Ethical Instruction of the letter begins with 4:1 and ends in 5:11. There are four ethical instructions in this section. We will discuss the four ethical instructions, then the section as a whole.

Following a general lead-in to this section in 4:1-2, the four instructions are to avoid *porneia* ("fornication" or "sexual immorality")[120] in 4:3-8; the instruction to live quietly in brotherly love, in 4:9-12; the instruction about grieving, with a reason for hope, in 4:13-18; and the instruction to stay alert, in 5:1-11.

The first two of these are a single section and need to be considered together,[121] because *peripateite* ("to walk") in 4:2 opens an *inclusio* which is closed by *peripatête* in 4:12.[122] They stand as separate topics because the *Peri de* ("Now concerning") in verse 9 indicates a change of subject. It will be necessary to suggest why Paul discussed these two topics within this *inclusio*.

1. Lead-in

Paul's words

    1   As for the rest, dear ones, we make this request of you
         and encourage you in the Lord Jesus
         that just as you have received from us
         how it is necessary for you to walk and to please God,
         that you walk in that way
         so that you please God abundantly.
    2   For you know what commandments we gave you
         on behalf of the Lord Jesus.

Rhetorical analysis

This is a forthright instruction. They are to walk as they have been previously instructed, in a manner that will please God. Furthermore, being both

---

120. The Greek word *porneia* is often translated "fornication." Fornication is defined as voluntary sex between unmarried persons or persons who are not married to each other; the translation of *porneia* as "sexual immorality" casts this idea as generally as possible, on the grounds that it is not possible to know precisely what Paul had in mind. *Porneia*, however, is closely related to the Greek word for prostitute. There is much more discussion of 4:3-8 in Part III, chapter 2.

121. See the discussion in Malherbe, *Letters*, 236-39, of Yarbrough, *Not Like the Gentiles*.

122. Malherbe, *Letters*, 237.

necessary and a commandment, it is very important that they do so.

The first two words of this chapter, *loipon oun* ("finally then") are difficult to interpret. My translation, "As for the rest," interprets it as a significant
transition.[123] The first word, *loipon* ("finally") has cognates meaning "remain-
ing" or "surviving," or "the remainder;"[124] we could translate it as "finally" or
"then." In Phil 4:8 and in 2 Cor 13:11, Paul used *loipon* to mark a closing. If
Paul had closed the letter here after 1 Thess 4:1, it would be a closing word.
However, he did not move into a closing after 1 Thess 4:1.[125] The second
word, *oun* ("then," "therefore"),[126] serves to mark a step in an argument or
resume after an interruption. It would make a certain amount of sense to
translate the two words as "Then, then" or "Therefore, then." It appears that
Paul has used *loipon* to indicate a conclusion of some kind. It appears that he
has used *oun* to indicate that there is some logical or rhetorical connection between the subject being concluded and the subject that he will take up next.

Even so, that does not explain the double expression *loipon oun*.[127] This
apparently redundant and difficult expression is used only this once in the

---

123. Schubert, *Pauline Thanksgivings*, 25, identifies *loipon oun* as a *properans ad finem.* Schubert
suggests that if the epistle went immediately to 5:22, we would not sense that anything was
missing.
My sense is that Paul has now exhausted the things he can say before getting to the point of what
he must say and that this *properans ad finem* means that he must now, finally, get down to the
point.
Malherbe, *Letters*, 218, argues that *loipon* might be temporal, meaning "finally" and suggests
that Paul is moving into a closing, or inferential, meaning "therefore" and suggests that Paul is
drawing a conclusion. Since *oun* is inferential, Malherbe argues that the combination introduces
paraenesis.

124. Liddell and Scott, *Greek-English Lexicon*, 417a.

125. Richard, *Thessalonians*, 179, as previously noted, argues that First Thessalonians is two
letters. He suggests that the *loipon oun* ends the letter that is basically chapters 1-3, just as the
word *loipon* signals the ending at 2 Cor 13:11 and Phil 4:8.

126. Liddell and Scott, *Greek-English Lexicon,* 505b-506a: The word *oun* is a logical expression,
such as "therefore" and means that Paul is about to draw a conclusion from what he has just been
saying.
See also Frederick William Danker, *The Concise Greek-English Lexicon of the New Testament*
(Chicago: University of Chicago Press, 2009), 259, which, curiously, does not cite this instance.

127. Malherbe, *Letters*, 218, observes that *loipon* and *oun* can have the same meaning, expressing
that connection. We might use "therefore," "then," "in conclusion," or "finally" for either of
them. We would not, however, say "finally, finally," or even "therefore then," although we might
combine some of the other expressions, such as "therefore in conclusion" or "finally then."
Malherbe offers the translation "Well, then" as a succinct version; he also offers "And now,
brethren, to apply more directly what we have been saying" as an accurate translation.

New Testament.[128] The "finally" of *loipon* and the double "finally finally" of *loipon oun* expresses something more, perhaps of exasperation and of a sense that he has laid all the groundwork he can and now must get down to the difficult subjects. It strongly suggests a transition to a subject that he has postponed.

Paul's use of *erôtômen* ("we ask" or "we make this request of you") and *parakaloumen* ("we encourage") have been identified as expressions Paul used to state his purpose in writing.[129] They often mark a transition to an important ethical instruction. In combination with *loipon oun*, it appears that Paul is moving into important material.

2. The instruction to avoid sexual immorality

Paul's words

 3   For the will of God is this: your sanctification,
     that you abstain from sexual immorality,
 4   that each of you know how to acquire a wife
     in holiness and honor,
 5   not in an emotional experience like those who do not know
     God,
 6   and how not to trespass against and cheat each other in this
     matter;
     for the Lord carries out justice for all these things,
     just as we have told you before and witnessed continually.
 7   For God has not called us for uncleanness
     but for holiness.
 8   Therefore whoever refuses, refuses—not man but—God
     who is giving you his own holy spirit.

---

128. Richard, *Thessalonians*, 179.

129. Malherbe, *Letters*, 218 f.
Richard, *Thessalonians*, 179-80.
Margaret M. Mitchell, *Paul and the Rhetoric of Reconciliation: An Exegetical Investigation of the Language and Composition of 1 Corinthians* (Louisville, KY: Westminster/John Knox Press, 1991), 199, footnote 79, says that Dahl noted that *parakalô* is Paul's word to announce that he is stating his main point in a letter.

Rhetorical analysis

This segment addresses sexuality and marriage. These verses are difficult to understand. There is no scholarly agreement, for example, on the exact meaning of *porneia* ("sexual immorality" in my translation) or on the correct translation of *skeuos ktasthai* ("to acquire a wife" in my translation). Nor is there broad agreement whether the instructions in verses 4, 5, and 6 are all on the same subject or are three different topics. While we are always open to the possibility that such disagreement comes naturally out of the two thousand years of cultural change between Paul's world and ours, this passage seems to be more obscure than most ancient passages, and although Paul is often difficult for us to understand, this passage is outstanding for its obscurity. Therefore we need to allow for the possibility that this segment was difficult for Paul and his hearers as well as for us.

What is clear, however, is that whatever Paul meant in this segment, it was something he said that he had told them before, of utmost importance. In verse 2 he said they knew what commandments he gave them, implying that he had told them before; and in verse 6c he said, "just as we have told you before and witnessed continually," giving the same impression. Furthermore, his words about sanctification in verse 3, holiness and honor in verse 4, justice in verse 6, holiness in verse 7, and God's gift of the holy spirit in verse 8 underscore and set these instructions in bold print. The instruction that he gave them in this segment is extremely important (I discuss the possibility that this teaching on sexuality was new, despite Paul's claim that it was not new, in Part III, chapter 2).

This ethical instruction that they should marry does not obviously continue the discussion of love. The ancients did not speak of marriage as a loving relationship.[130] Nevertheless, marriage is an intimate relationship in which it is appropriate for persons to consider the well-being of their partners. When Paul spoke in 4:4 of treating marriage with holiness and respect, he comes close to making it a loving relationship. It fits in the category of respect, even

---

130. Amy Richlin, *The Garden of Priapus: Sexual Aggression in Roman Humor* (New York: Oxford University Press, 1992), *passim*.
Kirk Ormand, *Controlling Desires: Sexuality in Ancient Greece and Rome* (Westport, Connecticut and London: Praeger, 2009), *passim*.
Yarbrough, *Not Like the Gentiles*, see chapter 2 "Marriage Precepts in the Greco-Roman Moral Traditions," especially pages 53-59.

if it does not imply affection. When he continues by saying not to trespass against or cheat each other in this regard, this is behavior consistent with the commandment to love one another. Therefore it is reasonable to include the instruction to marry under the heading of love.

Paul treated the emotionally positive aspect of love first, in his two statements of the precipitating events, stressing the quality of the relationship between him and his hearers. Only after that did he move on to a more difficult conversation about the intimate relationship of marriage.

3. The instruction to live quietly

Introduced as a new topic of brotherly love, verses 4:9-12 instruct them to live inconspicuously and to work with their hands.

Paul's words

9   Now concerning brotherly love,
      you do not need us to write you,
      for you are God-taught to love one another,
10   For you are doing this towards all the dear ones
      in all of Macedonia. We encourage you, dear ones,
      to excel even more.
11   Be ambitious to live quietly,
      to mind your own business,
      and to work with your hands,
      just as we commanded you,
12   in order that you walk worthily of respect from outsiders,
      and not depend upon others.

Rhetorical analysis

This brief instruction to live quietly announces itself as a comment on *philadelphia* ("love between brothers"). However, after commending them for already loving others as they have learned from the gospel, Paul segued to an instruction to work responsibly and keep a low profile in the community. Just exactly how minding their own business and working with their hands are connected with love may not be obvious to us, but it should be clear that to Paul they were related subjects.

While the Paul most often used *agapê* ("selfless love") in this letter, rather than *philia* ("friendship love"), the description here fits as well with *agapê* as it would with *philia*. Living quietly and working with one's hands so as to be respectable and not to be needy express a responsibility toward others as well as towards oneself.

It is clear from the *peri de* that begins this passage that 9-12 represents a separate subject from verses 3-8. They are joined, however, by both being about concern and care for oneself and others. This linkage, that both are part of Paul's discussion of love, is the reason for the *inclusio* formed by the *peripateite* in 4:2 and the *peripatête* in 4:12.

Therefore, the entire stretch, from 2:17 to 4:12, appears to come under the topic love. Paul has arranged the three discussions of love so that the two statements of the background discuss and illustrate his love for them and their love for him, the instruction to avoid sexual immorality discusses an unusual need for holiness and honor and for not taking advantage of one another, and the instruction to live quietly celebrates the out-pouring of their love for each other through appropriate responsibility for themselves. The first two are affirming, the third may be challenging, and the fourth is comfortable.

4. The instruction about grieving

Paul turned in the next passage to discuss hope.

Paul's words

¹³ I do not want you not to know, dear ones,
about those who are sleeping,
so that you do not grieve like others who do not have hope.
¹⁴ For since we believe that Jesus died and rose,
so also God will through Jesus
lead with him those who have fallen asleep.
¹⁵ This, of course, we say to you in accordance with the gospel.
that we the living who are being left behind
will not precede those who have fallen asleep
when the Lord arrives;
¹⁶ that with a commanding shout
with an archangel's call,
and with the trumpet's call to arms,
the Lord himself will step down from heaven,
and the dead shall rise in Christ first,

¹⁷   then we the living,
        who are being left behind,
        will be snatched up in the clouds along with them
        for the meeting with the Lord in the air;
        in this way we shall always be with the Lord.
¹⁸   Encourage each other just so, in these words.

Rhetorical analysis

Paul instructed his hearers not to grieve like others who do not have hope, and then gave them reason to hope. When Paul, just previously in 1 Thess 3:10, said he wished to make up what was lacking in their faith, probably referring to the missing element in Timothy's report of their faith and love (1 Thess 3:6), he pointed ahead to the hope that the dead will be raised. Paul, then, has moved on from his discussion of faith and love to his discussion of hope.

The most natural reading of the first phrase, "I do not want you not to know," is that Paul is going to tell them something they have not heard before. The point of the passage as a whole is that those who have died will not be neglected but will be resurrected to participate in the *parousia*. The question is whether the resurrection of believers was something that they did not know and therefore whether or not it was a new idea. The sense in which the resurrection of believers was new to Paul's Thessalonian hearers has been much debated (and will be further discussed in Part III, chapter 2).

In addition to the simple fact that the resurrection of believers was new in some sense, we need to note also the use of sounds. In verse 16, there is a commanding shout, an archangel's call, and the trumpet's call to arms. This use of clanging sounds is distracting. Paul's listeners, just like modern readers, quite naturally focused on these sounds. If indeed the resurrection of believers was a new doctrine at the time of the writing of this letter, this use of such a noisy distraction was an excellent rhetorical technique. These sounds would distract listeners from the newness of the doctrine. This rhetorical role is consistent with the interpretation that there is something new in this passage.

5. The instruction to stay alert

In 5:1-11, Paul addressed our not knowing when the Day of the Lord will come and focused on the need to stay alert for it.

Paul's words

1 Now concerning hours and opportunities, dear ones,
  you do not need to be written to,
2 for you yourselves know accurately
  that the day of the Lord comes as a thief in the night.
3 Whenever they say, "Peace and Security,"
  their destruction comes on them suddenly,
  just like labor-pains surprise a pregnant woman,
  and no way will they escape.
4 But you, dear ones, you are not in the dark,
  such that the day might take you by surprise, like a thief.
5 By belonging, you have become daylight.
  We are not of the night or of the dark;
6 Therefore let us not sleep like others,
  but be sober and alert.
7 For those who sleep sleep at night,
  and those who get drunk drink at night;
8 but we being of the day stay sober
  putting on the breastplate of faith and love
  and the headgear of hope for salvation.
9 God has not set us up for wrath
  but for the acquisition of salvation
  through our Lord Jesus Christ
10 who died for us so that
  whether we keep watch or sleep
  alike we might live with him.
11 Therefore encourage one another and build each other up,
  one to another, just as you are doing.

Rhetorical analysis

Paul began this segment with comments on the future. Like the preceding passage, this passage is oriented toward the future and consequently is part of Paul's discussion of hope. Then, almost immediately, he changed the subject to the character of his Thessalonian hearers: by "belonging, you have become daylight."[131] Because of that character they may have confidence when the "day of the Lord" arrives. Then in the closing of this passage, Paul returned to expectation for the future. The acquisition of salvation appears to be something that they will experience in the future, and thus is a subject for hope.

This whole passage is full of expressions not common to Paul but appearing elsewhere throughout the New Testament. Paul's language for this passage taps into a very early layer of Christian teaching. Every word appears to be a word that his hearers have heard before.[132] It is comforting to hear truth expressed in words that are familiar, so Paul might well have chosen familiar and comforting words to speak these truths, in order to make his listeners comfortable. Besides, who would object to being told that they belong to the light and to the day? Who would argue with being told to be watchful and alert, waiting for the promised day to arrive? This passage is quite the opposite of controversial.

This coherent segment concludes Paul's discussion of hope. By being oriented to the future, it is all about hope. Paul, then, has discussed the three virtues in the same order in which he named them in both the opening of the *inclusio* in 1:3 and its closing in 5:8. There must be some reason why he not only stated them in this sequence but also followed this sequence for his development. It would make most sense to suggest that he put them in this order in the opening and closing *inclusioi* because that was the sequence in which he wanted to discuss them.

Analysis of the Ethical Instruction as a whole

For the analysis of 4:1-5:11 as a whole, the important questions are why Paul raised these four topics, whether there is an alternation in the energy sur-

---

131. The Hebrew behind this expression means to be a member of a class: a "son of man" literally means "a human being." A "son of light" is a person who belongs to the enlightened. I have abstracted the sense of "belonging" from the idea of belonging to a class. Perhaps to the Greek-hearing ears of the Thessalonians, it conveyed something more of the family relations implied by "sons."

132. Matthew 24.36-44 includes *hêmera ekeinê* (that day), *parousia*, and *gregoreite* (stay awake). Mark 13.32-37 includes *hêmera ekeine* and *kairos*. 2 Peter 3.10 *hêxei de hêmera kyriou hôs kleptês* the day of the Lord will come as a thief. Revelation 3.3 so if you do not keep awake. I will come as a thief. And Revelation 16.15. Behold, I am coming as a thief.
Richard, *Thessalonians*, 250-251, refers to this as Q-like or pre-synoptic material.
Richard also uses the word "proverbial."

rounding them, and if there is alternation, what is its effect on this segment of the letter.

Scholars have offered three suggestions as to why Paul brought up these four points: A first theory is that Paul was responding to questions in a letter or questions which Timothy brought back from the Thessalonians.[133] A second theory is that these are points Paul discussed on every occasion.[134] A third theory sees that the "Marriage Mandate" would function so as to help the members of the ecclesia develop strong community boundaries.[135] To these three, I add a fourth possibility that the alternation of energy in the four topics suggest a sophisticated presentation of controversial material.

First, the impression that in First Thessalonians Paul was responding to points in a letter from them[136] is largely based on a similar interpretation of First Corinthians. In First Corinthians Paul mentioned their letter, and it appears that he used *Peri de* ("Now concerning") to move from one subject in their letter to another.[137] Consequently, it has been suggested that Paul used *peri de* in First Thessalonians, in 4:9 and in 5:1 to refer to points in their letter.[138] However, the expression *peri de* is also used to move from one point, without there necessarily having been a letter.[139]

Paul's expression of his pleasure in 3:6 that they remembered him has been offered as evidence of a letter, on the grounds that he said this upon reading in their letter that they remembered him.[140] Paul's expression of plea-

---

133. Hurd, *Earlier Letters*, 59-61; Richard, *Thessalonians*, 15; Malherbe, *Letters*, 75-77.

134. Hurd, *Earlier Letters*, 75-76.

135. Yarbrough, *Not Like the Gentiles, passim*, but particularly 87.

136. Both Hurd, *Earlier Letters*, 59, and Chalmer E. Faw, "On the Writing of First Thessalonians." *Journal of Biblical Literature* 71 (1952) 217-25. and Malherbe, *Letters*, 75-76, credit J. Rendell Harris, who wrote in 1898, with the idea that Timothy brought back a letter or an oral communication, in which these Thessalonians asked Paul questions on these four topics. This article by Faw cites a wide range of evidence for a letter to which Paul was responding, but it is not convincing.

137. In First Corinthians Paul used *peri de* six times, in 7:1, 7:25, 8:1, 12:1, 16:1, and 12. He spoke of "their letter" in 7:1.

138. This suggestion runs through all of the literature cited. Hurd, *Earlier Letters*, 59-60 is a good illustration.

139. Malherbe, *Letters*, 209, 217, 288. Mitchell, *Rhetoric*, 191.

140. Harris reportedly thought that when Paul expressed his pleasure (3:6) that they remembered him, it would have been because he was reading their letter in which they said that they remembered him.

sure comes more logically, however, as a response to Timothy's report. Likewise, each time Paul said "as you know" or similar phrases, it could mean that
he knew they knew because they had mentioned it in their letter. It is not
necessary, however, to postulate a letter in order to explain these references.
We have already suggested that Paul used phrases such as "as you know" when
he was referring to events in their memory and knowledge, in order to build
a series of Yes answers in their minds. Furthermore, the uses of "you know" in
4:2 and 5:2 are different from all the others.

All the others are used without an object; they say that "you know," but
do not specify what they know. In 4:2, however, Paul said "you know what
commandments we gave you;" the "you know" has the object "what commandments." In 5:2 he said "you yourselves know accurately that the day of
the Lord comes as a thief in the night;" the object is the clause "that the day of
the Lord, *etc.*" Therefore, the phrase "you know" does not indicate that Paul
spoke to these four points because of a letter that they wrote him. So far, the
argument for a letter does not appear convincing.

The instruction on sexual morality could conceivably be a precise response to some specific question, although it is not obvious what question
might have elicited this exact response. The difficulty of generating a question
behind this passage argues against its being a response to a question.

Second, the suggestion that these four topics are part of a standard list
which Paul regularly addressed is based on the impression of Paul's skill and
control as a writer; he chose the topics about which he wrote. Paul may have
addressed these same four topics in letters that have not survived, and there
could conceivably have been many of his letters that discussed these topics.
However, these four topics do not commend themselves as usual topics.[141]

Furthermore, it does not make sense that Paul would introduce a customary topic with "I do not want you not to know." If the topic in 4:13-18
were a standard theme, he would probably not have used a formula that he
typically used to introduce new material. Therefore, the suggestion that Paul
raised these four topics because they were his standard topics does not seem
to be satisfactory either.

Third, Paul's choice of the Marriage Mandate is accounted for on the

---

141. Hurd, *Earlier Letters*, 76, observes that the four topics do not commend themselves as stock
themes. If you were the preacher, to what themes would you keep returning? Probably not these
four.

basis of twentieth-century perception of how social groups are formed. In the diaspora, Jews found it important to reinforce their differences from the people of their surrounding communities. This reinforcement of their differences created a boundary between the Jewish and the gentile communities. Paul's marriage mandate had a similar function of providing a boundary for and strengthening the ecclesia. Paul wrote about the marriage mandate in order to strengthen the ecclesia as a community.[142]

This explanation has force as a basic reason why Paul would enforce a marriage mandate for his fledgling community. However, it does not explain the relationship of this topic to the other three topics or why Paul brought up the other topics.

The fourth possible explanation for Paul's choice of these four topics is based on the way that the alternation of the four topics contribute to the first and third topics. There are four peculiarities that expose this alternation: the use of *peri de*, Paul's statement that he did not need to write on certain topics, the non-controversial nature of the second and fourth topics, and the potential for controversy about the first and third topics.

Of these four passages, the second and fourth both begin with *peri de*. Some scholars have suggested that the third topic in the Ethical Instruction also uses *peri* to make a change of subject. That passage, however, does not begin with *peri de* as transition words; it begins with the phrase, "I do not want you not to know . . . about [something]," which itself marks the transition to a new subject. The *peri* clause identifies the subject. He did not want them to be ignorant **about** those who sleep. Therefore the usage of *peri* in 4:13 differs from the *peri de* in 4:9 and 5:1. In those two places, *peri de* marks the transition, clearly and abruptly.

The second peculiarity is that in both of these passages Paul said he did not need to write them on the named subject. It was a literary convention to say that it was not necessary to discuss a subject on the grounds that the recipients of the letter already knew enough on that subject, and then to proceed to discuss the subject.

If they were points in a letter from the Thessalonians, Paul's saying that he did not need to write them is particularly unattractive. If Paul began to ad-

---

142. Yarbrough, *Not Like the Gentiles, passim.*
See also Meeks, *Urban Christians, passim.*

dress a point or question in their letter by saying that it was not necessary to write on that subject, his comment amounts to an implication that they were asking a question to which they perfectly well knew the answer. If we take his statement at face value, it is a rebuke. It appears as if Paul was scolding them for having asked the question. However, the rest of the letter is very warm. Nowhere else in this letter does Paul appear to criticize them. Therefore, it seems highly unlikely that we should take this statement at face value.

This expression implies that Paul will not be saying anything new. Paul seems to be saying that, since they do not need to be written to, he will be telling them what they already know. Following 4:9, in the section on brotherly love, his use of the unique expression that they are God-taught, reinforces the same point. What he is going to say next will be familiar material—it clearly is. He next said that they were already doing what they needed to do regarding this subject, and that they just needed to excel more. This is a conventional expression, and it could be that Paul was simply following the convention. However, it is very striking that the instructions are familiar material, old stuff, such that Paul could quite rightly expect that no one would argue with him on this subject. If Paul thought they already knew it, then he did not expect any argument on these topics.

Paul developed the passage about brotherly love by telling his hearers to be ambitious to live quietly and mind their own business. Paul's statement in 4:11 "just as we commanded you" indicates that this instruction is not a new topic. This instruction also seems to be in line with the example Paul said he himself gave in 3:9, of working night and day so as not to be a burden on anyone. Since he commended his work ethic to them in 3:9, in a context that suggests they would not disagree, for him to commend his work ethic in 4:9-12 probably was not controversial.

Likewise, as mentioned, the passage of the coming of the day of the Lord shares language with several other books of the New Testament, so that Paul appears to be using words that were customary to this subject. That feature, in combination with Paul's saying that they did not need for him to write them about this subject, strongly suggests that Paul did not expect them to disagree with him on this topic. This passage would not have been controversial.

The two passages which are introduced by *peri de* and "you do not need to be written to" are non-controversial. However, the other two segments in

this section, if we cannot say with absolute certainty that they were controversial, nevertheless have the potential of being controversial. Both the first
and the third passages could have given Paul reason to be concerned that they
might stir an argument. It is perhaps a curiosity that these two passages are
the subject of some controversy for us; we shall have to look more closely to
see if they might have been controversial for Paul and his hearers.

Twentieth-century translators, like their predecessors, find the word *porneia* and the words *skeuos ktasthai* difficult to translate. As mentioned, we can
translate *porneia* as "fornication" or "sexual immorality," but it is difficult to
know exactly what Paul meant. Some translators take *skeuos ktasthai* to mean
that Christians should marry: that is, that every Christian man ought to have
a Christian wife. Other translators interpret this phrase as a reference to a
man's control of his own sexuality.[143]

Perhaps we should expect that any discussion of sexual morality would be
uncomfortable. It is certainly more possible for us to discuss sexual morality
than it was for our Victorian ancestors. Quite possibly, it was comfortable
for first century Thessalonians and Jews, but we know that Jews thought
that Greeks were sexually loose,[144] so that for a Jew like Paul to be speaking
to Greeks about sexual morality would probably have a subtext of criticism.
Criticism of their sexual behavior has always been likely to upset people. It
would not take exceptional pastoral sensitivity to realize that telling a congregation to clean up their sexual behavior would provoke resistance. Therefore,
we ought to say on an *a priori* basis we would expect this topic to be controversial, and that we would expect Paul to be aware of this topic's potential for
controversy.

Furthermore, we have the evidence of Paul's discussion of the same topic
with the ecclesia in Corinth. In 1 Cor 7:2, Paul said that every Christian man
should have a wife and every Christian woman should have a husband.[145] Paul
then spent the rest of Chapter 7 of First Corinthians exploring how to apply

---

143. Malherbe, *Letters*, 227-240, takes it as an injunction to marry: Richard, Thessalonians, 198,
takes it as an imperative for self-control over one's sexuality.

144. See Part III, chapter 2 for discussion and references.

145. The question, of course, is how to understand the flow of thought between 7:1 and 7:2.
Hurd discusses this question in Chapters 5 and 6 of *The Origin of I Corinthians*, suggesting that
the maxim in 7:1 was a quote of a position taken by the Corinthians, and that 7:2 represents a
position Paul took, distinct from theirs.
Mitchell, *Rhetoric*, 236, takes a more complex position that Paul's apparent inconsistency

this general principle to specific situations. It may be that he was responding to a large number of specific questions. If, however, Paul said, "Christians should marry," and the Corinthians reminded Paul that he himself was not married, what we have is an argument. Paul was in the unenviable position of giving advice that he himself did not follow. This observation makes Chapter 7 of First Corinthians sound like a controversial topic. If the topic was controversial in the context of First Corinthians, we ought to be open to the possibility that it was controversial in the context of First Thessalonians.

Perhaps when Paul was preaching for the first time in Thessalonica and in Corinth, Paul had urged his converts to stay single.[146] If indeed this passage is an instruction that members of the ecclesia ought to marry, then it would represent a reversal of that earlier position and would have been controversial for that reason. If it meant that Paul was reversing his earlier position, it is easy to see that he might have some difficulty in bringing up the subject. How was he to convince his hearers of something on which he was reversing his position?

The problem with the third topic, the resurrection of believers, is not with understanding the meaning of the words that Paul spoke. There is no question about what the words mean. Our problem today lies in understanding why Paul discussed this topic. The controversy today is whether or not the resurrection of believers was a new doctrine. Some scholars conclude that Paul had originally preached that Jesus would return in the lifetime of the believers; it had not originally occurred to him that any believers would die before Jesus arrived, so Paul discovered the truth about the resurrection of believers only after some of them had died.[147] Others have suggested that Paul was in Thessalonica for such a brief time that he was able to instruct them only in the most important beliefs of this new religion, and that there had not

represents a single nuanced position. Seeking a reconciliation between two sides, Paul agrees as much as he can with both.

146. The best evidence that Paul at one time preached that members of the movement should remain single is in 1 Cor 7. Since that document is not at issue here, we can go no further than to say that it is possible that Paul once took that position.

147. Hurd, *Origin*, 229, concludes that Paul brought up the resurrection of believers for the first time in First Thessalonians and in the Previous Letter to the Corinthians.
Buck and Taylor, *St. Paul*, 38, argued that during the founding visits to Thessalonica and to Corinth, Paul preached that the *parousia* would come during their lifetime.
Luedemann, *Apostle*, 238, suggests that by the time Paul wrote First Thessalonians enough of the followers of Jesus had died that Paul needed to deal with this problem.

been enough time to tell them about the resurrection of believers.[148] Still others have suggested that he had told them about the resurrection of believers, but that they had not been able to connect the doctrine-in-the-abstract with the real deaths of their friends in the ecclesia.[149] Thus, there is controversy today about whether this doctrine was new to Paul's hearers.

One passage in the Gospels (which are later than First Thessalonians) explains that the Sadducees did not believe in the resurrection.[150] Since the Sadducees were Jews, there were some Jews who believed in ressurection and some who did not. Therefore, at the time when the followers of Jesus were writing the Gospels and Acts, there was disagreement about the resurrection within Judaism.

There is evidence that the idea of resurrection was not commonly accepted throughout first century Judaism. Three books from the two centuries before Christ disagree about it. Second Maccabees was written by an author who believed in the resurrection. First Maccabees was written by an author who did not. Daniel does not indicate any belief in the resurrection.

Furthermore, the concept of resurrection presented in Second Maccabees is not that of a general resurrection. In Second Maccabees, participation in the resurrection appears to be a special reward for exceptional service. It is the resurrection of heroes. A belief such as this works to account for the belief in the resurrection of Jesus, who was no less a hero than the Maccabees, but it does not automatically extend the offer to all the faithful.

To be precise, we have to say that belief in the resurrection of the dead was in the air, in the literature, and available to Paul and other early followers of Jesus.[151] However, we cannot say that they all believed everyone would be raised from the dead. The first generation followers of Jesus may not have included it in their beliefs. The statement in 1 Thess 4:13-18 may be Paul's creative adaptation of the idea of resurrection to apply to all the believers. The

---

148. Richard, *Thessalonians*, 231-232, enumerates five proposals why Paul had not preached the resurrection of the dead to the Thessalonians or why they had not fully understood the promise; lack of time is one of the five.

149. Malherbe, *Letters*, 284, suggests that some particular problem in Thessalonica got in the way of their being able to apply the resurrection of believers to their situation.

150. Mark 12:18 and parallels Matthew 22:23 and Luke 20:27 describe Sadducees as not believing in the resurrection and reports their bringing to Jesus a question that is designed to ridicule the resurrection. Acts 23:8 also reports that the Sadducees did not believe in the resurrection.

151. Malherbe, *Letters*, 282, says belief in immortality was widespread in the ancient world.

resurrection of believers likely was a new idea to the believers in Thessalonica.

Would this doctrine, then, have been controversial? If the statement was actually a new doctrine, it seems likely that it would be controversial. If, however, this statement merely clarified a doctrine that the members of this ecclesia had not fully understood, does it still seem that they would find it controversial? It is possible to say something that changes people's understanding and have them be happy accepting the change. However, this is often not the case in religious belief. Usually when one attempts to change people's beliefs, some of them become unhappy about the change. Whenever there is change in the church, it is reasonable to expect the change to be resisted. If Paul was telling them something they had not heard before, it is reasonable to expect some to object. If they had heard it before but had not absorbed it, it is still reasonable to expect resistance.

Likewise, we have evidence that the resurrection of believers was controversial when Paul discussed it with the Corinthians. There are three pieces of evidence in First Corinthians that the doctrine was controversial.

First, in 1 Cor 15:35, Paul restated the question, "How are corpses raised? What kind of body will they have?" This appears to be a question raised by the Corinthians, which Paul then proceeded to answer in verses 36-58. His care in answering means that he took their question seriously.

Those questions in 1 Cor 15:35, however, may have been meant to be unanswerable questions, reducing belief in the resurrection to absurdity. If this latter is the correct interpretation of these questions, then the controversy was a rather serious one.

Second, in 1 Cor 15:12, Paul acknowledged that some of them said there was no resurrection of the dead. There are two ways to take their statement. We could interpret it that there is no resurrection of the dead, period. Paul appears to have taken it in that sense, as a denial that would include the denial of Christ's resurrection, because he countered their statement by appealing to the resurrection of Jesus. We could, however, take it as a denial of the resurrection of believers, that is, as a specific argument against the position Paul has taken in 1 Thess 4:3-8. If that is the case, the argument between the Corinthians and Paul was, again, rather serious.

Third, Paul said, in 15:3, "I delivered what I received." Commentators have generally accepted Paul's statement at face value, that Paul placed himself in the context of a tradition in which the truth was passed on from one believer to another. However, I find it hard to imagine a conversation in which this expression occurs where it is not part of an argument. It sounds defensive. Paul may have meant, "I did not make this up! I passed on what I received from others." This is Paul's denial that he added to the tradition, or it could simply be an appeal to the authority of the Apostles who saw the risen Lord. In either case, it appears that this statement is a transaction in a rather serious argument.

These three statements in First Corinthians (15:3, 12, and 35) imply controversy about the resurrection. At the very least, the second of these (15:12) may mean that the Corinthians disagreed with Paul about the resurrection.

If it was controversial in the context of First Corinthians, we need to be open to the possibility that it was controversial in the context of First Thessalonians. It is not unreasonable to conclude that the topic of the resurrection of believers was a surprising and disturbing topic when it was first brought up with the ecclesia of the Thessalonians, nor would it take exceptional pastoral sensitivity to know that pronouncing a doctrine that has not been heard previously might elicit a negative response.

Therefore, it is a strong possibility that the two topics of resurrection and sexuality were controversial, and further that Paul was alert to that possibility. Then, the four topics in 1 Thess 4-5 are in a sequence of alternating potentially controversial and non-controversial material. It is less clear that the first and third would have been controversial. It is more clear that Paul did not expect disagreement regarding the second and fourth topics. That contrast is enough to indicate an alternation of energy between them. The sequence is the high-energy topic of sexuality, the much less-controversial topic of brotherly love, the high-energy topic of the resurrection of believers, and the much less-controversial topic of the future "day of the Lord."

Paul, then, can be seen as having structured chapters 4-5:11 so that each controversial topic is followed by a non-controversial topic, expressed in familiar words. Each time Paul finished what he had to say about one of the potentially controversial topics, he changed the subject, using *peri de* to make an abrupt transition. In each case, however, Paul not only changed the subject but he also changed it to a subject that was familiar, which he discussed in familiar, comfortable words. These transitions into conventional thoughts, expressed in conventional language, distract from the explosive issues that precede them, soothe and disarm his hearers.

These abrupt transitions[152] seem designed to distract his hearers from being upset about the previous topic. Changing the subject is a very effective technique in a social context where one needs to persuade others. Paul did this twice. He has distracted his hearers from their potential objections to his discussion of marriage and brought them back to a position of agreeing with him. Then he repeated the same process for the second controversial topic. The net result is that he has covered both controversial topics and left his hearers thinking Yes.

If this is the correct interpretation, then there appears to have been a rhetorical reason for Paul to use the second and fourth topics as a way of increasing acceptance of the first and third. This brings forward the conclusion that the first and third topics were the ones that were important to Paul and that he was under some stress to express them in a way that would convince his hearers.

This view also suggests that Paul took up the topics of resurrection and sexual morality not because he wanted to but because there was some reason why he had to. If this is the case, then we need to be alert to any clues that will tell us why he had to bring up these subjects. The analysis of the alternating energy in this section leads to the conclusion that there may have been some external pressure that moved Paul to discuss these subjects.

The passages in 4:3-8 and 4:13-18 are the points Paul needed to make. In addition to expressing his concern and relief that the ecclesia of the Thessalonians still existed, Paul wrote this letter to express these points. It still is not clear, however, why he needed to make these points.

---

152. Hurd, *Earlier Letters*, 60, characterizes the transitions at 4:9, 4:13, and 5:1 as abrupt.
Referring to Faw, he says, that the abrupt transitions at 4:9, 13; 5:1, 12 suggest something not visible to us has chosen the topics.
Malherbe, *Letters*, 75-76, says the same thing.
Malherbe, *Letters*, 208-209, again referring to Faw, says that the strongest evidence for a letter is Paul's use of *peri de*.
Allowing for 4:13 being a different use of *peri*, the uses of *Peri de* in 4:9 and 5:1 are abrupt.

The closing of the letter

Paul's closed the letter with "instructions" that are really a series of blessings, a blessing prayer, and a final serious instruction.

Paul's words

12 We make this request of you, dear ones,
     to hold your leaders in respect,
     those who are standing up in front of you
     and admonishing you in the Lord

13 and to think of them so much more in love because of their work.
     Be at peace among yourselves.

14 We encourage you, dear ones, to admonish the unruly,
     give cheer to the faint of heart,
     be patient with the weak,
     think the best of everyone.

15 See that no one gives back evil for evil,
     but in everything pursue the good towards each other and
     towards all.

16 Rejoice always,

17 Pray without ceasing,

18 Give thanks for all things—for this is God's will for you in Christ,

19 Do not quench the spirit,

20 Do not belittle prophecy.

21 Look for the true character of all things: hold tight what is good

22 And hold apart from every appearance of evil.

23 May God, the very God of peace,
     make you entirely holy,
     and may your entire spirit—and your life and your body—
     be kept protected,
     blameless when our Lord Jesus Christ arrives.

24 He is faithful, the one calling you, and he will do it.

25 Dear ones, pray for us.

26 Greet all your dear ones with a holy kiss.

27 I solemnly charge you in the Lord to read this letter to everyone in
     the ecclesia.

28 The grace of our Lord Jesus Christ be with you.

Rhetorical analysis

The instructions that begin this passage are a way of bringing a communication to an end. We today might say, "have a nice day" or "drive safely" or "take care." We do not really mean to be issuing directions as to what the other person needs to do. We are offering them our good wishes for their happiness and well-being, as a way of closing the letter or conversation. Paul's use of the expression, "We make this request of you,"[153] might lead us to think that this is a major ethical instruction, but that would be incorrect. Although these "instructions" may apply to specifics of the situation in Thessalonica, they are part of the closing.

The instructions in the first portion may be organized around the well-being of a community. Paul asked them to be aware of those who were doing the work, having positions of leadership and responsibility for instructing them (5:12) and asked them to regard these leaders lovingly because of their work. Such practices help make communities function happily.

Among these instructions, the injunction to "be at peace among yourselves" in verse 13 seems anticlimactic. There are always disruptive people who need to be admonished, faint of heart who need to be cheered, and weak with whom we must be patient, but Paul's request that they be at peace with one another suggests that he was concerned with the possibility that they might not be at peace with one another. This adds weight to our interpretation that Paul feared that some of his teaching in this letter might be controversial and cause division.

The second portion of this closing, verses 16-22, has a parallel in Philippians 4:4-9. The tight parallelism of these two passages suggests that Paul often used a similar set of words. He may often have pronounced a blessing on people similarly, with creative variations.

The third portion of this closing, verse 23, is a prayer of blessing. Then, after that, Paul asked them to pray for him and reminded them to greet one another with a holy kiss.

Then comes a most peculiar statement. Paul asked them to read the letter to everyone in the ecclesia. Some have supposed that the ecclesia of the Thessalonians was made up of more than one house-church, and that Paul meant

---

153. See the discussion of *erôtômen* in 4:1, page 142.

that the letter should be read aloud in all of the house-churches.[154] It is also possible that he meant them to seek out those people who were absent when the letter was read and read it to them. However, he not only **asks** them, he **solemnly charges them in the Lord**. These words are the equivalent of making them swear an oath, such as one would swear as a witness in court. Therefore, this request is of the greatest importance, and therefore in turn, we are confronted with the question, what was so important about this letter that Paul demanded it be read to everybody?

Analysis of the letter as a whole

There are very significant differences between the Introduction and the Ethical Instruction. The primary difference is style. The first three chapters are chatty, warm and friendly, reminiscent of good things in the past and expressive of strong emotions, both positive and negative. These chapters feel like one side of a conversation between old friends.

The last two chapters are much more direct. In them, Paul told his hearers what they ought to do. He said they should abstain from *porneia*, that they should be ambitious to lead quiet lives and mind their own business, that they should not grieve like people who have no hope, and that they should be sober and vigilant. These instructions are direct statements rather than personal examples to be imitated. People would not miss what Paul was telling them to do.

In the Introduction, Paul talked about their relationship and their shared history. Consequently he used the first person pronouns and first person verbs an exceptional number of times. In the Ethical Instruction, Paul used the first person pronouns and first person verbs relatively few times (see Tables 3 and 4).

One possibility is that Paul's abundant use of first person pronouns and first person verbs in chapters 1-3 implies that he was self-conscious, that he was overly focused on himself, and perhaps that he was embarrassed. In addition, several phrases where first person pronouns stand out as unnecessary may indicate Paul's excessive attention to himself.

First, the phrase "our gospel" in 1:5 is the most outstanding of these three. It is the gospel of Jesus Christ, and yet Paul referred to it as "our gospel." It

---

154. Malherbe, *Letters*, 344-45.

refers to the proclamation that Paul made when he arrived in Thessalonica, the preaching that he preached. The "our" refers to his act of preaching. Still, the word "gospel" would, even this early in the history of this religion's development, have stood on its own. It was not really necessary for Paul to qualify the "gospel" as the one which he preached; his doing so constitutes an excessive self-reference.

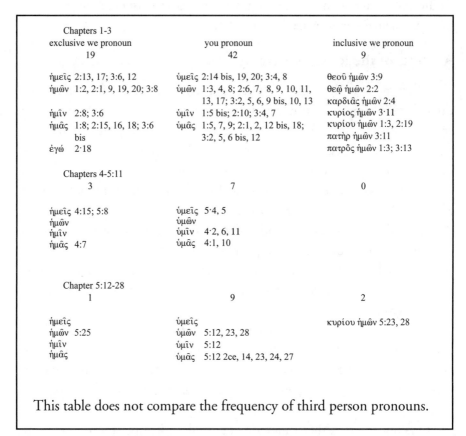

Chapters 1-3 exclusive we pronoun 19	you pronoun 42	inclusive we pronoun 9
ἡμεῖς 2:13, 17; 3:6, 12	ὑμεῖς 2:14 bis, 19, 20; 3:4, 8	θεοῦ ἡμῶν 3:9
ἡμῶν 1:2, 2:1, 9, 19, 20; 3:8	ὑμῶν 1:3, 4, 8; 2:6, 7, 8, 9, 10, 11, 13, 17; 3:2, 5, 6, 9 bis, 10, 13	θεῷ ἡμῶν 2:2 καρδιᾶς ἡμῶν 2:4
ἡμῖν 2:8; 3:6	ὑμῖν 1:5 bis; 2:10; 3:4, 7	κύριος ἡμῶν 3·11
ἡμᾶς 1:8; 2:15, 16, 18; 3:6 bis	ὑμᾶς 1:5, 7, 9; 2:1, 2, 12 bis, 18; 3:2, 5, 6 bis, 12	κυρίου ἡμῶν 1:3, 2:19 πατὴρ ἡμῶν 3:11
ἐγώ 2·18		πατρὸς ἡμῶν 1:3; 3:13
Chapters 4-5:11 3	7	0
ἡμεῖς 4:15; 5:8 ἡμῶν ἡμῖν ἡμᾶς 4:7	ὑμεῖς 5·4, 5 ὑμῶν ὑμῖν 4·2, 6, 11 ὑμᾶς 4:1, 10	
Chapter 5:12-28 1	9	2
ἡμεῖς ἡμῶν 5:25 ἡμῖν ἡμᾶς	ὑμεῖς ὑμῶν 5:12, 23, 28 ὑμῖν 5:12 ὑμᾶς 5:12 2ce, 14, 23, 24, 27	κυρίου ἡμῶν 5:23, 28

This table does not compare the frequency of third person pronouns.

Table 3. We and You pronouns.

Second in 2:3 he said "our word of encouragement." The sense is that the message that he spoke did not proceed out of trickery or flattery. The "our" is not absolutely necessary. It indicates that Paul may have been thinking, not about the gospel as any evangelist might speak it, but as he spoke it. There is a self-consciousness that he is the one who spoke it. Third, in 2:13 he spoke of "the word of our preaching." Again the "our" may imply that he was quite self-involved at this moment.

Furthermore, there are two cases where Paul said "of us" and then seems to catch and correct himself. In 1:6 he said, "You have become imitators of us and of the Lord." It is ambiguous whether we should read this as if Paul caught himself after saying "imitators of us" and then added "of the Lord" as an afterthought, or whether he thought of his own behavior and the Lord's behavior as a single entity. Paul made exactly the same self-correction in 3:6. When Timothy reports on their faith and love, it is all "your love for **us**" and "your good memory of **us**," and that "you desire to see **us** as much as we you." It is not until verse 3:8 that Paul shifted the focus from himself and his team to the Lord: "Now we can live, since you stand firm **in the Lord**." It is possible to read these passages as implying that Paul's focus was very much on himself.[155]

However, he also used the pronoun "you" more frequently in the Introduction of this letter than in the Ethical Instruction. This brings up a second possibility, that Paul was not overly focused on himself but on his relationship with his hearers. Paul's words kept reminding his hearers of their shared history, their shared warmth, the way they had become related because of their faith in Christ.

He also used other language that evokes family relationships, like father (2:11) and nurse (2:7), and *adelphoi*. As Paul used the word, he probably meant both men and women. My translation of *adelphoi* as "dear ones" lacks the implication that members of the ecclesia belong to the same family unit. The ecclesia was a new social way of relating one to another. It was to be a society of people who loved one another.

We have to consider that the concentration on the relationship and on its depth and warmth in the Introduction of the letter had a rhetorical function. They are in fact an extraordinary preparation for the Ethical Instruction, with the apparent intention of making the material in the Ethical Instruction as persuasive as possible.

155. Malherbe, *Letters*, 133-134. who otherwise is highly respectful of Paul and always presents him in the most favorable light (and who complains about others who are less respectful of scripture), observes that it is their love for Paul that meant the most to Paul and acknowledges that in this section Paul's focus stays on Paul. See also 77, where, although he states it very positively, Malherbe appears to admit Paul's level of self-involvement in the first three chapters.

Chapters 1-3

1st person	2nd person	3rd person
count: 23	count: 16	count: 14

1st person	2nd person	3rd person
δεδοκιμάσμεθα 2:4	ἐγενήθητε 1:6; 2:5, 14	ἀπαγγέλλουσιν 1:9
δυνάμεθα 3:9	ἐδέξασθε 2:11	γένηται 3:5
ἐγενήθημεν 1:5, 2:5, 7, 10	ἐπάθετε 2:14	γέγονεν 2:1
ἐκηρύξαμεν 2:9	ἐπεστρέψατε 1:9	ἐγένετο 3:4
ἐπαρρησιασάμεθα 2:2	ἐστε 2:20	ἐγενήθη 1:5
ἔπεμψα 3:4	ἔχετε 3:6	ἐνέκοψεν 2:18
ἐπεπέμψαμεν 3:2	οἴδατε 1:5, 2:1, 2, 5, 11; 3:3, 4	ἐνεργεῖται 2:13
ἐσπουδάσαμεν 2:17	στήκετε 3:8	ἐξελήλυθεν 1:8
ἔσχομεν 1:9		ἐξήχηται 1:8
ευδοκήσαμεν 3:1		ἐπείρασεν 3:5
εὐδοκοῦμεν 2:8		ἔστιν 2:13
εὐχαριστοῦμεν 1:2; 2:13	Inclusive we verbs	ἔφθασεν 2:16
ζῶμεν 3:8	2	ἤγειρεν 1:10
ἠθελήσαμεν 2:18		θάλπῃ 2:7
ἦμεν 3:4	κείμεθα 3:3	
λαλοῦμεν 2:4	μέλλομεν 3·4	
παρεκλήθημεν 3:7		
προελέγομεν 3:4		
χαίρομεν 3:9		

Chapter 4-5:11

count: 8	count: 16	count: 16
διαμαρτυράμεθα 4:6	ἐστε 4:9; 5:5 ἐστὲ 5:4	ἀθετεῖ 4:8
ἐδώκαμεν 4::2	ἔχετε 4:9; 5:1	ἀναστήσονται 4:16
ἐρωτῶμεν 4:1	ἔχητε 4:12	ἀνέστη 4:14
θέλομεν 4:13	λυπῆσθε 4:13	ἄξει 4:14
λέγομεν 4:15	οἴδατε 4:2; 5:2	ἀπέθανεν 4:14
παρακαλοῦμεν 4:1, 10	οἰκοδομεῖτε 5:10	ἔθετο 5:9
παρηγγείλαμεν 4:11	παρακαλεῖτε 4:18; 5:10	ἐκάλεσεν 4:7
προείπαμεν 4:6	παρελάβετε 4:1	ἐκφύγωσιν 5:3
	περιπατῆτε 4:12	ἔρχεται 5:2
	ποιεῖτε 4:10; 5:10	ἔστιν 4:3
Inclusive we verbs		ἐφίσταται 5:3
count: 9		καθεύδουσιν 5:7
		καταβήσεται 4:16
ἁρπαγησόμεθα 4:12		καταλάβῃ 5:4
γρηγορῶμεν 5:6, 10		λέγωσιν 5:3
ἐσμὲν 5:5		μεθύουσιν 5:7
ἐσόμεθα 4:17	νήφωμεν 5:6, 8	
ζήσωμεν 5:10	πιστεύομεν 4:14	
καθεύδωμεν 5:6, 10	φθάσομεν 4:15	

Chapter 5:12-27
Count 3   count 17   count 2

ἐνορκίζω 5:27   ἀντέχεσθε 5:14   ποιήσει 5:24
ἐρωτῶμεν 5:12   ἀπέχεσθε 5:22   τηρηθείη 5:23
παρακαλοῦμεν 5:14   ἀσπάσασθε 5:26
                                     διώκετε 5:15
                                     δοκιμάζετε 5:21
                                     εἰρηνεύετε 5:13
                                     ἐξουθενεῖτε 5:20
                                     εὐχαριστεῖτε 5:18
                                     κατέχετε 5:21
                                     μακροθυμεῖτε 5:14
                                     νουθετεῖτει 5:14

Table 4: 1st, 2nd, and 3rd person finite verbs

The social message that they belonged to one another as a family was the subject matter of the first part of the letter. The subjects of the second part, however, are what Paul had to say. He wrote the letter in order to convey the new information in chapters 4-5.

These differences of subject (the social message, the faith, and the shared history of part one, in contrast to the new information to be conveyed in the second part) account for much of the differences of style. The difference of style underscores the importance of what Paul said in the second part.

The unusual size and structure of the first three chapters can be construed as one piece of evidence for an interpretation congruent with the idea that Paul was wading into controversy. What we have said about chapters 1-3 being preparation for the topics which he was reluctant to discuss fits together with his perception of the trouble he was about to get into. Paul avoided getting to the things he had to say as long as he could.

Perhaps, on one hand, Paul developed his fighting strength in the years after the writing of this letter. Perhaps, on the other, what he developed was a certain skill that gave him an air of being comfortable fighting but that always cost him great effort. This latter possibility changes our image of him, portrays him as always stretched to his limit, reaching deep within himself for strength and love when he had to take controversial positions.

The alternation of energy in the Ethical Instruction of the letter highlights the significance of the instruction on *porneia* and the doctrine of the resurrection.

The extraordinary shape and size of the Introduction, with its extreme focus on the relationship between the apostolic team and the ecclesia functions as an extraordinary preparation for these two teachings. The focus on relationship causes its function as preparation to outweigh its function as paraenesis. This conclusion underscores the importance and sensitivity of these two main points of ethical instruction. They are the points that Paul needed to make, and they were extremely important to him. It was most important to him that he make these points as persuasively as he possibly could.

CHAPTER 2

THE TWO POINTS AT ISSUE

PAUL, then, had an agenda to present two topics: the resurrection of believers and the marriage mandate. The examination of these two topics will lead us into questions about why these topics were urgent.

The resurrection of believers

The resurrection of believers is part of the message of 4:13-18. There is more to the passage in a way that adds other content to the message and that also distracts from the newness of the doctrine.

Analysis of the verses one at a time will lead to some clarity about how Paul developed this passage and perhaps to why he developed it this way.

Paul's words

13a I do not want you not to know, dear ones,
about those who are sleeping.

Transactional Analysis

Paul began this passage with a standard Pauline phrase: "I do not want you not to know." Some interpreters say that this phrase generally "points to a misconception that needs to be clarified or dismissed."[156] Paul used this phrase five other times (see Table 5a). Those other times that Paul used this exact phrase, he introduced something new to his hearers. Some interpreters demur that we can hardly know what Paul's hearers knew or what he thought they knew, so caution is necessary. Since all five other uses of this phrase are in letters written somewhat later than our letter, we need to question whether Paul had already established the way he would use this phrase.

---

156. Richard, *Thessalonians*, 233.

```
Romans 1:13
οὐ θέλω δὲ ὑμᾶς ἀγνοεῖν, ἀδελφοί,
    ὅτι πολλάκις προεθέμην ἐλθεῖν πρὸς ὑμᾶς, καὶ ἐκωλύθην ἄχρι τοῦ δεῦρο, ἵνα τινὰ
    καρπὸν σχῶ καὶ ἐν ὑμῖν καθὼς καὶ ἐν τοῖς λοιποῖς ἔθνεσιν.


2 Corinthians 1:8
οὐ γὰρ θέλομεν ὑμᾶς ἀγνοεῖν, ἀδελφοί,
    ὑπὲρ τῆς θλίψεως ἡμῶν τῆς γενομένης ἐν τῇ Ἀσίᾳ ὅτι καθ᾽ ὑπερβολὴν ὑπὲρ δύναμιν
    ἐβαρήθημεν ὥστε ἐξαπορηθῆναι ἡμᾶς καὶ τοῦ ζῆν·

Romans 11:25
οὐ γὰρ θέλω ὑμᾶς ἀγνοεῖν, ἀδελφοί,
    τὸ μυστήριον τοῦτο, ἵνα μὴ ἦτε παρ᾽ ἑαυτοῖς φρόνιμοι, ὅτι πώρωσις ἀπὸ μέρους τῷ Ἰσραὴλ
    γέγονεν ἄχρι οὗ τὸ πλήρωμα τῶν ἐθνῶν εἰσέλθῃ καὶ οὕτως πᾶς Ἰσραὴλ σωθήσεται,
    καθὼς γέγραπται·

1 Corinthians 10:1
οὐ θέλω γὰρ ὑμᾶς ἀγνοεῖν, ἀδελφοί,
    ὅτι οἱ πατέρες ἡμῶν πάντες ὑπὸ τὴν νεφέλην ἦσαν καὶ πάντες διὰ τῆς θαλάσσης διῆλθον
    καὶ πάντες εἰς τὸν Μωυσῆν ἐβαπτίσθησαν ἐν τῇ νεφέλῃ καὶ ἐν τῇ θαλάσσῃ καὶ πάντες τὸ
    αὐτὸ πνευματικὸν ἔπιον πόμα·

1 Corinthians 12.1
οὐ θέλω ὑμᾶς ἀγνοεῖν
    Περὶ δὲ τῶν πνευματικῶν, ἀδελφοί,
```

Table 5a: I do not want you to be ignorant, brothers,

Paul used a similar expression, "I want you to know," in First Corinthians and in Philippians (see Table 5b). In the Philippians passage, Paul was talking about local current events; if the developments were news to his hearers, Paul would have been telling them something they did not know. If, however, rumor had already reached them, Paul might have been putting his spin on the events. In the First Corinthians passage, what he said next is theology. They probably already knew this theology. The phrase implies, in a backhanded sort of way, that they knew it; it is almost as if Paul were daring them to say that they did not know this theology.

Paul used another similar phrase, "I make known to you," twice in First Corinthians and once in Galatians. These three instances seem to me, in each case, to be keystones in his argument in those letters. In each case, the following statement is one that Paul would defend; in each case, the statement that follows is passionate (see Table 5c).

---

1 Corinthians 11:3
Θέλω δὲ ὑμᾶς εἰδέναι

ὅτι παντὸς ἀνδρὸς ἡ κεφαλὴ ὁ Χριστός ἐστιν, κεφαλὴ δὲ γυναικὸς ὁ ἀνήρ, κεφαλὴ δὲ τοῦ Χριστοῦ ὁ θεός.

Philippians 1:12-13
Γινώσκειν δὲ ὑμᾶς βούλομαι, ἀδελφοί,
ὅτι τὰ κατ᾽ ἐμὲ μᾶλλον εἰς προκοπὴν τοῦ εὐαγγελίου ἐλήλυθεν, ὥστε τοὺς δεσμούς μου φανεροὺς ἐν Χριστῷ γενέσθαι ἐν ὅλῳ τῷ πραιτωρίῳ καὶ τοῖς λοιποῖς πᾶσιν, καὶ τοὺς πλείονας τῶν ἀδελφῶν ἐν κυρίῳ πεποιθότας τοῖς δεσμοῖς μου περισσοτέρῳ τολμᾶν ἀφόβως τὸν λόγον λαλεῖν.

Colossians 2:1-3
θέλω γὰρ ὑμᾶς εἰδεναι
ἡλίκον ἀγῶνα ἔχω ὑπὲρ ὑμῶν καὶ τῶν ἐν Λαοδικείᾳ καὶ ὅσοι οὐχ ἑόρακαν τὸ πρόσωπόν μου ἐν σαρκί, ἵνα παρακληθῶσιν αἱ καρδίαι αὐτῶν συμβιβασθέντες ἐν ἀγάπῃ καὶ εἰς πᾶν πλοῦτος τῆς πληροφορίας τῆς συνέσεως, εἰς ἐπίγνωσιν τοῦ μυστηρίου τοῦ θεοῦ, Χριστοῦ, ἐν ᾧ εἰσιν πάντες οἱ θησαυροὶ τῆς σοφίας καὶ γνώσεως ἀπόκρυφοι.

Table 5b: I want you to know, brothers,

---

1 Corinthians 12:3 (cf. 1)
διὸ γνωρίζω ὑμῖν
ὅτι οὐδεὶς ἐν πνεύματι θεοῦ λαλῶν λέγει Ἀνάθεμα Ἰησοῦς, καὶ οὐδεὶς δύναται εἰπεῖν Κύριος Ἰησοῦς, εἰ μὴ ἐν πνεύματι ἁγίῳ.
It is unique that Paul says διὸ γνωρίζω ὑμῖν here immediately after saying οὐ θέλω ἀγνοεῖν in 12:1.

1 Corinthians 15:1
Γνωρίζω δὲ ὑμῖν, ἀδελφοί,
τὸ εὐαγγέλιον ὃ εὐηγγελισάμην ὑμῖν, ὃ καὶ παρελάβετε, ἐν ᾧ καὶ ἑστήκατε, δι᾽ οὗ καὶ σῴζεσθε, τίνι λόγῳ εὐηγγελισάμην ὑμῖν εἰ κατέχετε, ἐκτὸς εἰ μὴ εἰκῇ ἐπιστεύσατε.

Galatians 1:11
Γνωρίζω γὰρ ὑμῖν, ἀδελφοί
τὸ εὐαγγέλιον τὸ εὐαγγελισθὲν ὑπ᾽ ἐμοῦ ὅτι οὐκ ἔστιν κατὰ ἄνθρωπον·

Table 5c: I make known to you, brothers,

Another possible meaning of this phrase in First Thessalonians, "I do not want you not to know," is that Paul meant to emphasize what he will say next. When people are told that they are about to hear something new, they might expect something they had not heard before. This expression of Paul's probably alerted them. For him to alert his hearers that he is about to say something new would raise their expectations. Thus, this expression is a build-up to the point he is going to make. This expression means that what he will say next is important, worth the emphasis this opening comment gives to it.

Paul's saying "I do not want you not to know" adds nothing to the content of what he is going to say. It is a meta-comment. Paul needed to tell them the content of 4:13-18; he did not need to tell them that they did not know it.

Paul's opening statement may be his reflection, the dawning of the realization that his listeners do not know something. In this case, this expression would represent Paul's realization that he needs to tread carefully.

Another consideration comes from what he does not say. In both the passage before this (1 Thess 4:9-12) and in the following passage (5:1-11), Paul said there was no need to write to them on those subjects. However, he does not repeat that expression in this passage. This omission underscores the importance of what he says here.[157] There was need to write them on this subject! This positive conclusion, based on the omission, is suggestive and adds to the cumulative weight.

In exactly the same way, Paul did not say "as you know" or "as I told you before" here. In comparison with the number of such comments in the Introduction, Paul's decision not to use even one such comment in this passage is striking; it suggests, even though it does not prove the point, that he is telling them something new.

Therefore, Paul's expression, "I do not want you not to know," tends to confirm that Paul thought he was about to tell them something they did not know, and that it would lead his hearers to expect something that they had not heard before. However, it would not do to overemphasize this single phrase.

Paul used the expression "those who are sleeping" as a common euphemism for death. Paul may have used this euphemism here because it was the one that his friends in Thessalonica were using. Paul may have echoed their euphemism in verse 13 as part of his pastoral strategy. Perhaps they used it because they were in the denial stage of grief. Those who have hope, surely, can speak of death explicitly; those lacking hope might use the euphemism. Paul used the same expression twice more in this passage, except he changed it from the aspect of "those who are continuing to be sleeping" in verse 13 to

---

157. Luedemann, *Apostle*, 213: Unlike 4:9-12 and 5:1-11, which are declared to be unnecessary, 4:13-18 is not declared unnecessary; the absence of this disclaimer underlines the importance of this segment.

"those who have fallen asleep" in verses 14 and 15. It is only in verse 16 that he uses a more explicit expression, and there he uses an in-your-face word for the dead, *nekroi*.

Paul's words

¹³ᵇ so that you do not grieve like others who do not have hope.

Transactional Analysis

When people die who are close to us, we experience a shock that feels like a physical blow, and indeed, it may take place on a bodily level. We react to the loss of persons from our daily lives the way we react to any other loss, with both surprise and pain.

This half-verse, "so that you do not grieve like others who do not have hope," does not say that they should not grieve.[158] Paul's purpose was that they not grieve in a specific manner, that is, not grieve as others who do not have hope. There is a specific way of grieving to be avoided.

The use of the words "like others" suggests that Paul has some specific people in mind, whom he counsels his hearers not to imitate. Paul did not name the others. The word translated "others" is *loipoi* ("the rest"). Perhaps Paul meant the rest of the world outside the ecclesia.[159] Perhaps he meant all those who do not have hope. Perhaps he meant those who do not have the hope that belongs to the followers of Jesus.

Nevertheless, if his hearers are not to "grieve like others who do not have hope," perhaps we should understand the passage to mean that they are to grieve **with hope**. Hope is a catalyst that changes the grieving process. Grieving with hope permits us to complete the process of working through the emotional experience of loss without descending into despair.

Paul's words

¹⁴ For since we believe that Jesus died and rose,
so also God will through Jesus
lead with him those who have fallen asleep.

---

158. *pace* Malherbe, *Letters*, 263-264.

159. It is possible that not grieving like others is a cultural comment, on the grounds that Hellenistic grieving was an industry; however, the commotion described in Hebrew contexts, in Mark 5:38, because of the death of Jairus' daughter, and in Luke 7:11-12, at the procession with the widow of Nain, sound equally excessive.

Transactional Analysis

This verse anticipates Paul's argument, with a number of curiosities. It is even more awkward in Greek than this translation shows. One commentator describes it as a "stylistically awkward construction that is singular among Paul's creedal formulations."[160] Another describes it as "somewhat disjointed."[161] Another refers to "grammatical awkwardness."[162] Yet none of them raised the further question why Paul expressed himself so awkwardly.

Perhaps the awkwardness of this verse indicates that Paul was struggling with a new thought. Perhaps it suggests he was aware that this new doctrine might cause controversy. The combination of these two could explain the logical problems with this verse.

The verb "rose" is unusual; rather than saying that Jesus rose, Paul usually says that God raised Jesus. Here he waits until the second clause to introduce God. If he had said, "Since God raised Jesus from the dead, God will also raise those who have died," the two clauses would have been parallel. Nevertheless, he did not say that. What he says is much more awkward than that.

The first clause says "we believe that . . ." The "we believe" construction is unnecessary to Paul's point and complicates things. We might expect the second clause to parallel it by beginning with "we believe that." Paul might have said, "Since we believe that Jesus died and rose, we may in the same way believe that God will raise those who have died." That would retain the perspective that both clauses are what we believe.[163]

We could just as easily remove the belief-perspective by saying, "Since Jesus died and rose, God will in the same way raise those who have died." Jesus rose from the dead whether or not we think he did. Whatever logic is involved here, the resurrection of Jesus' followers depends upon Jesus' resurrection. The logic is not dependent upon the belief of the ecclesia.

The "through Jesus" and "with him" phrases seem redundant and are im-

---

160. Luedeman, *Apostle*, 219.

161. Richard, *Thessalonians*, 225.

162. Malherbe, *Letters*, 265-266.

163. On two technicalities, this statement of belief is not a creedal statement. First, all of the creeds that can be dated before the fourth century are singular: "I believe . . ." Second, the creeds are statements of "belief in . . ." and not statements of "belief that . . .", which this statement is. The creeds are statements of confidence in a person or God rather than an assent to a proposition. The use of the conjunction *hoti* identifies this as a proposition: *pisteuomen hoti Iêsous apethanen kai anestê* asserts the proposition that Jesus died and rose.

portant to distinguish. These two phrases are confusing because they appear close together. The phrase "through Jesus" is sometimes taken as modifying "those who have fallen asleep." The interpretation that Paul meant those who have fallen asleep through or because of Jesus has led some commentators to think that Paul meant martyrs, those who have died because of Jesus, giving their lives as testimony to their faith.[164] Except for Stephen,[165] however, the great numbers of those who would die because of their commitment to Jesus were still in the future.[166]

The correct interpretation is to take "through Jesus" as modifying the verb "will lead." The idea is that God will lead the deceased as a result of Jesus or because of Jesus. Paul's use of the preposition *dia* ("through") suggests a principle or precedent. "Through him" is the means employed. The implicit thought is that Jesus has established the foundation or principle or precedent by which God has become able to bring the dead with Jesus. Because of Jesus, God is now able to bring the dead into the *parousia*. We could wish that Paul had been more explicit, because it would have been valuable theology.

This means that we are free to take "with him" literally. "With him" means a joining together, that he and they will be together. The result of God's leading will be a gathering of the saints, both dead and alive, with Jesus, in his arrival and in the inauguration of his reign.

Paul was dealing with six realities: Jesus' death, his resurrection, and his *parousia*, and the deaths of members of the ecclesia, their resurrection, and their being gathered into the *parousia*. In the first half of this verse, Paul referred to the first two: the death and resurrection of Jesus. In the second half he spoke of the death and *parousia* of believers, since the expression "will... lead with him" refers to the *parousia*, when the faithful will meet Christ in the air. The progression of thought is from the death and resurrection of Jesus to the *parousia* of deceased believers, but the resurrection of believers is not explicitly stated in this verse. In such a progression, the death of Jesus corresponds to the death of members of the ecclesia. The term that corresponds to the resurrection of Jesus, then, is the resurrection of believers, which is not

---

164. Luedeman, *Apostle*, 217.

165. If the story of the martyrdom of Stephen is historical, it happened before the writing of this letter.

166. *Pace* Donfried, *Thessalonian Cults*, 349-350. Donfried thought that those who had fallen asleep are Christians who died in persecution.

explicit. He appears to have skipped a step that would tie Jesus' resurrection to his *parousia*. He left out the step that would tie Jesus' resurrection to the resurrection of believers. Then he left out a step to tie the death and resurrection of believers to their *apantêsis* with Jesus.

Paul's omission in this verse of the resurrection of believers means that his hearers were free to draw that conclusion. Indeed, since he mentions the death and resurrection of Jesus and implies Jesus' *parousia*, and mentions the *parousia* of the believers, he has engineered his hearers into drawing that conclusion. As we shall see, a later verse states the resurrection of believers explicitly, but this verse has already led his hearers into it.

Of these six realities, Paul has placed "with him" last. In English what comes at the end of a sentence is usually its most important thought. Greek, by way of contrast, often ends sentences with words of remarkably little importance. We have, however, mentioned previously a case where it seemed that Paul ended a sentence with its most important words. So it is a question whether these words are an instance of this sort of sentence structure or not. If so, then the most important part of this future, when God will lead those who have fallen asleep, is that they will be with Jesus.

Paul's words

¹⁵ᵃ This, of course, we say to you in accordance with the gospel.

Transactional Analysis

Like verse 13, this verse is also a meta-comment. It does not add directly to what Paul was saying. It is usually taken as a claim of the Lord's authority for Paul's point. Both the first words and the last words of this verse have caused discussion and disagreement. What did Paul mean by *touto gar*, the first words, and what does he mean by *en logôi kyriou*, the last words?

The literal translation of *en logôi kyrioi* is "in the word of the Lord." That seems to refer to something that Jesus said. Three possibilities have been suggested: (1) something Jesus said before he was crucified, (2) something that was said by a Christian prophet speaking in the name of Jesus, or (3) something that the risen Jesus said to Paul.

Where Paul referred to what Jesus said about divorce (1 Cor 7:10), it is easy to guess that he meant a saying similar to the one in Mark 10:7-8. Paul also referred to traditions that he received and passed on in 1 Cor 11:23-26 and 15:3-8. In the former, which is Paul's tradition of the Lord's supper, he includes the words that Jesus said. Therefore, Paul attributed some sayings to the earthly Jesus and considered them distinctive. In this case, however, several passages from the four Gospels have been proposed and none of them appears to fit exactly with Paul's reference (see Table 6). There is, therefore, no evidence one way or the other that he had one of them in mind when he wrote 1 Thess 4:15a.

Perhaps a Christian prophet spoke these words and Paul was referring to such a saying. Paul respected Christian prophecy. In First Thessalonians he says, "Do not quench the spirit; do not belittle prophecy" (5:19-20). In 1 Cor 12-14, he argued at great length for the value of prophecy. However, we are not able to consider this as more than a suggestion, because there is no evidence to suggest that Paul was here referring to a prophecy spoken by a Christian prophet.

If we are committed to reading *en logôi kyriou* as referring to a saying of Jesus, and we do not have that saying, then perhaps it was something the risen Jesus said to Paul directly.[167] If Paul meant that he himself received a revelation from the Lord, to the effect that God will lead the deceased to be with Jesus, then it would appear that the resurrection of believers was in fact a new doctrine, based upon that revelation given to Paul. If so, we would not say that Paul came up with it as a new idea, but that it was given to him as a revelation. As a revelation, it might have been just as new, but with dominical rather than human authority.

However, when Paul spoke about information that was given to him as a revelation, he used the word *apocalypsis* ("the revelation of a hidden truth").[168] He did not use the word *apocalypsis* here, which implies that he did not mean *en logôi kyriou* to refer to a revelation.

---

167. Malherbe, *Letters*, 268: Malherbe is very cautious; but it is a good guess that he thinks *en logôi kyriou* refers to a revelation given personally to Paul.

168. Galatians 1:12 and 2:2. He also speaks of a revelatory experience in Second Corinthians 12:1-4. These verses may make it clear that Paul himself had ecstatic, revelatory experiences; since the Second Corinthians passage refers to an event of fourteen years previous, we are confident that Paul had at least one such experience prior to the writing of First Thessalonians.

1) The two uses of λόγος κυρίου in 1 Thess.
   "the Lord's discourse" , "the gospel" , "a saying of the Lord"
   1 Thess. 1:8 ἀφ' ὑμῶν γὰρ ἐξήχηται ὁ λόγος κυρίου is almost a parallel.
                 ὁ λόγος κυρίου = the gospel
   1 Thess 4:14 λέγομεν ἐν λόγῳ κυρίου. Liddell and Scott, 221a, ἐν 6. according to, in
                 accordance with.
                 ἐν λόγῳ κυρίου = in accordance with the gospel
2) Paul's references to actual statements made by Jesus.
   1 Cor 7:10   Τοῖς δὲ γεγαμηκόσιν παραγγέλλω, οὐκ ἐγὼ ἀλλὰ ὁ κύριος, γυναῖκα ἀπὸ
                ἀνδρὸς μὴ χωρισθῆναι,
   1 Cor 9:14   οὕτως καὶ ὁ κύριος διέταξεν τοῖς τὸ εὐαγγέλιον καταγγέλλουσιν ἐκ τοῦ
                εὐαγγελίου ζῆν.
   1 Cor 11:23 ἐγὼ γὰρ παρέλαβον ἀπὸ τοῦ κυρίου, ὅ καὶ παρέδωκα ὑμῖν, ὅτι ὁ κύριος
                Ἰησοῦς ἐν τῇ νυκτὶ ᾗ παρεδίδετο ἔλαβεν ἄρτον
3) Candidate phrases from the Gospels.
   Matt 10:39   ὁ εὑρὼν τὴν ψυχὴν αὐτοῦ ἀπολέσει αὐτήν, καὶ ὁ ἀπολέσας τὴν ψχὴν αὐτοῦ
                ἔνεκεν ἐμοῦ εὑρήσει αὐτήν.
   Matt 16:25   ὅς γὰρ ἐὰν θέλῃ τὴν ψυχὴν αὐτοῦ σῶσαι ἀπολέσει αὐτήν· ὅς δ᾽ ἂν ἀπολέσῃ
                τὴν ψυχὴν αὐτοῦ ἔνεκεν ἐμοῦ εὑρήσει αὐτήν.
   Matt 16:28   ἀμὴν λέγω ὑμῖν ὅτι εἰσίν τινες τῶν ὧδε ἑστώτων οἵτινες οὐ μὴ γεύσωνται
                θανάτου ἕως ἂν ἴδωσιν τὸν υἱὸν τοῦ ἀνθρώπου ἐρχόμενον ἐν τῇ βασιλείᾳ
                αὐτοῦ.
   Matt 24:31   καὶ ἀποστελεῖ τοὺς ἀγγέλους αὐτοῦ μετὰ σάλπιγγος μεγάλης, καὶ
                ἐπισυνάξουσιν τοὺς ἐκλεκτοὺς αὐτοῦ ἐκ τῶν τεσσάρων ἀνέμων ἀπ᾽
                ἀπκρων οὐρανῶν ἕως τῶν ἄκρων αὐτῶν.
   Matt 24:34   ἀμὴν λέγω ὑμῖν ὅτι οὐ μὴ παρέλθῃ ἡ γενεὰ αὕτη ἕως ἂν πάντα ταῦτα
                γένηται.
   Matt 25:6   μέσης δὲ νυκτὸς κραυγὴ γέγονεν· ἰδοὺ ὁ νυμφίος. ἐξέρχεσθε εἰς
                ἀπάντησιν αὐτοῦ.
   Matt 26:64   λέγει αὐτῷ ὁ Ἰησοῦς· σὺ εἶπας. πλὴν λέγω ὑμῖν· ἀπ᾽ ἄρτι ὄψεσθε τὸν υἱὸν
                τοῦ ἀνθρώπου καθήμενον ἐκ δεξιῶν τῆς δυνάμεως καὶ ἐρχόμενον ἐπὶ τῶν
                νεφελῶν τοῦ οὐρανοῦ.
   Luke 13:30   καὶ ἰδοὺ εἰσὶν ἔσχατοι οἳ ἔσονται πρῶτοι καὶ εἰσὶν πρῶτοι οἳ ἔσονται
                ἔσχατοι.
   John 5:25   ἀμὴν ἀμὴν λέγω ὑμῖν ὅτι ἔρχεται ὥρα καὶ νῦν ἐστιν ὅτε οἱ νεκροὶ
                ἀκούσουσιν τῆς φωνῆς τοῦ υἱοῦ τοῦ θεοῦ καὶ οἱ ἀκούσαντες ζήσουσιν.[1]
   John 6:39-40 τοῦτο δέ ἐστιν τὸ θέλημα τοῦ πέμψαντός με, ἵνα πᾶν ὃ δέδωκέν μοι μὴ
                ἀπολέσω ἐξ αὐτοῦ, ἀλλὰ ἀναστήσω αὐτὸ ἐν τῇ ἐσχάτῃ ἡμέρᾳ. τοῦτο γὰρ
                ἐστιν τὸ θέλημα τοῦ πατρός μου, ἵνα πᾶς ὁ θεωρῶν τὸν υἱὸν καὶ πιστεύων
                εἰς αὐτὸν ἔχῃ ζωὴν αἰώνιον, καὶ ἀναστήσω αὐτὸν ἐγὼ ἐν τῇ ἐσχάτ ἡμέρα.

---

[1] John 5:25 seems pretty close to me; I don't know why scholars have not selected it. If we are correct that there was
a time when the resurrection of believers became a new belief in the Jesus movement, then John 5:25 and First
Thessalonians 4:13-18 might offer testimony to the same moment.

Table 6. Sayings of Jesus which might lie behind 1 Thess 4:15a.

The Greek word *logos* had a broader meaning than "word." It customarily has a broad range of meaning, from "saying," "meaning," and "discourse" to "argument." We have a hint of what Paul might have meant by his other use of *logos kyriou,* in 1 Thess 1:8, where he says that "the *logos kyriou* has gone out from you throughout Macedonia and Achaia." There Paul used *logos kyriou* to mean the good news or gospel of Jesus Christ. If Paul meant the same thing in 4:15a, we would translate, "This, of course, we say to you in the good news."

The preposition *en* is usually translated "in," "with," or "by"; but it is a stretch to translate it "as." The translation "We say this to you **as** a word of the Lord" distorts the preposition *en*. In classical Greek, however, *en* can also mean "according to" or "in accordance with." Therefore, we translate the phrase *en logôi kyriou* as "in accordance with the gospel."

For Paul, the gospel meant the equality of all in Christ. It meant the kenosis of Jesus, who humbled himself to crucifixion (Phil 2:5-10). It meant a reversal of status-in-the-world. "The last shall be first and the first shall be last" (Mark 10:31 and parallels Matthew 19:30 and Luke 13:30). So for Paul to assert that even those who are most disadvantaged by death will be raised to participate in the *parousia* is in accordance with the gospel. The good news of the gospel is always that those who appear to be disadvantaged are to be given the advantage. It is at the heart of all that he says.

The other problem with this verse is the opening two words, *touto gar* (see Table 7). The word *touto* ("this") may refer to the previous verse (verse 14), the clause in the second half of 15 (verse 15b), or the mini-apocalypse in the following verse (verse16).[169] *Touto* was often used to refer back to what has just been said, and Paul often used it that way. If Paul meant *touto* in verse 15a to refer to what he has just said, then he is asserting authority for the preceding statement that through Jesus, God will lead with him those who have fallen asleep. However, *touto* may refer to the second half of this verse, which begins with a subordinating conjunction, *hoti* ("that"). The second half of verse 15 states "that we the living who are being left behind will not precede those who have fallen asleep at the Lord's *parousia*." Because of the subordinating conjunction, *hoti*, the *touto* at the beginning of verse 15 may refer to this clause. If Paul intended the verse this way, we might paraphrase his meaning: what Paul says about the living not preceding the deceased at the *parousia* is in accordance with the gospel.

---

169. The experts disagree. Luedemann, *Apostle*, 221, suggests that *gar* looks back and *touto* marks the beginning of a new section. Richard, *Thessalonians*, 240, says that the initial *touto* refers to what follows. Malherbe, *Letters*, 267: "The *touto* points forward to the explanation that begins with *hoti* ('that')."

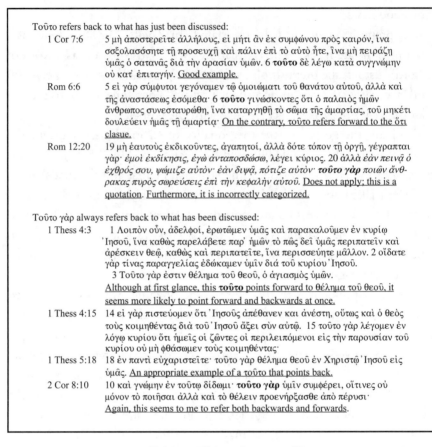

Τοῦτο refers back to what has just been discussed:
  1 Cor 7:6   5 μὴ ἀποστερεῖτε ἀλλήλους, εἰ μήτι ἂν ἐκ συμφώνου πρὸς καιρόν, ἵνα
                 σσξολασόσητε τῇ προσευχῇ καὶ πάλιν ἐπὶ τὸ αὐτὸ ἦτε, ἵνα μὴ πειράζῃ
                 ὑμᾶς ὁ σατανᾶς διὰ τὴν ἀρασίαν ὑμῶν. 6 **τοῦτο** δὲ λέγω κατὰ συγγνώμην
                 οὐ κατ᾽ ἐπιταγήν. Good example.
  Rom 6:6   5 εἰ γὰρ σύμφυτοι γεγόναμεν τῷ ὁμοιώματι τοῦ θανάτου αὐτοῦ, ἀλλὰ καὶ
                 τῆς ἀναστάσεως ἐσόμεθα· 6 **τοῦτο** γινώσκοντες ὅτι ὁ παλαιὸς ἡμῶν
                 ἄνθρωπος συνεσταυρώθη, ἵνα καταργηθῇ τὸ σῶμα τῆς ἁμαρτίας, τοῦ μηκέτι
                 δουλεύειν ἡμᾶς τῇ ἁμαρτίᾳ· On the contrary, τοῦτο refers forward to the ὅτι
                 clasue.
  Rom 12:20   19 μὴ ἑαυτοὺς ἐκδικοῦντες, ἀγαπητοί, ἀλλὰ δότε τόπον τῇ ὀργῇ, γέγραπται
                 γὰρ· ἐμοὶ ἐκδίκησις, ἐγὼ ἀνταποδώσω, λέγει κύριος. 20 ἀλλὰ ἐὰν πεινᾷ ὁ
                 ἐχθρός σου, ψώμιζε αὐτόν· ἐὰν διψᾷ, πότιζε αὐτόν· **τοῦτο γὰρ** ποιῶν ἄνθ-
                 ρακας πυρὸς σωρεύσεις ἐπὶ τὴν κεφαλὴν αὐτοῦ. Does not apply; this is a
                 quotation. Furthermore, it is incorrectly categorized.

Τοῦτο γὰρ always refers back to what has been discussed:
  1 Thess 4:3   1 Λοιπὸν οὖν, ἀδελφοί, ἐρωτῶμεν ὑμᾶς καὶ παρακαλοῦμεν ἐν κυρίῳ
                 Ἰησοῦ, ἵνα καθὼς παρελάβετε παρ᾽ ἡμῶν τὸ πῶς δεῖ ὑμᾶς περιπατεῖν καὶ
                 ἀρέσκειν θεῷ, καθὼς καὶ περιπατεῖτε, ἵνα περισσεύητε μᾶλλον. 2 οἴδατε
                 γὰρ τίνας παραγγελίας ἐδώκαμεν ὑμῖν διὰ τοῦ κυρίου Ἰησοῦ.
                 3 Τοῦτο γὰρ ἐστιν θέλημα τοῦ θεοῦ, ὁ ἁγιασμὸς ὑμῶν.
                 Although at first glance, this **τοῦτο** points forward to θέλημα τοῦ θεοῦ, it
                 seems more likely to point forward and backwards at once.
  1 Thess 4:15   14 εἰ γὰρ πιστεύομεν ὅτι Ἰησοῦς ἀπέθανεν και ἀνέστη, οὕτως καὶ ὁ θεὸς
                 τοὺς κοιμηθέντας διὰ τοῦ Ἰησοῦ ἄξει σὺν αὐτῷ. 15 τοῦτο γὰρ λέγομεν ἐν
                 λόγῳ κυρίου ὅτι ἡμεῖς οἱ ζῶντες οἱ περιλειπόμενοι εἰς τὴν παρουσίαν τοῦ
                 κυρίου οὐ μὴ φθάσωμεν τοὺς κοιμηθέντας·
  1 Thess 5:18   18 ἐν παντὶ εὐχαριστεῖτε· τοῦτο γὰρ θέλημα θεοῦ ἐν Χηριστῷ Ἰησοῦ εἰς
                 ὑμᾶς. An appropriate example of a τοῦτο that points back.
  2 Cor 8:10   10 καὶ γνώμην ἐν τούτῳ δίδωμι· **τοῦτο γὰρ** ὑμῖν συμφέρει, οἵτινες οὐ
                 μόνον τὸ ποιῆσαι ἀλλὰ καὶ τὸ θέλειν προενήρξασθε ἀπὸ πέρυσι·
                 Again, this seems to me to refer both backwards and forwards.

Table 7: This, of course,[170]

Verse 15b, about the living not preceding the deceased at the *parousia*,
restates and only slightly modifies the statement in verse 14, that God will
lead the deceased to be with Jesus. If we consider that verses 14 and 15b are
saying almost the same thing, then *touto* in 15a points in both directions at
once. It points backwards to the preceding phrase and forwards to the following phrase.

The third possibility is that *touto* may point to verse 16a, the mini-apocalypse, which describes the sounds that will be heard when the Lord steps
down from heaven. The mini-apocalypse is introduced by the same result

---

170. These seven citations come from the passage in Richard, *Thessalonians*, 240, just cited.
I have sequenced them in the order in which the letters were written, and the underlined
comments are mine.

conjunction, *hoti,* so that the grammatical structure gives it a sense parallel to verse 15b. Because of the repetition of *hoti,* it is possible that Paul intended to refer to this mini-apocalypse when he wrote the word *touto* at the beginning of verse 15. It seems likely then, that the three grammatical considerations add together. The *touto gar* points backwards but the two *hotis* point forward. Probably Paul's hearers would not have heard the word "this" as referring to only one of the three; they likely heard it as referring to all three phrases.

Touto gar, then, refers to the previous verse, that God will lead with Jesus those who have fallen asleep. It also refers forward to the reassuring news that the deceased will go ahead of us the living. At the same time it refers ahead to the commanding shout and stirring trumpet, announcing the Lord's arrival. *Touto gar,* then, means that all of this is in accordance with the gospel.

Likewise, when he stated that what he said is in accordance with the gospel, or that it is based on a saying of the Lord, however we understand that phrase, he asserted authority for his communication. This statement is not part of the communication; it is an external buttress to it.

Paul's words

15b that we the living who are being left behind
      will not precede those who have fallen asleep
      when the Lord arrives.

Transactional Analysis

The key thought of this verse is expressed in its verb *phthasomen.*[171] In Paul's time this verb had come to mean "to arrive" and was used intransitively. However, here, Paul used it in a somewhat antique sense, with an object, so that it means "to arrive ahead of" or "precede" something else. The transitive use with the object, "those who have fallen asleep," is the clue to Paul's using the verb *phthasomen* in its older sense. He used it to say that we the living will not arrive ahead of those who have died.

This is a direct answer to the concern about the dead: God will lead them to be with Jesus. The living will not precede the deceased in the *parousia.* When God leads the living and the dead into the *apantêsis* at Christ's *parousia,* the dead will not be assigned a lower status. They will not be disadvantaged. According to Paul's unusual transitive use of the verb *phthasomen,*

---

171. See the discussion of *ephthasen* on page 95.

the dead will actual go ahead of those who are still alive; they will be the ones with the advantage.

Paul turns the tables with *perileipomenoi* ("who are being left behind"). If the Thessalonians were afraid that upon Jesus' return, the living would go to meet him and the dead would be left behind, Paul reversed the field by identifying those who are still alive as the ones who are being left behind. The deceased will be gathered up first and only afterwards the living; momentarily, the living will be left behind. Not only did Paul make his focus clear by his choice of the word *phthasomen*; he also made it subtly with the participle "being left behind." There is something witty about the way he does this, and perhaps there is a bit of a tease as a gentle way of encouraging these Thessalonians to think differently about their deceased friends.

Like the statement of verse 14, that God will lead the dead into the *parousia*, this statement that the living will not precede the dead into the kingdom of heaven is theological. It says something about the nature of God: God is capable of following through on the promise of love made in the gospel; and God does not disadvantage any of those to whom the promise has been made.

Paul's words

> ¹⁶ᵃ that with a commanding shout
>   with an archangel's call,
>   and with the trumpet's call to arms,
>   the Lord himself will step down from heaven.

Transactional Analysis

As we have seen, the *touto gar* of the previous verse (15a) points both backward, to the statement in verse 14 that God will lead with Jesus those who have fallen asleep, and forward to the *hoti* clauses in 15b and 16a. Verse 16a is a mini-apocalypse that rings with impressive sounds. It is not often noticed, however, just how noisy this passage is.

It is unusual for Paul to use imagery and unusual (though not unique)[172] for him to refer to sound effects. The phrase *en keleusmati* ("with a commanding shout") appears nowhere else in the New Testament.[173] The phrase

---

172. The uncertain trumpet in 1 Cor 14:7-8 is another audible metaphor.

173. *keleusma* "shout of command" or "command." Richard, *Thessalonians*, 229, says this is a technical military term, quoting Thucydides 2.92.1 and Josephus *Jewish Antiquities* 27.140. He

en phonê archangelou ("with an archangel's call") appears nowhere else in the New Testament, although Paul used *phonê* in other contexts, and *archangelos* is also found in Jude 9. The *salpigx* of *en salpiggi* ("with the trumpet's call to arms") appears elsewhere only in First Corinthians 15:52, where it has the same apocalyptic function as here.[174] The trumpet, being an instrument with a piercing tone, was used by Roman armies to communicate instructions: the soldiers would learn whether to advance or retreat from the sound of the trumpet. Paul's hearers, familiar with the ancient battlefield, would also hear, in their minds, the clang and confusion of battle.

Since Paul did not use these phrases elsewhere, it has been suggested that he is quoting from a source.[175] If that is the case, it is a spot-on quotation, exactly appropriate to make an appealing image. However, the fact that he does not repeat a word in such a small *oeuvre* does not necessarily mean that it is part of a quotation from somebody else.[176]

Paul's words

[16b] and the dead shall rise in Christ first,

Transactional Analysis

This half-verse comes right after the mini-apocalypse. If the mini-apocalypse is a quotation, these words might be part of the same quotation. It is be hard to know where the quotation ended. Likewise, if we are thinking that *en logôi kyriou* introduced something Jesus said, the saying of Jesus might include both the mini-apocalypse and this verse. Nevertheless, the expression here is *hoi nekroi*, a word Paul used earlier in this letter. It therefore seems more likely that this verse is Paul's own composition, because of *hoi nekroi*, and also because of the way the word "first" echoes the "will not precede" of verse 15. This last word of this phrase, *prôton* ("first"), points to Paul's focus. It is not a focus on the resurrection of believers, but on the order in which they rise. The dead go first. Without the interruption of the mini-apocalypse, Paul would be saying, "The living will not precede the dead; the dead will go

---

refers to Euripides *Iphigenia in Tauris* 1483 as a divine command and Philo, *On Rewards and Punishments*, 117, for a gathering of God's elect.

174. The identification of all three *hapax legomena* are from Luedemann, *Apostle*, 223.

175. Luedemann, *Apostle*, 230-37, discusses a Jewish apocalyptic substratum.

176. Hurd, *Earlier Letters*, 101, discusses the use of *hapax legomena* as a witness against Pauline authorship.

first." Paul has emphatically moved them to the front of the line. This focus echoes Jesus' saying that the last shall be first, and it also is profoundly in accordance with the gospel as Paul understood it, a gospel of love that humbled itself.

Paul's words

17a then we the living
     who are being left behind
     will be snatched up in the clouds
     for the meeting with the Lord in the air;

Transactional Analysis

Paul has given us a scenario of a two stage *apantêsis*. He set the scene with his use of the verb *phthasomen*, "will not precede," and then emphasizes it with the adverb *prôton*, "first." Now, by the use of *epeita* ("then"), he makes the *apantêsis* of the living into a subsequent stage. The use of these words, one after another, makes it clear that his focus is on **this sequence**. The *parousia* seems to be the point; but Paul's attention was really on how the deceased will participate in it. They will not be disadvantaged in the *parousia*. In fact, they will be given the advantage of going first.

Incidentally, it is worth noting that the word *harpagêsometha* ("snatched") does not refer to both the living and the deceased. It refers only to the living. This word has the mildly violent connotation of thievery. Perhaps Paul is suggesting that the deceased go to meet the descending Lord *naturally*, while there is something violent and unnatural about the way the living are to be gathered to him. This usage once again underlines the advantage given to the supposedly disadvantaged, and the reversal of status that is the gospel.

Paul's words

17b in this way we shall always be with the Lord.

Transactional Analysis

Paul has here restated the goal of this whole event: we shall, both living and dead, be gathered to the Lord. However, with one word, *houtôs* ("thus" or "in this way"), he shifted the focus from the goal to the manner in which we shall be gathered. It is hard to capture the impact of this word in the translation. We tend to read the English clause as a statement that we will be with the Lord forever. The Greek emphasizes the manner by which we are joined with the Lord. The word *houtôs* looks back at the two-stage movement of the dead and the living in verses 16 and 17. It is by means of this double parade that we will be gathered to be with him.

Analysis of this passage as a whole

The proposal that the resurrection of believers was an addition to the Gospel when Paul wrote this passage has been rejected by most scholars, most significantly on the grounds that Paul was making a point, not introducing a new doctrine. However, Paul's use of the intransitive verb, "rose" calls attention to this doctrine. The creedal structure singles out the resurrection. The manner in which verse 14 leads the hearer to draw a conclusion accentuates it. Paul's use of the expression, "being left behind" gives prominence to the resurrection. Finally, the distraction provided by the sounds of the apocalypse suggest some sleight of hand, that Paul is both introducing something new and distracting his hearers from what he is doing.

On the grounds that Paul and those who formed the ecclesia originally expected that Christ would return to reign during their lifetimes, it has been suggested that the resurrection of believers was not part of Paul's original proclamation and that the death of some members was a problem.[177] According to this suggestion, adding the resurrection of believers to the expectation of Christ's return was a solution to this problem. First Thessalonians marks the historical moment when the resurrection of believers was added to the content of Christianity, and Paul can be credited with the creative solution of adapting an available idea to the theological needs of his communities.

Today the resurrection of believers is so much an accepted part of Christianity that it is hard to think of a milieu when it was not part of the gospel. If it was a new thought as late as the 50s, then the Christian message developed; the message was not complete when Jesus gathered his community of disciples. It seems to me that it is difficult for many people to accept that Christianity's system of belief has gone through several stages of development, even a stage of development as early as during the first twenty years after Jesus' death.

Furthermore, if the resurrection of believers was a new thought at this time, then Paul changed his mind about the gospel and preached a differ-

---

177. Buck and Taylor, *St. Paul*, 46-47.

ent gospel later than he had preached earlier, and a different gospel than he preached when he was part of a ministry team with Barnabas in Antioch. Most scholars, however, do not believe that there was any change or development in Paul's theology, partly on the grounds that his thinking was already mature when he began writing the letters which are part of our New Testament, and because the letters were written over a period of too few years for there to have been development in his thinking.[178]

Nevertheless, it appears that the first generation of Paul's followers of Jesus expected Christ to return in their own lifetimes. A belief system based on this premise has the capacity to be mature and complete, even if it was headed toward a change in expectation. For Paul to have changed his mind about the immediacy of Christ's return is not a matter of immaturity or incompletion. It is a matter of responding to reality, to the real life situation of the followers of Jesus and their religious needs.

The conclusion that Paul was fully mature and that the development of his theology was complete by the time he wrote this letter is based on evidence other than examination of his letters. This needs to be rethought. The evidence of the letters may be telling or it may be inconclusive; yet it is not correct, based on other evidence, to foreclose the issue of development before the letters have been examined completely and in isolation.

What hope is offered to Paul's hearers in this passage? Our first impression might be that they lacked hope that the dead would be raised. For the last several hundred years, Christians have focused on the promise of eternal life. We would thus expect that the focus would be their inclusion in the kingdom of God. Did they fear that when Christ came, the deceased would be left behind in their graves?

Did they, alternatively, fear that the deceased would have some lower status in the kingdom than those who lived until Christ's arrival? If Paul's hearers expected as the meaning of the gospel they embraced, to rule with Christ in his *parousia*, and if they expected that Christ would return in their lifetimes, then what would happen to those who had died? Would they be able to reign with Christ?[179] Or would they be relegated to some lower status

---

178. Malherbe, *Letters*, 13, states this as a positive affirmation of his conclusions. Hurd, *Origin*, states it repeatedly as a criticism.

179. Richard, *Thessalonians*, 231-45. Richard's essay covers both the issues of the status of the deceased and their participation in the reign of Christ.

in the kingdom?

According to these arguments, Paul had a specific intention for this passage. If the problem to which Paul was responding was their grieving without hope, his intent was to give them a ground on which they may change their conduct.[180] By giving them the hope that the dead would be raised, he gave them an alternative to grieving. If his purpose was to give them an alternative to grieving, then it was not his intention to introduce a new teaching.

This passage suggests, not only that the deceased will not be disadvantaged when Christ arrives; but that they will have the advantage of going first. Therefore, the passage makes it quite clear that Paul's primary purpose was to clarify the status of the deceased; and since this is so, it was not his primary purpose to propose a new doctrine.

Neither of those arguments is conclusive. Whether it was his stated purpose to provide them hope, to assure his hearers that the deceased would not be disadvantaged in the *parousia*, or to give them a ground on which they might change their behavior from grieving to rejoicing, it could also have been his purpose to present a new doctrine. Whether or not Paul was introducing a new doctrine is independent of his stated purpose. Paul may have introduced a new doctrine ancillary to his real purpose of giving hope for the dead and reassurance regarding their status in the *parousia*.

At issue is whether Paul could do two things at once. Could he both introduce a new doctrine and encourage his hearers to have hope? If he was presenting a new doctrine, it was not to his advantage to say so. Saying that he was presenting a new doctrine would invite controversy. For him to say that he was doing something else was to his advantage.

It is more likely that he was doing both. If Paul introduced a new doctrine here, and if he knew or suspected that it would be controversial, it is an effective rhetorical technique for him to concentrate on stating the principle that the deceased will not be disadvantaged while leaving it to his hearers to draw the conclusion, new to them, that the dead will be resurrected. It was an advantage to Paul that he introduced the new idea while he was calling attention to something else, while he was doing everything he could to call attention to the primary message of hope.

---

180. Malherbe, *Letters*, 279. The point of 4:13-18 is not to give them new theology but to change their behavior, i.e., they are not to grieve.

If the resurrection of believers was not a new idea, then it should be possible to show evidence that it was already part of Paul's preaching. Since First Thessalonians is the oldest of the letters that are agreed to have been written by Paul, such evidence would have to be in First Thessalonians. Some passages have been suggested: 1:10, 2:12, 3:13, and 5:10.[181] Each of these mentions the *parousia*. The question whether the *parousia* assumes resurrection is precisely the question at issue. These references to the *parousia* cannot be proof that the resurrection of believers was already an established part of Paul's doctrinal belief, because Paul used *parousia* to mean a coming historical event.

Scholars who have thought that the resurrection of believers was a new idea are the same scholars who wanted to establish a chronology for Paul's ministry based on the letters alone. It helps to know in which camp scholars stand, because it helps us understand their position. However, this is not a valid argument against the newness of the doctrine. The value of a historical interpretation does not depend upon which particular school of thought promotes it.

It is peculiar that Paul said Jesus "rose" from the dead. It would also make sense if "Jesus died and rose" were already a traditional statement. If that is the case, then Paul used the word "rose" here because it was an expression familiar to his hearers.

Beyond that, however, it is striking that Paul used the same active, intransitive form of the verb "rise" in verse 16. He could have used the transitive verb; he could have said, God will raise them, just as easily as he might have said, God raised Jesus. So we are once again faced with the question of why Paul used the verb "rose" in both of these places. He must have wanted to emphasize what will happen to them, and he must have thought that the agency of their resurrection was for the moment less important.

In either case, it then makes sense that, having used the intransitive verb in verse 14, Paul can use it again in verse 16. It seems more likely, however, that Paul planned to use the intransitive verb in verse 16 and used it in verse 14 because he was already thinking of it. The effect of the repetition is to make the second use more dramatic and emphatic than it might be otherwise. The emphasis is on the statement that the dead shall rise, but its effect is to

---

181. Richard, *Thessalonians*, 232.

tie the resurrection of believers very closely to the resurrection of Jesus. By echoing his word choice, he asserts for a second time that the resurrection of believers is connected to Jesus' resurrection. If this is a new idea, then he is very cleverly slipping it in and tying it to what is already an older idea.

We have already noted the awkwardness of verse 14. Paul's use of the active verb "rose" is a part of that awkwardness. However, his second use of the same verb in verse 16 makes the passage as a whole seem less awkward and better planned as a whole passage. The repetition underscores how important it was to Paul to state what will happen to those believers who have died.

Paul has made this expression that "Jesus died and rose" into an object of belief: "We believe that Jesus died and rose." We have already noted that this "we believe" is an unnecessary complication to the phrase. Since Paul's point is that the dead will be raised just the same as Jesus was raised, our belief adds something to that statement. One way of interpreting this addition is to say that Paul is referring to a traditional creedal statement as a way of giving depth to his argument. If the statement that "Jesus died and rose" is a premise, leading towards a conclusion, then it is highly desirable to state the premise in a form that will have weight with the listeners. The assertion that "we believe," then, adds or identifies the weight of the premise in the argument.

Paul's structuring of verse 14 so that it leaves it to his hearers to draw the conclusion that the dead would be raised places a significant amount of emphasis on that idea. If the resurrection of believers is a conclusion Paul has drawn, thinking about the resurrection of Christ and about his *parousia*, then it is also to Paul's advantage for his hearers to draw the same conclusion themselves. If he can lead them to think of it as their own idea, they are most likely to accept it. There is also sleight of hand here, as Paul communicated something that he did not say, and the idea is emphasized because his hearers thought of it.

Our text has the phrase "who are being left behind" twice, in verse 15b as well as in this clause. Once might have been enough. Paul may have used it both times because it appealed to him to turn the tables on those who feared that the dead would be left behind. By its emphasis, however, he highlights the advantage being given to the dead in the *parousia*.

Finally, throughout two millennia, readers of this passage have focused on the sound effects of Jesus' arrival. These sound effects are riveting, the most attention grabbing of anything in the passage. If we think that Paul's focus on the status of the deceased, that they will not be left behind or disadvantaged in the *parousia*, had a rhetorical function of distracting his hearers from potential controversy around the newness of the doctrine of the resurrection of believers, then we also might notice the distraction that is provided by the echoing sounds. The excitement of Christ's arrival more than distracts us from the potentials for controversy.

The rhetoric of the passage both highlights and distracts from the newness of the doctrine, which is an effective use of persuasive technique. There are the two asides; one underscores that there is something new to them in what he said here, and one asserts that it agrees with the gospel. If Paul had been merely modifying the chronology of the *parousia*, these comments would not be needed. If he is introducing a new doctrine, however, they become intelligible and a measure of his discomfort with what he is about to unleash. Verse 14 is so awkward that it draws attention to the fact that Paul was in some difficulty in this passage. Paul was everywhere else such a skillful writer of prose, that we need to look for an explanation of all of these peculiarities.

Where there is rhetoric, there is an attempt to convince someone. This leads to the question, whom was Paul trying to convince? Is it possible that he was trying to convince himself? Some—and perhaps a majority—of Jews believed in resurrection, so the doctrine was available in Judaism. However, if it had not been part of Paul's kerygma, if he was in the process of convincing himself that the resurrection of believers should be added to the kerygma, that would be enough to account for the awkwardness of this verse.

If Paul himself was already convinced that through Jesus the dead would be raised, then perhaps the purpose of the argument would be to convince his Thessalonian hearers.

As a missionary Paul must have known that people are upset by changes in doctrine. If the resurrection of believers was a new doctrine, introduced in these words in First Thessalonians, Paul knew in advance that people would be challenged by it. New doctrine will excite some people, and it will upset others. We should underestimate neither the difficulty of persuading people of any change in religion, nor Paul's skill in persuading. In the history of religion, it often takes more than a generation for a doctrinal change to take effect.

It can be very distracting, at least for some writers, to know what they are saying will be surprising to their audience. It makes it difficult to write perfect and balanced sentences. If Paul knew that some people would be disturbed by his introduction of new material, that knowledge would account for both the care with which he repeated "rose" and the awkwardness of verse 14.

The interpretation, then, that the resurrection of believers was new, being an addition to the kerygma, is congruent with the exegesis of this passage. The fact that Paul's statement of the doctrine is awkward can be explained by supposing that Paul was uncomfortable with the doctrine, either because he was struggling with it himself or because he feared that it might be controversial.

There is, however, no evidence that these Thessalonians were disturbed by Paul's new doctrine of the resurrection of believers. For the evidence that some ancient people found Paul's new teaching controversial, we have to look at a later letter (which we have already done in the discussion of the individual verses). There is reasonable supposition, however, that some of the Thessalonians were disturbed by it. There is even more reason to guess that Paul anticipated the possibility that they would not be easily convinced.

Analysis of this passage as persuasion reveals Paul's subordination of the resurrection to the *parousia,* his use of meta-comments, and his introduction of his new material as subservient to his pastoral goals. By subordinating the resurrection to the *parousia*, Paul included the resurrection in his statement but then passed over it. The *parousia* was the familiar term. By making the resurrection subservient to the *parousia*, Paul distracted his hearers from its newness. If he had announced the resurrection of believers nakedly, they might have been more struck by its newness and might have raised more opposition to it. By stating the new in the context of the old and underscoring the importance of the old, he undercuts the potential for controversy.

Similarly, if this is a new idea, nevertheless Paul introduced it as being in service to his pastoral goal. His goal was to comfort those who grieve. By introducing the new idea of resurrection in the process of giving them hope, Paul again used excellent persuasive technique.

These considerations show that Paul's argument was well designed to minimize fallout and bring his hearers along. The whole picture is congruent with the idea that Paul was presenting a new doctrine and is genuinely aware of how much controversy he might have been stirring up. His approach in this passage seems both to argue cogently for the resurrection of believers, and, at the same time, take as many steps as possible to avoid controversy.

If this is correct, that Paul was under stress because he had to introduce a new doctrine that had not been part of the original kerygma, the recognition of the stress contributes to explaining the shape of the rest of the letter. After this statement, Paul went on immediately to a non-controversial subject, the issue of *chronos* and *kairos*, which he explicated in the totally non-objectionable terms of being of the light and of the day. He moved from the potentially controversial material in 4:13-18 to the non-controversial material of 5:1-11 in order to fend off controversy.

The stress of 4:13-18 also led Paul to prepare for it with the extraordinary rehearsal of their relationship in chapters 1-3. Whether this unique Thanksgiving was consciously organized as the best way to prepare for the potential controversy of introducing the resurrection of believers, or an unconscious result of the stress Paul was feeling, the new teaching accounts for the unusual shape of the letter.

Therefore, *mutatis mutandi*, the unique size of the Thanksgiving and the shift of subject in 5:1 contribute to the argument that the resurrection of believers was a new doctrine, introduced by Paul at this very moment. That he was under stress about introducing the new doctrine accounts for his unusual preparation for it, the unusual build-up of their relationship so that he might ask them to take the new in stride. His rhetorical sophistication, likewise, accounts for the abrupt change of subject, as a reminder of something old, to take away any sting of the new. The shape and construction of the letter as a whole, then, points to the newness of this doctrine.

The peculiarity of the statement on sexuality

Marriage and sexuality, the topic of 4:3-8, appears to be the other topic on which the letter is focused.

Some of the verses

We need to look at some of the verses to explore the strange features of the passage.

Paul's words

> 4:3 For the will of God is this: your sanctification
> that you abstain from sexual immorality,

Transactional Analysis

The difficult word in this clause is *porneia*, which was translated into Latin as *fornicatio*, which in turn became the English word "fornication," with a dictionary sense of sexual relations between persons who are not married. This English word, however, is not an adequate translation of Paul's term. Paul's term represents the beachhead of a standard for sexual behavior that was new to Europe.

How did the sexual morality of the Greeks differ from the sexual morality of the Jews? More to the point, what were their perceptions of each other's sexual morality?

The Greek moral standard for sex condemned *moicheia*, which was the sexual violation of respectable women. The concern was not whether the behavior was consensual; *moicheia* was a criminal act whether the woman was willing or not. The concern was her status. Her status was defined by whether or not she was acceptable as a marriage partner for a citizen, and whether when married to a citizen she might produce children who would be eligible to become citizens. The issue of respectability, then, turned on citizenship. Sex relations with such a woman was *moicheia*.[182]

With *moicheia* identified as the criminal sexual act, other sexual acts were less important. Greek society was able to tolerate all other sexual acts. Given the one characteristic of respectable women, that of being marriageable,

---

182. In the recent past we have understood ancient people were concerned with adultery because they wanted to know who was the father, casting society's concern with sexual morality as patriarchal. However, in ancient Greece the concern was the concern of the *polis*, the city-state, and on its need to identify its future citizens.

Greek society fostered a range of available women, from slaves to courtesans. The Greeks even admired and valued well-educated, mannerly, and beautiful *hetairai* ("companions"). They used *porneia* to refer to sexual acts other than those between citizen husband and wife, but they did not necessarily disapprove of sexual relations outside of marriage. They considered the use of prostitutes to be a protection of marriage.[183] In short, *porneia* bordered on being a good thing.

Both Greek civilization and Judaism condemned adultery, rape, and incest. Both of these civilizations articulated high standards for sexual morality. In Greek literature and philosophy, there are calls by the Pythagoreans, by Plato, and by the Stoics for a monogamous sexual morality.[184] The sexual moral standards of Rome were similar to those of Hellenism. Yet even Augustus' marriage laws of 18 B.C.E. and 9 C.E., which encouraged Roman citizens to have more babies and which discouraged prostitutions, did not limit a young male citizen from finding opportunities for sexual relations.[185]

In Greek literature, however, one does not find condemnations of the sexual customs of other people, which is exactly what one does find in the Hebrew literature. In the prohibitions of homosexual acts in the book of Leviticus, part of the instruction is a comparison with the sexual behavior of other people. The Lord God displaced the people of Canaan, allowing the Hebrews to conquer them, because of their homosexual behavior; the scripture says, do not act sexually in the manner of the conquered people of Canaan, because it is precisely because of their behavior that God has displaced them (Lev 18:22 and 20:13). There has been an attempt to explain Canaanite homosexuality as a cultic ritual,[186] but the point is that the prohibition is not absolute: it is relative to the behavior of specific people. There is a qualification to the prohibition: "Do not do what those other people are doing."

This qualifying clause raises an epistemological question and a historical

183. Kyle Harper, "*Porneia*: The Making of a Christian Sexual Norm," *Journal of Biblical Literature*, 131, No. 2, (2012): 363-383. I am indebted to Harper for the distinction between *moicheia* and *porneia*.

184. William Loader, *The New Testament on Sexuality* (Grand rapids, MI: Eerdmans, 2012), 91-98.

185. Loader, *NT Sexuality*, 93, refers to Plato's concession in Laws that men may have extramarital sexual relations if they are discrete, and 103-04 refers to an observation that Augustus' laws did not intend to end extramarital intercourse.

186. Loader, *NT Sexuality,* 91-98.

question. The epistemological question is, How did the Hebrews know what was the sexual practice of those people? The historical question is "What was the sexual practice of those people?" The historical question determines exactly what practice was condemned and determines what practice is to be condemned today.

If we assume that scripture was written by an omniscient narrator, then the narrator knew what was the practice of the previous occupants of the promised land. Even an omniscient narrator, however, cannot make the case that the people being given the commandment actually knew what the behavior of the Canaanites was. The Romans bragged about their sexual activity, and if the Canaanites did so too, that would be one way for the invading Hebrews to know what their behavior was. Otherwise, rumor would have to be a large factor. Rumor always leaves much to the imagination, so the exact nature of the sexual acts would have been left to the Hebrews' imaginations. Furthermore, if the narrator is not omniscient, then we are dealing with even more misinformation and projection. Nevertheless, the point here is the fact that it was the behavior of some other people that was condemned.

The same contrast between "our" morality and "their" morality is found in passages by the first-century C.E. Hellenistic Jewish philosopher Philo. In a passage where Joseph is explaining to Potiphar's wife why he will not have sexual relations with her, Philo put these words into Joseph's mouth:

> We descendants of the Hebrews use special customs having lawful weight. To other men it is permitted, after the age of fourteen, to use prostitutes without restriction, and sex-workers and those who earn wages by the use of their bodies, but it is not permitted for a courtesan to live among us; justice sets a penalty of death for harlotry. Before the lawful union, we do not come together sexually with any other woman, but marry as inexperienced men with inexperienced girls, not cherishing sexual pleasure but the issue of legitimate children.[187]

From a twenty-first century point of view, this is a commendable stan-

---

187. I used the Greek text in *Philo: with an English translation by F. H. Colson, M.A.* vol. VI (Cambridge, MA: Harvard University Press, 1935 [reprint 1966]) and compared my translation with Colson's.

dard. What we should have learned from the sexual revolution of the mid-twentieth century is that there is a value to faithful marriage, and that the greatest aspects of that value are to one's self-respect and to consideration for the other person in one's marriage. The next thing to observe about this passage, however, is the comparison between "we descendants of the Hebrew" and "other men." Not only do the Hebrew tribes hold a high standard against adultery, not only do they not tolerate any form of harlotry among themselves, but it is especially significant that they consider their intolerance of prostitution dissimilar to the practices of other people.

What are we to make of this contrast? For some, it will appear to be a simple statement of fact. The Greeks and Romans not only tolerated prostitution, but also permitted sexual relations with persons of lower status than themselves, specifically with slaves. Jewish communities, if we take Philo's comment as representative, did not. Thus, for some contemporary readers of history, these ancient civilizations had different customs.

For other contemporary observers, perhaps the important thing is the Jewish attitude. Whether or not the behavior difference was a fact, the Jews, or perhaps some of the Jews, thought it was. If they were wrong, if for example the majority of Hellenized people eschewed prostitution as much as the Jews did, perhaps there was some psychosocial reason for their perception. Perhaps, in the case of the Canaanite tribes, men projected behaviors they were forbidden onto the people they were conquering. Perhaps in the case of Hellenistic people, Jews projected onto others freedoms they did not have. Regardless of whether or not the attitude was true or false, it was their attitude. Members of the Jewish community of the First Century appear to have thought of themselves as sexually moral and of other people as sexually immoral.

Some dimensions of that attitude are particularly important. From Philo and other literature we know that the Jews of the First Century considered themselves moral in comparison with other peoples in terms of using their sexuality for procreation and not for excessive sexual pleasure, of allowing their passions to sweep them away and being out of control during their sexual activity, in terms of homosexual behavior. As a measure of the attitude of moral disapprobation, Jews avoiding staying in inns run by gentiles, avoided lodging their animals with gentile innkeepers, and avoided apprenticing their sons to gentiles.[188]

Paul's position on *porneia* and the use of prostitutes mirrors the position of First Century Jews. In particular, his words in 1 Cor 6:12-20 make it clear that he was very much opposed to relations with a prostitute. In that passage, Paul interpreted the saying that "the two become one flesh" (Genesis 2:24) as referring to sexual intercourse. He reasoned that a person who belongs to the body of Christ and has relations with a prostitute joins the body of Christ to the prostitute. This is strong language against prostitution, which we should expect from a First Century Jew.

However, there is another aspect to Paul's opposition to *porneia*. Since *moicheia* as a standard for sexual behavior depends on the status of the woman, and since we have already suggested that Paul understood the gospel as obliterating status, his opposition to *porneia* can be likewise understood as an opposition to status. He may have perceived that sex with courtesans, no less than with other prostitutes and especially with slaves, was an oppression of persons of lower status, taking advantage of misfortune. Such oppression, if indeed we see it as operative in the system of prostitution, is contrary to the gospel. We know just enough about Paul's perception of the equal status of all who are baptized to understand why he condemned *porneia* as oppression of persons of lower status.

Paul's words

> 4:4 that each of you know how to acquire his own wife
> in holiness and honor,

Transactional Analysis

The phrase translated "to acquire [a] wife" is *skeuos ktasthai*. I have no doubt that this translation is what Paul intended by this phrase. Earlier interpretations have, correctly, translated *skeuos* as "vessel" and understood it as a rabbinic expression for "wife." The English translations have gotten the sense right, because we have received the correct interpretation from tradition and

---

188. Yarbrough, *Not Like the Gentiles*, 7, 10, 12, 17-19, 20, 22-23, 27-29. Yarbrough suggests that the claim to moral superiority and the warnings against sexual relations with others protected the identity of the diaspora Jewish community.
Malherbe, *Letters*, 226, says teaching against lustful pagan impurity was a part of basic Jewish moral instruction.

have always inferred what Paul meant and translated accordingly.[189] It is only relatively recent scholarship that has discovered how these words actually can take this meaning.[190]

In this interpretation, the words that follow and precede *skeuos ktasthai* take on great importance. They are *eidenai* ("to know") and *en hagiasmôi kai timêi* ("in holiness and honor"). We ought to understand the full phrase of 4:4 is "that each of you know how to *ktasthai* his *skeuos* in holiness and honor." It emphasizes both "to know how" and "in holiness and honor." They do not need to marry; they just need to know how. In particular, they need to know how to marry in a holy way.

However, it is more significant that this correct translation finds confirmation in relation to the Greek spoken in Jewish communities, a Jewish *Koinê* surviving primarily in the Septuagint. To be sure, *skeuos* appears in the Septuagint in a least one place where it refers to the male sex organ,[191] but the two-word phrase, *skeuos ktasthai*, is used to translate a two-word Hebrew expression meaning "to acquire a wife."[192] Paul was thinking in Jewish *Koinê* when he wrote this passage; he meant that Christians should marry.[193]

If Paul had been speaking to Jewish Christians, they probably would have had no problem with his choice of words. It appears, however, that he was thinking of them rather than of his Thessalonian audience. A native Greek speaker, such as Paul's hearers in Thessalonica, would have heard the expression differently. *Ktasthai* more commonly means to "have" or "keep" rather than to "acquire," and *skeuos* is a common word that could be used for any "thing" for which the speaker does not want to use a more precise name. It can be a "thing" or a "tool" or an "instrument," or, yes, it might refer to a vessel. It could refer to the "body" as contrasted with the "soul."[194] It was, however, used in some situations as a slang word for penis.[195] Therefore, it appears

---

189. The Revised Standard Version follows this line of thought.

190. Yarbrough, *Not like the Gentiles, passim.*

191. Malherbe, *Letters,* 226, refers to 1 Sam 21:5.

192. Malherbe, *Letters,* 227. Yarbrough, *Not Like the Gentiles,* 70-71, makes a very convincing case, although Richard, *Thessalonians,* 187-88, and William Loader, *NT Sexuality,* 154, 160, are not convinced.

193. Malherbe, *Letters,* 227.

194. Liddell, and Scott, *Greek-English Lexicon,* 638b.

195. Donfried, *Thessalonian Cults,* 342.

that Paul's hearers might have thought that he meant "that each of you know how to keep his tool in holiness and honor." Following through on this sense of *skeuos* as "thing" or "tool" or "male sexual organ," the verse becomes "that everyone of you know how to maintain possession of his sexuality in holiness and honor,"[196] which is a second possible way to translate this phrase.

A third possible translation of *skeuos ktasthai* involves an explanation that Paul was thinking of a chaste semi-marriage. In First Corinthians (1 Cor 7:36-38), Paul gave instructions regarding members of the ecclesia who were "engaged," that is, they were living in chaste relationships (1 Cor 7.36-38). Although the meaning of that text is not entirely clear, the relationships of such couples may have brought them some of the legal advantages of marriage, but they nevertheless intended to refrain from sexual relations. The construction of such chaste relationships is one possible interpretation of the passage in First Corinthians, and the logic is that if Paul knew about and possibly promoted such relationships in Corinth, he might also have fostered them in Thessalonica. In that case, his words here in First Thessalonians might be addressed to couples in such relationships.

If in this verse, Paul was thinking about that kind of chaste relationship, his concern was that his followers know how to behave appropriately in their chaste relationships, which may well mean that their sexual relations would be considered proper as a part of their marriage. Those scholars who believe this is the correct interpretation of *skeuos ktasthai* prefer to leave it in this ambiguous language, that men know how to "maintain their vessels" appropriately, concluding that Paul and his parishioners understood perfectly well, because they had already been using these words in their discussions.[197]

This suggestion that Paul had previously defined *skeuos ktasthai* is entirely consistent with the rest of the letter. The phrase, which seems peculiar to us, would have been clear to them, because it had been defined. In that case, it would make perfectly good sense in the context of the letter. There is nothing in First Thessalonians that would rule out this interpretation.

However, that interpretation does seem like special pleading when it is applied to this passage in First Thessalonians. The words *skeuos ktasthai* take

---

196. The New Revised Standard Version follows this set of decisions.

197. E. Elizabeth Johnson, "A Modest Proposal in Context" in *The Impartial God: Essays in Biblical Studies in Honor of Jouette M. Bassler* (Calvin J. Roetzel and Robert L. Foster, eds. Sheffield Phoenix Press, 2007), 232.

their most obviously correct interpretation from the context of the Septuagint. Understanding it as a referrence to chaste relationships is a different interpretation than the one from the context of the Septuagint; since the explanation invoking the Septuagint is adequate, it is not necessary to suppose this other definition. The most likely interpretation of *skeuos ktasthai* is to take it back to the Hebrew which the Septuagint translated, and understand it "to acquire a wife." The strongest case for translating *skeuos ktasthai* as "to acquire a wife" is it would have been understood in that way in Jewish circles.

The reason *skeuos ktasthai* does not work in Greek is that it is a calque, an idiomatic expression in another language that has been translated literally into Greek.[198] This is the equivalent of translating "it is raining cats and dogs" into French "*il pleut chats et chiens.*" The French would never understand! We cannot quite reproduce the calque in an English version of this verse; we have to smooth it over and make the verse somewhat more intelligible in English than it is in Greek. If Paul meant one thing and his hearers heard another, the result is rather awkward. It is not clear to us and very likely was not clear to them. Paul has been clumsy in thinking in terms that he would use with a Jewish audience, when he was addressing an audience of native Greek speakers. Very likely it was not clearly intelligible to his Thessalonian hearers, and very likely it was offensive to them. Can we explain his clumsiness? Can we find an explanation why Paul took a position in this letter that was all but guaranteed to produce controversy?

There is second century (and later) literature that strongly associates Paul with celibacy. The promise of freedom from sexual relations has a long history in Christian tradition,[199] and apparently had some appeal to Christians and others in the Roman Empire. This interpretation of Paul puts his preference for freedom from sexual relationships in parallel with the same preference in the larger culture. Perhaps understanding Paul in this way helps us to understand the origin of a high valuation of chastity.

Because of evidence in First Corinthians, it is sometimes held that when he planted the ecclesiae in Thessalonica and in Corinth, Paul advocated celi-

---

198. Malherbe, *Letters*, 227. Malherbe does not use the word "calque," but he does say that *ktasthai* is difficult to translate, on grammatical grounds.

199. Elisabeth Schüssler Fiorenza, *In Memory of Her: A Feminist Theological Reconstruction of Christian Origins*, (Tenth Anniversary Edition, Crossroad, New York, 2000), 144. The comparison of heaven to the angels' manner of existence has long been interpreted as freedom from sex.

bacy as the appropriate Christian life-style.[200] Paul said that people who were already married should stay married, but that people who were single should stay single, because the Lord Jesus would return soon and there would not be enough time to get engaged. If that is true, 1 Thess 4:4 as a commandment to marry represents a reversal of Paul's position.

There is nothing in First Thessalonians, however, to suggest that Paul was reversing himself regarding chastity and marriage. The evidence of reversal is in First Corinthians, if, indeed, that is what it is. We cannot conclude, based on First Thessalonians alone, that Paul reversed himself in 1 Thess 4:4. However, if 4:4 amounts in some sense to a reversal along these lines, that would be consistent with several features of this letter.

- The stress would account for the awkward choice of words *skeuos ktasthai*.
- It would account for the long build up in chapters 1-3 before he finally gets to this point.
- It may account for the peculiar ingratiating character of chapters 1-3.
- The self-centered defensiveness of chapters 1-3 is congruent with seeing Paul as reluctant to take up some distressing issue.
- Stress would also account for the finality of the unusual expression *loipon oun* when he finally gets to what he needs to say.

The theory of self-reversal gives us a perspective to understand why Paul was under great stress when he wrote this letter.

Why would Paul have reversed himself on such a position? The Jewish provenance of the expression *skeuos ktasthai* leads us to suspect that he was under pressure from Jewish Christians.

The primary reason for preferring the translation "to acquire a wife" for *skeuos ktasthai* is that it opens the possibility that Paul expressed the marriage mandate in Jewish *Koinê* because he was thinking in the same words in which

---

200. The reference is to 1 Cor 7:7. Paul may have recommended an unmarried life-style because of his dislike of sexual involvement (1 Cor 7:1) or because of a concern for the shortness of time before the *parousia*. Buck and Greer Taylor, *St. Paul*, 37. On the contrary, Mitchell, *Rhetoric*, 236, suggests that Paul's position on celibacy and on marriage in 1 Cor was conditioned by his attempt to agree as much as he could with both sides of the issue and call for people on both sides to live in unity.

the concern was expressed to him. If so, Paul introduced the marriage mandate because he was seeking to meet the expectations of Jewish Christians and because he was under pressure from them to do so.

This is not to say that those concerns were untrue. The fact that these were the concerns of Jewish Christians in Judea about the sexual morality of non-Jews in Thessalonica does not mean that the concerns were misplaced. Thessalonians may have behaved exactly as Jews thought they did. Paul's Thessalonian congregants may have been looser in their sexual morality than members of the Judaean ecclesiae could tolerate. Paul's motive to satisfy complaints about his gentile congregations may have been occasioned by their misbehavior. Nevertheless, the answer appears to lie in the Jewish perception of gentile sexual behavior.

Since *moicheia* set the standard for Greek sexual morality, *porneia* was always a practice of unequal status, in which persons (males) exploited persons of lower social status (both male and female, both slave and free). The exploitation of unequal status is contrary to Paul's vision of our equal status before God our Father. This perception of *porneia* as exploitation is radical; however, it rings true.

Why did Paul wade into this controversy? He had to have known that the marriage mandate would disturb his non-Jewish church members, so why did he not simply avoid pronouncing it? Paul has been accused, both by readers today and by his contemporaries, of trying to please everybody (1 Cor 9:18-23). In addition, in other places he appears to refer to Jews as his relatives (Rom 11; 16-7, 11, 13). It appears that he was trying to please those relatives. It is likely that they actually put pressure on him to announce the marriage mandate. But beyond that, it does appear that he himself agreed with this higher vision of sexual morality.

Paul was attempting to act in the best interest of the whole church. It is the best interest of the church that congregations have good opinions of each other, that they get along. To ask non-Jewish ecclesiae to accept the marriage mandate in order to satisfy Jewish ecclesiae would seem like a reasonable step to a Jew. Paul, then, most likely waded into the controversy thinking that he was right but also that he was acting in the best interests of the entire international body of Christ.

This fact that he used words appropriate to his Judaean critics when speaking to native Greek speakers in Thessalonica indicates that he was under stress. He appears not to have been thinking clearly about how these Thessalonians used words. This indicates that he was not functioning up to his full potential at this point. It is quite possible that he knew that this marriage mandate might not be well received and that this perception, even if it were subconscious, would add to his stress as he approached this subject.

The evidence of the awkwardness of *skeuos ktasthai*, then, suggests that Paul was under stress. The unique shape of the first three chapters agrees. It appears that Paul knew this would be controversial. The alternation between controversial and non-controversial subjects in the Ethical Instruction suggests that Paul deliberately composed the letter in such a way as to distract his hearers from potential controversy.

The evidence of the awkwardness of *skeuos ktasthai*, then, suggests that Paul was under stress. It appears that Paul knew this would be controversial. The alternation between controversial and non-controversial subjects in the Ethical Instruction suggests that Paul deliberately composed the letter in such a way as to distract his hearers from potential controversy. The unique shape of the first three chapters agrees.

Paul's words

4:5 not in an emotional experience like those who do not know God,

Transactional Analysis

The expression *en pathei epithymias* ("in an emotional experience") to which Paul added "like those who do not know God" is another problem. The word *pathos* ("suffering," "experience") is the same root we have met before with the sense of passive experience. A *pathos* is something that happens to a person without the person's doing anything; it could conceivably be a good experience, but the word has a connotation reflecting a cultural attitude that bad things happen to people.

The word *epithymia* ("desire," "longing," "lust," "passion") was built on the word *thymos* ("soul," "heart"). It is related to a verb meaning "to produce smoke;" the connection appears to be that sometimes breath is a visible mist. Thus, it refers to the movement of breath in and out of the lungs. The lungs and chest become excited when a person is passionate. Therefore the three word phrase means, "in an experience of passion" or "in an emotional experience." From a first-century Jewish perspective, such passion would be an overwhelming experience, and their cultural desire would be to stay in control and not be overwhelmed by the experience, i.e., stay in control of themselves.[201]

Paul may have thought that the sexual relations that were part of the Greek Dionysian and other cult activities were acted out while people were emotionally out of control. There was an active Dionysian cult in Thessalonica at the time, and this phrase is one of several that indicate that Paul was thinking of that cult when he wrote this letter.[202] His warning, then, "not in an emotional experience like those who do not know God" means "do not have sex as the gentiles do **in their cults**, being overwhelmed by passion."

It is also possible to build an interpretation of this verse around the final phrase of the clause. Those who do not know God have only their own knowledge on which to make moral judgments. In our age, the expression, "If it feels good, do it," implies that there is no other standard for making moral judgments than a person's own personal perceptions. However, those who know God have more information to use in making decisions than physical perceptions alone; we might, for example, take into account how our actions affect other people, and whether or not our actions reflect our love of others. Those who know God put value upon not being swept away by fleeting impressions, but on maintaining a divine perspective.

If one takes "those who do not know God" absolutely, the clause suggests that there is a link between not knowing God and being overwhelmed by sexual passion.[203] To know God is to put the created being into proper relationship with the creator. Human beings should not be swept away with their emotions when they are properly and seriously mindful of their creator.

However, it seems more likely that by "those who do not know God," Paul simply meant non-Jews. It was in his experience and in the experience of his hearers, that gentiles tended to get swept away by their emotions, particularly in their practice of the Dionysian cult. Paul was admonishing his hearers not to act that way.

Paul's words

⁴:⁶ and how not to trespass and cheat each other in this matter;

---

201. Loader, *NT Sexuality*, 98, indicates that Greek arts portray sexual passion as an irresistible burden inflicted by the gods. Ormand, *Controlling Desires, passim.*
202. Donfried, *Thessalonian Cults*, 341-42.
203. Richard, *Thessalonians*, 190-92.

for the Lord carries out justice for all these things,
just as we have told you before and witnessed continually.

Transactional Analysis

Likewise, the expression *to mê hyperbainein kai pleonektein* ("not to trespass against and cheat"), to which Paul added "each other *en tôi pragmati*" ("in this business") is another problem. The word *pleonektein* ("take advantage of," "be greedy," "cheat") most often refers to business, and *en tôi pragmati* literally refers to commerce. Thus one can apply this phrase to business dealings as an issue of social justice.[204]

This phrase, *hyperbainein kai pleonektein*, suggests that we not take advantage of one another. Taken as continuing the same thought as the previous verse, it means that Christians ought not harm other people by their sexual practice. Some commentators have thought the act of having sexual relations with a man's wife would be a violation of that man's property rights in her. Adultery with a married woman harms her husband.[205]

However, Paul might have been thinking of the harm done as harm to the violated sexual partner. Roman society was an aggressive society, and rape was portrayed as a manly activity.[206] The Roman way was to take advantage of barbarians and slaves. If Paul was thinking of that kind of greediness and advantage taking, these two expressions are about the same topic: immoral and inappropriate sex.

In this passage, Paul spoke of the one being abused as *adelphos* ("brother"); throughout the rest of the letter, we have thought of his use of *adelphoi* as including females. It makes good sense to translate *ton adelphon autou* ("your brother") here in a gender-inclusive way: "each other."

The final words, *en tôi pragmati*, may be translated "in this matter." The word *pragmati* ("business") does not restrict its meaning to commerce. It is just as general as "business" is in English. The expression "in this matter," then, is a broad reference to the previous subject. All three phrases can be interpreted as boundaries for sexual behavior. It is possible, then, to read the

---

204. Richard, *Thessalonians*, 194.

205. Richard, *Thessalonians*, 200.

206. Crossan and Reed, *Search*, 242. Roman art associates martial conquest with sexual conquest. Amy Richlin, *The Garden of Priapus, passim*. The message of the garden statue with the huge erection is "Trespassers will be violated!" Clearly the Romans enjoyed their *priapi*, but the *priapi* are not funny.

section as the statement of a single principle.

There are three arguments for taking these four verses as expressing a single principle. One is Paul's use of the *inclusio*. The section is delineated by the *inclusio* of the word *hagiasmos* in verse 3 and verse 7.[207] Verses 3 through 7 are a unit of thought.

Second, this segment speaks specifically to aspects of how first century Jews thought about sexual morality. The admonition against *porneia*, the suggestion that marriage could be a defense against prostitution, and the stricture against being carried away by passion all reflect and match up with first century Jewish perceptions of non-Jews.

Third, taking these instructions in 4:3, 4:4, 4:5 and 4:6 as the same subject is reasonable on the grounds that this is the simplest interpretation of the passage. If this were written prose, 4:3, 4:4, 4:5 and 4:6 could be interpreted as four separate moral issues.[208] We readers of a printed text are able to read a passage as many times as we like, to plumb its depths, but Paul dictated his letters expecting that most of his hearers would listen to the letters only once. Hearers who are accustomed to oral communication would be listening for the simplest and most connected meaning; Paul, as an oral communicator, most likely composed with the objective of communicating the most simple meaning.

Therefore, the *inclusio*, the coherence of the instructions in the Jewish perception of the sexual moral behavior of non-Jews, and the considerations of oral communication all argue for the same point: that 4:3-8 as a whole section is about a single subject: sexual morality.

The passage as a whole

Apparently, then, Paul has addressed one subject in this passage. He meant the phrase, *skeuos ktasthai*, to urge and encourage sexual morality, whichever way we take it. The rest of 4:3-8 enlarges that thought. Several features of the rest of the letter suggest that Paul was experiencing some stress around bringing up this subject: he had an emotional outburst in 2:14-16, he treated this material as having potential for controversy, he presented what was new as if it were something old, he presented it abruptly, and he was clumsy in his

---

207. Richard, *Thessalonians*, 194.

208. Richard, *Thessalonians*, 187-88.

expression. Beyond that, it begins to appear that Paul was under the influence of other persons to bring up this subject.

The clumsiness in Paul's expression lies in his choice of the words *skeuos ktasthai*. As previously discussed, unless this expression had been previously defined, it is a calque of a Hebrew expression and his Thessalonian hearers probably would not have been understood it as he intended.

This paragraph is abrupt. Paul moved into the subject quickly and used few words. In comparison with other passages, this one is short and includes little explanation. We could certainly wish that Paul had said a great deal more here. He has left us disagreeing with each other and probably misunderstanding what he meant. He has said far too little to have communicated effectively with us, quite possibly too little to have communicated effectively with his Thessalonian hearers; and we need to take an interest in the reason why he is so abrupt.

Paul said that this teaching was not new three times. First, Paul's statement, 'For you know what commandments we gave you," asserted that the commandments that follow were the same as those which they already knew. Paul's statement, "For you know" looks similar, on first analysis, to the expressions such as "you know," "just as you know," and "just as we have told you before" with which he has peppered this letter. This "For you know" expression, however, has the object that they know what commandments Paul has already given them. Therefore, he implies, they already know the commandment that he will give them next.

Second, the expression in 4:3, the Greek translated "For the will of God is this" begins with *touto gar* ("for this"), which points backwards to what Paul has just said and forward to what he said next, as we have discussed, indicating that the two statements are equivalent. In this case, it points backward to the instructions that Paul gave them on how to walk and please God. It points forward to their sanctification, meaning that they should abstain from sexual immorality.

Third, in the midst of this passage, in verse 6c, Paul said, "just as we have told you before and borne witness." That statement also asserts that what Paul said in this passage is a repetition of what he said earlier. If the implication of this verse is true, then what Paul said here about sexual morality is not new. The expression in 6c, "just as we have told you before and borne witness," follows the statement in 6b, "for the Lord carries out justice for all these things."

It is not clear whether the "just as" refers to 6a or to 6b, whether Paul meant that he had previously told them the statement of 6a, which is the prohibition of trespassing against one's brother in this matter, or that he had previously told them the statement in 6b, that God repays such behavior. He could have meant that he told them either of these statements, either not to trespass or that God repays such behavior. It makes sense that what Paul had previously told them is that the Lord carries out justice for all these things. Paul did say *toutôn* ("these things"), not *toioutôn* ("similar things"), so it appears that he meant *skeuos ktasthai, mê en pathei epithymias,* and *mê hyperbainein kai pleonektein.* However, the import of 6c is persuasive, not propositional. We should take it that Paul says "just as we have told you" in order to persuade them to adopt the sexual morality appropriate for followers of Jesus.

Nevertheless, it was new. This new-with-its-newness-denied character, a paradigm of partial truth, is very peculiar.

In our paradigm of partial truth, we would say that Paul certainly had given them commandments about how to walk and to please God. What he went on to say, spelling out the requirements of sexual morality, explicates how they should walk so as to please God, but in our paradigm that explication went beyond what was originally communicated.

His claiming that it is not new is defensible on the grounds that the new teaching is consistent with what Paul had taught previously. As we have said, Paul's original teaching called for a change in behavior based on the commandment to love one another. Treating one's body with respect and not harming others through one's sexual behavior explicate the implications of love for one another. Since it is the implication of a proposition previously stated, it is justifiable to say that this implication is not new. Even though the instruction itself is new, the proposition behind it is not new. Saying that the implication is not new likely makes the newness of the explication more acceptable and less objectionable. This is a rhetorical device of great wisdom. For Paul to say that it is not new heads off objections to its newness.

Since Paul was a Jew, it is likely that he had discussed sexual morality with his gentile converts. However, even if Paul might have previously discussed sexual morality with them, he appears now to be adding something more specific: the instruction to marry. As a specific, it still was consistent with the previous teaching. Both statements are true: the marriage mandate was new, and Paul had told them before. The "I already told you" and "you know" statements are both at least partly true, because he had already given them general instruction. However, there was something new in the teaching in this letter.

Paul's surrounding the instruction about *porneia* and marriage with statements that deny any newness may be a rhetorical technique. Paul's disclaimer of newness distracts from the novelty of the instruction. It heads off any objection to its newness. If Paul needed to introduce a new commandment, then it was effective for him to disclaim its novelty and make it appear as an old idea.

The subject had a potential for controversy. Not only did Paul bring up the subject of sexual morality, it appears that he brought the subject up as part of a call for a change in behavior; that is, his discussion calls for a change in his hearers' sexual behavior. While it is possible that the phrase, "that each of you know how to acquire his own wife in holiness and honor," is a reminder of standards that Paul had previously discussed with his hearers, it is more likely that the phrase asks for some change in their behavior.

The words, "abstain from sexual immorality," suggest that they have been caught, found to be immoral, and warned to cease their immoral behavior. It implies that Paul objected to their behavior. The word *apechesthai* ("abstain") implies that they should **stop doing something**. They are likely to have heard the word "abstain" as implying that they have been caught at doing something wrong. While it is possible that they were eager to be corrected, to be told exactly what they were doing wrong, it is more likely that they heard it as criticism. Therefore, it seems that Paul was giving them a new instruction that they have not heard before.

Why did Paul bring up this subject of sexual morality? Four potential answers have been suggested. One possibility is that the transition from gentile morality to Christian morality was too difficult, and some scholars have felt that the Pauline standard of chastity before marriage required a major change of behavior for persons raised in Hellenistic culture.[209] Such changes take more than a little time and are not accomplished the first time the subject is mentioned. Paul needed to remind and encourage them to make a major

---

209. Arthur Darby Nock, *St. Paul* (London: Thornton Butterworth Ltd., 1938), 114, suggests that since they had regarded use of prostitutes an indifferent matter, these converts needed to be told more than once.

change. If this is the case, Paul's statement is still mystifying.

If he had originally told them that a change in their sexual behavior was a requirement, then he might have reminded them of the requirement in a more forthright manner, such as by saying that he had heard that some of them were misbehaving and that they should meet the standard. Furthermore, if he had told them of the requirement while they were face to face, surely he would have had enough practice to develop a straight-forward expression of the issue, such as "Christian men should have wives and Christian women should have husbands" (1 Cor 7:2).

Both the expression of the issue in Jewish *Koinê* and the awkward abruptness of the issue argue against Paul's having expressed it previously, during his original delivery of the gospel. Therefore, it seems that the choice of words and their abruptness and their context in the rest of the letter argue for the marriage mandate's being a new requirement.

A second possibility is that Timothy might have learned of some *porneia* during his fact-finding mission. He is listed in verse 1:1 as one of the senders of the letter, so it appears that he was a member of the team that planted the ecclesia. Therefore he would be familiar with the standard of chastity that had been preached during that earlier period. If Timothy had discovered some failure of chastity, and if the instruction to avoid *porneia* was part of the original kerygma, then Timothy ought have been able to speak to the problem himself. If Timothy did not speak to the problem, or if he spoke to the problem and also needed to refer it on to Paul, then we might expect that Paul would speak, here, with more anger, and certainly not in an abrupt and clumsy fashion. If Timothy had referred the problem on to Paul for any reason, then Paul's joy at Timothy's report is overblown. Timothy's report did hint that something was lacking, as we have noted; but what was lacking was hope. If Timothy had brought back some report of sexual immorality, then perhaps Paul might have indicated that there was something lacking in their faith. However, not only is there no indication that Timothy's report contained any issue of sexual morality, but also the reference to that report is distorted if it did. On the whole, it seems unlikely that Timothy's report was the origin of the issue of sexual morality and, therefore, it seems less likely that the marriage mandate as expressed in 4:3-8 is a reminder of something that had been taught during the initial mission.

A third possibility is that Paul has introduced the marriage mandate here in order to strengthen the boundary between the world and the ecclesia. There was some *thlipsis,* some difficulty (1 Thess 2:14), which caused Paul to be concerned that this ecclesia might be no more (1 Thess 3:5). In that context, it is quite appropriate for Paul to remind the members of the ecclesia of the boundaries between them and the social world in which they lived. Among those boundaries, sexual morality is predominant; the members of the ecclesia differed from the society around them because of their sexual morality, so when Paul was concerned about the existence and well-being of his ecclesia, it makes sense for him to stress the importance of their sexual morality.[210]

A fourth possibility is that Paul was discussing the institution of chaste relationship between fiancés. If knowing how to marry in holiness and honor is a reference to betrothal, then it clearly is a matter that Paul had previously discussed with his Thessalonian hearers.

If, as has been suggested, the Thessalonians were practicing some sort of betrothal that was not marriage, it is possible that their fellow-citizens ridiculed them for it. If that were the case, then Paul's instruction that they "know how to acquire a wife in holiness and honor" makes sense.

The instruction that follows this one (1 Thess 4:10-12) makes equally good sense in this social context. If the members of the ecclesia are being publicly ridiculed for their differences from the conventional behavior of Greeks in Thessalonica, it makes sense that they should keep a low profile.[211] This observation makes it attractive to read 4:3-8 and 9-12 as closely related subjects.[212]

These four possible explanations of why Paul wrote about sexual morality all fail to explain the clumsiness of the passage, its abruptness, or its claim not to be new. They do not explain the immediate way Paul follows this passage with the non-controversial material about *philadelphia.* They do not explain the extreme preparation in chapters 1-3, and they do not explain why Paul might have been so upset that he took the globalized digression in 2:14-16. Therefore we need to look for another answer.

Paul's focus in the first three chapters on the existence of the ecclesia and

---

210. Yarbrough, *Not Like the Gentiles, passim.*

211. Johnson, *Modest Proposal,* 245.

212. Johnson, *Modest Proposal,* 234 and footnote 14. Yarbrough, *Not Like the Gentiles,* 65.

its character as a faith response of an all-gentile community is a clue to what
was going on. There was, as observed in Part II, an intercontinental network
of communication among the ecclesiae of Jesus. When Paul planted ecclesiae
in Macedonia that were exclusively made up of non-Jews, the ecclesiae of Jesus in Judaea learned very soon about these novel congregations. Given what
we know about the contemporary Jewish appraisal of gentile sexual morality,
the followers of Jesus in Judaea must have experienced considerable anxiety
about the sexual morality of all-gentile ecclesiae, rightly so. They communicated to Paul their concerns about the sexual morality of these gentile Christians, probably immediately.

Spurred by their concern and thinking from their point of view, Paul felt
impelled to write First Thessalonians and pronounce the marriage mandate.
Listening to Jewish followers of Jesus, because he was seeking to meet their
expectations, he was thinking in the words that they used, and expressed himself in the same Jewish *Koinê*. The fact that it was a problem distracted him
from the need to fully translate the marriage mandate into words that would
be intelligible to Greeks in Thessalonica. Because he was under pressure from
the ecclesiae of Jesus in Judaea, he did not realize how confusing and offensive
his words might be to his native Greek ecclesia in Europe.

Paul's three level instructions on sexual morality appear to be precisely
tailored to what Jews thought non-Jews were doing. That they should know
how to marry and avoid sexual relations outside of marriage meets the Jewish
criticism. That they should not have sex in the heat of passion fits exactly with
the common Jewish prejudice about how gentiles had sex. Third, that they
should not harm one another by their sexual practice is a more subtle correlation with Jewish morality, which often values concern for others. So the three
injunctions together represent the Jewish criticisms of the sexual morality of
others quite well. This triple correlation is the most telling evidence that this
section owes its origin to Jewish Christians who were concerned about Paul's
creation of all-gentile ecclesiae.

This possibility that Paul brought up the marriage mandate under pressure from others is another reason for his pithy exposition. Paul was abrupt
here because he was dealing with somebody else's material. His shortness of
answer has to do with meeting the requirements of the Jewish followers of
Jesus in Judaea who were pressing him, and he wanted to get through the
subject as quickly as possible.

Paul's perception of this instruction's potential for controversy, whether or not it was conscious, accounts for his use of the pattern of alternating energy. Just as he did in 5:1, Paul made the transition in 4:9 to lower energy topics by using the abrupt *peri de* and saying they did not need for him to write about this topic. This topic, then, was a distractor, designed to divert attention from the controversial issue.

Likewise, this possibility that Paul introduced the marriage mandate at the request of others accounts for the possibility that it might have been a reversal of his previous support of celibacy. That it might be a reversal is consistent with the awkwardness and abruptness of expression.

The origin of the marriage mandate in those complaints gives weight to Paul's statement in 2:16 that some Jews were trying to prevent him from preaching to the non-Jews. If we recognize that Judaean Christians objected to Paul's Macedonian and Greek congregations, then there were some Jews, probably meaning Jewish Christians, who opposed the establishment of all-gentile congregations altogether.

Given that perspective, it would be entirely understandable for Paul to say that some Jews opposed him. However, rather than make such a precise statement, i.e., that **some Jews** opposed him, he globalized the statement, implying that **all Jews** stood against him. It would make sense that he made this misstatement because he was under stress and because he resented the pressure that was being put upon him.

In that mix and recognizing that Paul was feeling the pressure, it becomes quite understandable that he lost his temper in 2:14-16. If a major part of the motivation for writing First Thessalonians is to appease Judaean critics, this outburst is intelligible as a side vent. Furthermore, if Paul was being pressured to change his position from the support of celibacy, a position he had taken when he planted the ecclesiae, some of that pressure spilled out.

Observing 2:14-16 in this interpersonal context and reading First Thessalonians as a concession to his critics underscores our decision that it represents Paul's sentiment and is not an interpolation. It fits together with the conclusions we have drawn concerning the entire letter. The letter bears the marks of Paul's having been pressured and of having felt the stress.

Therefore Paul had three reasons to write First Thessalonians. As I concluded in a previous section of this chapter, Paul wrote First Thessalonians because he needed to announce the new doctrine of the resurrection. He also needed to ask, on behalf of those who pressured him, for a new higher level of morality. Those two concerns had been building for some time. The precipitating event that led to this letter was Timothy's news upon return from his mission: Paul was overjoyed to learn that his congregation still existed and was still faithful to the Lord Jesus. And so he wrote, expressing his joy and relief that they still existed, and dealing with the two issues that were causing his stress.

CHAPTER 3

EPILOGUE, NARRATIVE, AND THE WHOLE LETTER

THE gospel Paul originally preached, when he founded the ecclesia in Thessalonica, was a religion of the heart, a religion that focused on each person's inner attitude, calling each one to a standard of faith and exclusive loyalty to the one true and living God, of love for each other and for all people, and not incidentally of hope for the future that would justify their continuing readiness for the arrival of Jesus from heaven. This religion of the heart called for them to make significant changes in their behavior, including responsibility for themselves, respect for their leaders, and a willingness to discern the true nature of all things and make changes as needed. Paul's original preaching included many of the theological propositions that came to be represented in the church's creeds, but not all; it has been a particular surprise that the future arrival of Jesus was more important in Paul's early preaching than Jesus' resurrection, which is almost neglected in this letter. Furthermore, it appears quite possible that Paul and his Thessalonian converts expected, not only that Jesus would return during their own lifetimes, but also that his return would be a political event, replacing the Roman Empire at least in part with a network of self-governing assemblies of loving people.

It has been surprising that a document written so few years after the life of Jesus already referred to him as God's son and described his death as on our behalf; but whereas later generations have come to understand these terms theologically, we have been able to suggest what may have been a very early stage in the development of Christology, when Jesus was being given the Emperor's titles in an attempt to say where our true loyalty lies and where our true citizenship belongs. It is not with those whose armies conquer us but with those who give our lives meaning, the one God, and with Jesus who died and rose and will return.

Believing so, and loving so, and hoping so involves us in difficulties that will be caused for us, just by the nature of how our loyalty fits in the world. The sequence of events, which we can now modify slightly from the version at the end of Part II, chapter 4, show how Paul and his Thessalonian congregation were exposed to difficulties.

1. Paul may have been driven out of Asia by religious critics.
2. Speaking in tongues may have been experienced as a gift of the holy spirit and evidence that the receivers were qualified to be members of the ecclesia.
3. There was a network of communication between congregations, across provincial and continental boundaries.
4. From an undetermined beginning, some Jews—including Paul—abused the ecclesiae in Judaea.
5. From an undetermined beginning, some Jews hindered Paul from preaching to the non-Jews.
6. Paul was abused and treated outrageously in Philippi.
7. Paul preached in Thessalonica
   a. Some Thessalonians responded with power, holy spirit, and much conviction.
   b. He established an all-gentile congregation.
   c. At this time, Paul resented those Jews in Judea who opposed him.
   d. This prejudice was intelligible and shared.
8. When they heard about the establishment of all-gentile ecclesiae in Macedonia, some Jewish Christians communicated to Paul concerns about the sexual morality of non-Jews.
9. Paul went on to Achaia and beyond Achaia.
10. Some event in Judaea anticipated the wrath of the end time.
11. Some members of the ecclesia of the Thessalonians died.
12. As Paul became aware of concerns about whether and how deceased members of the ecclesiae would participate in the *parousia*, he searched for an appropriate answer.

13. Immediately before Paul wrote First Thessalonians, new trouble in Thessalonica gave Paul anxiety about the existence of the ecclesia.
14. Paul was in Athens when he learned of this trouble in Thessalonica.
15. Paul sent Timothy on an investigatory mission.
16. Upon Timothy's return, Paul wrote to them to rejoice. He wrote to express his joy, but he also wrote to present to them the instructions that followers of Jesus ought to marry and the hope that deceased members of the ecclesiae would rise from the dead in order to join the *parousia*.
17. Some indefinite time after the writing of the letter, Jesus' followers began to refer to Jesus as "Son of Man."

The following summary is a narrative version of how I believe this letter came to be written. It intends to bring together positions for which the more dispassionate argument has been given above. This statement does not include all of the **if**s that might constrain a more cautious approach; however, it represents the probable—most probable in my opinion—course of events.

When Paul called in his aide to write his dictation, he had been putting off writing about two subjects, but there was a precipitating event that made it the right moment for him to write, addressing three topics. Because there was some event, some difficulty affecting the ecclesia of the Thessalonians that gave Paul particular concerns for his people, he had sent Timothy to find out what was the condition of the ecclesia. In due time, Timothy returned and made his report. He reported on the constancy of their faith in Jesus and on their continuing love for Paul; he also probably reported the sad state of their hope, challenged as it was by the deaths of some of their members. That was the moment when Paul had to write. He wrote to express his love and care for them.

One subject he had to address was their lack of hope. Paul had originally proclaimed that Jesus would return during the original converts' lifetimes. Time had passed, and Jesus had not yet returned from heaven, and some of them had died. The deaths posed a problem, and not a local problem for the Thessalonians only. Others in other ecclesiae had died. The problem that they would not be still living to participate in the parousia faced the church generally. This problem had just been waiting for some impelling event to tip Paul over into speaking to it.

Paul had a second problem that members of the ecclesiae in Judaea were con-cerned about the sexual morality of the members of ecclesiae made up entirely of non-Jews, given what people in Judaea generally thought about the sexual mores of non-Jews. It was one thing for there to be some gentile members of the ecclesiae in Judaea; it was an entirely different matter for there to be all-gentile ecclesiae in Macedonia and Achaia. The all-gentile ecclesiae were a concern for the ecclesiae of Jesus in Judaea. Their concerns weighed on Paul.

Writing First Thessalonians was a devastating task. Paul needed to provide that which was lacking in their faith (3:10) and in particular provide hope in the face of the dashed hopes of those who had died. He also needed to speak in a way that would satisfy the moral concerns of his Jewish Christians in Judaea. He needed to lead the church in a way that would preserve the spiritual unity of the international church.

He was inspired by the Holy Spirit to speak of the resurrection of believers as the basis for hope on behalf of those who had died. This new doctrine was a crucial component in the emergence of this new Christian religion. He was inspired by the Holy Spirit to pronounce the marriage mandate for the benefit of the whole state of the church.

Paul's letter to the ecclesia of the Thessalonians

1:1 Paul and Silvanus and Timothy:
to the Thessalonians' ecclesia
in God the Father and in the Lord Jesus Christ:
grace to you and peace.

2 We give thanks to God always, concerning you all,
remembering you in our prayers without fail,

3 remembering your work of faith
and your labor of love
and your steadfastness of hope
before our Lord Jesus Christ in the presence of God our Father,

4 knowing, dear ones, that you are loved by God who chose you,

5 because our preaching the gospel did not come to you as mere words
but in power and in holy spirit, and in great conviction,
as you know what happened among you because of us.

6 And you have become imitators of us and of the Lord,
receiving the word in much conflict
with the grace of holy spirit,

7 with the result that you have become an example to all the believers
in Macedonia and as far as Achaia.

8 The word of the Lord has gone out from you
not only in Macedonia and in Achaia,
but in every place, your faith in God has been announced
so much that there is no need for us to tell others about you.

9 For others announce what sort of entrance we had among you
and how you turned towards God away from idols
to serve a living and true God,

10 and to await his son from the heavens,
whom he raised from corpses,
Jesus, who is rescuing us
from the coming wrath.

2:1 For you yourselves recall, dear ones, our entrance on your scene,
that it did not happen in vain,

2 but having previously been badly treated and insulted in Philippi
as you know,
we found courage in our God to speak to you the gospel of God,

in a great contest.

3 For our proclamation came
   neither to deceive or trick or manipulate,
4 but just as we have been entrusted by God to preach,
   just so we speak, not pleasing humans but God who discerns our hearts.
5 We never spoke in flattering words, as you know,
   nor as a pretext for greed, God is my witness,
6 and we were not seeking to impress people, neither you nor others.
7 Although we were entitled to use our authority as apostles of Christ,
   we were gentle among you
   as a nursing woman nourishes her own children.
8 Yearning, we choose to give you not only God's good news
   but our own selves, so dear had you become to us.
9 Of course you remember, dear ones, our toil and labor;
   working night and day so as not to be a burden on any of you
   we announced to you the Gospel of God.
10 You and God are witnesses
   how blameless, righteous, and pleasing to God we were
   with you the believers,
11 just as you know, we were to each one of you
   like a father to his own children,
12 encouraging you and cajoling you and giving you an example
   how to walk worthily of God
   who is calling you to his kingdom and glory.
13 And for this reason it is especially important for us in particular
   to give thanks to God
   that, taking possession of our preaching about God,
   you received it not as a human word
   but as what it really is, the word of God,
   who is at work in you, the believers.
14 For you have become imitators, dear ones,
   of the ecclesiae of God which are in Judea in Christ Jesus
   in that you have endured the same thing as they,
   you at the hands of your own countrymen,
   just as they from the Jews,
15 who killed the Lord Jesus and the prophets,

and chased us out, not pleasing God,

and opposing themselves to all people,

16 preventing us from preaching to save the gentiles,

as a way of filling up their sins.

The wrath of the end-time has already begun for them.

17 We, then, dear ones, being separated from you

for a long enough time,

physically, not emotionally,

became exceedingly eager to see you in person,

with a great desire.

18 So that we wanted to come to you,

I, myself, Paul, not once or twice,

but the satan hindered us.

19 For who is our hope or grace or wreath to boast of—

except you—before our Lord Jesus in his arrival?

20 You are our glory and grace.

3:1 When we could bear it no longer, we chose

to be left alone in Athens

2 and we sent Timothy, our dear brother

and God's co-worker in the good news of Christ,

to steady you and to encourage you in your faith

3 that you not be shaken in these current difficulties,

for you know that we can expect troubles;

4 we kept on telling you so ahead of time, when we were with you,

that we were going to have difficulties,

just as has happened and as you know.

5 Because of this, being no longer able to bear it,

I sent Timothy to learn of your faith,

lest the tempter had tempted you

and our work had been in vain.

6 Just now Timothy has returned from you to us

and has announced to us your faith and your love

and that you always have a good memory of us,

wanting to see us just as we want to see you.

7 Because of this we are encouraged, dear ones,

because of every effort and difficulty of ours on your behalf, to create your faith,

8   that now we live, since you are steadfast in the faith.

9   What thanksgiving we are able to return to God concerning you!
   We rejoice before God because of you,

10 night and day praying exceedingly to see you in person
   and make up what is lacking in your faith.

11 God himself, our Father, and our Lord Jesus,
   guide our path towards you;

12 the Lord fill and make you overflow
   with love for one another and for everyone,
   just as we love you,

13 in order to steady your hearts
   to be blameless in holiness
   before God our Father
   in the arrival of our Lord Jesus with all his saints.

4:1 As for the rest, dear ones, we make this request of you
   and encourage you in the Lord Jesus
   that just as you have received from us
   how it is necessary for you to walk and to please God,
   that you walk in that way
   so that you please God abundantly.

2   For you know what commandments we gave you
   on behalf of the Lord Jesus.

3   For the will of God is this: your sanctification,
   that you abstain from sexual immorality,

4   that each of you know how to acquire a wife
   in holiness and honor,

5   not in an emotional experience like those who do not know God,

6   and how not to trespass against and cheat each other in this matter;
   for the Lord carries out justice for all these things,
   just as we have told you before and witnessed continually.

7   For God has not called us for uncleanness
   but for holiness.

8   Therefore whoever refuses, refuses—not man but—God
   who is giving you his own holy spirit.

9   Now concerning brotherly love,

you do not need us to write you,

for you are God-taught to love one another,

10   For you are doing this towards all the dear ones

in all of Macedonia. We encourage you, dear ones,

to excel even more.

11   Be ambitious to live quietly,

to mind your own business,

and to work with your hands,

just as we commanded you,

12   in order that you walk worthily of respect from outsiders,

and not depend upon others.

13   I do not want you not to know, dear ones,

about those who are sleeping,

so that you do not grieve like others who do not have hope.

14   For since we believe that Jesus died and rose,

so also God will through Jesus

lead with him those who have fallen asleep.

15   This, of course, we say to you in accordance with the gospel.

that we the living who are being left behind

will not precede those who have fallen asleep

when the Lord arrives;

16   that with a commanding shout

with an archangel's call,

and with the trumpet's call to arms,

the Lord himself will step down from heaven,

and the dead shall rise in Christ first,

17   then we the living,

who are being left behind,

will be snatched up in the clouds along with them

for the meeting with the Lord in the air;

in this way we shall always be with the Lord.

18   Encourage each other just so, in these words.

5:1   Now concerning hours and opportunities, dear ones,

you do not need to be written to,

2   for you yourselves know accurately

that the day of the Lord comes as a thief in the night.

3   Whenever they say, "Peace and Security,"
    their destruction comes on them suddenly,
    just like labor-pains surprise a pregnant woman,
    and no way will they escape.

4   But you, dear ones, you are not in the dark,
    such that the day might take you by surprise, like a thief.

5   By belonging, you have become daylight.
    We are not of the night or of the dark;

6   Therefore let us not sleep like others,
    but be sober and alert.

7   For those who sleep sleep at night,
    and those who get drunk drink at night;

8   but we being of the day stay sober
    putting on the breastplate of faith and love
    and the headgear of hope for salvation.

9   God has not set us up for wrath
    but for the acquisition of salvation
    through our Lord Jesus Christ

10 who died for us so that
    whether we keep watch or sleep
    alike we might live with him.

11 Therefore encourage one another and build each other up,
    one to another, just as you are doing.

12 We make this request of you, dear ones,
    to hold your leaders in respect,
    those who are standing up in front of you
    and admonishing you in the Lord

13 and to think of them so much more in love because of their work.
    Be at peace among yourselves.

14 We encourage you, dear ones, to admonish the unruly,
    give cheer to the faint of heart,
    be patient with the weak,
    think the best of everyone.

15 See that no one gives back evil for evil,
    but in everything pursue the good towards each other and towards all.

16 Rejoice always,

17 Pray without ceasing,
18 Give thanks for all things—
   for this is God's will for you in Christ,
19 Do not quench the spirit,
20 Do not belittle prophecy.
21 Look for the true character of all things: hold tight what is good
22 And hold apart from every appearance of evil.
23 May God, the very God of peace,
   make you entirely holy,
   and may your entire spirit—and your life and your body—
   be kept protected,
   blameless when our Lord Jesus Christ arrives.
24 He is faithful, the one calling you, and he will do it.
25 Dear ones, pray for us.
26 Greet all your dear ones with a holy kiss.
27 I solemnly charge you in the Lord to read this letter to everyone in the ecclesia.
28 The grace of our Lord Jesus Christ be with you.

GLOSSARY

adelphos, adelphoi	literally "brother," "brothers," but here translated as "dear ones"
adialeiptôs	"without fail"
agapê	"selfless love"
agapê eis	"love for each other"
alpha	the first letter of the alphabet: "a"
amemptos	inflected as an adjective in 3:13 "blameless" or "without fault"
amemptôs	inflected as an adverb in 5:23: "{act} blamelessly"
anangkê	"necessity," "duress"
apantêsis	"meeting" or "going out to welcome"
apechesthai	"abstain"
apocalypsis	"the revelation of a hidden truth"
aporphanisthentes	"being separated"
apo tôn nekrôn	"from the corpses"
archangelos	"archangel"
asphaleia	"security"
ataktos	'unruly' or 'disorderly'
autoi	"themselves," "yourselves," or "ourselves"
basileia	"kingdom"
chara	"grace," "joy"
christos	"anointed"
chronos	"time"
dia	"through"
dia tês hymôn pisteôs	"because of your faith"
dia touto	"for this reason"
dokimazonti	"discerns"
doxa	"glory," "reputation"
eidenai	"to know"

eidotes	"knowing"
eirênê	"peace"
eisodos	"arrival," or "entrance"
eis telos	"for the end"
eis to agapan allêlous	"to love one another"
ekdiôkô	"chased out"
ekklêsia	"ecclesia"; "church," but "assembly" is better
eklogê	"election," "choice," "being picked out"
en	the preposition "in"
en dynamei	"in power"
en hagiasmôi kai timêi	"in holiness and honor"
en keleusmati	"with a commanding shout"
en logôi kyriou	"in accordance with a word of the Lord," "in accordance with the gospel"
en pathei epithymias	"in an emotional experience"
en phonê archangelou	"with an archangel's call"
en plerophoria pollei	"in great conviction"
en pollôi agôni	"in a great contest"
en salpiggi	"with the trumpet's call to arms"
en têi parousiai	"in the parousia"
en thlipsei pollei	"in much conflict"
en thlipsesin tautais	"in these difficulties," "in these troubles"
en tôi pragmati	"in this business"
eparresiasametha	"we found courage"
epathete	"experienced"
epeita	"then"
ephthasen	"has come"; antique sense: "has preceded"
êpioi	"gentle"
epiphaneia	"appearance"
epithymia	"desire," "longing," "lust," "passion"
erôtômen	"we ask" or "we make this request of you"
euangelion	"good news"
eucharistia	"thanksgiving"
eucharistoumen	"we give thanks"
euschêmonôs	"respectably," "with a good reputation"
ex akatharsias	"out of uncleanness"

gar	"for," "because," "what comes next explains what came before"
gregoreite	"stay awake"
hagios	"saint" or "holy one"
hagiasmos	"holiness"
hagiosynê	"holiness"
harpagêsometha	"we will be snatched"
hêmeis	First person plural pronoun: "We"
hêmera ekeinê	"that day"
hetairai	"companions"
hoi	a plural form of "the"
hoi nekroi	"the corpses"
hote	"when"
hoti	"that"
houtôs	"thus" or "in this way"
huios	"son"
hybristhentes	"having been insulted"
hymeis	Second person plural pronoun: "You"
hyperbainein	"trespass," "cross a boundary"
hyper hêmôn	"for us"
hypomonês	"steadfastness"
hypo tôn idiôn symphyletôn	"by" or "from your own countrymen"
idios	"private," "personal"
Ioudaioi	"Jews" or "Judaeans"
kai	may be the conjunction "and" or may add emphasis to the next word
kai hêmeis	"we in particular"
kairos	"the right time," "the fulness of time," "the opportune moment"
kateuthunai	"guide"
kathaper	"just as"
kathôs oidate	"as you know"
keimetha	"we lie" [as in a bed]
keleusma	"a commanding shout"
kôluontôn	"preventing"

kenos	"vain," "empty"
Koinê	"something shared": "the common dialect"
kopos	"toil"
ktasthai	"to own," "to acquire" in the sense of "begin to own"
kyrios, kyrioi	singular and plural of "Lord" or "Master"
logos	"word," "reason," "meaning"
logos kyriou	"a word of the Lord"
loipoi	"others," "the rest"
loipon	"finally"
martyr, martyres	a witness at a trial, witnesses
martyromenoi	"witnessing" or "giving an example"
mê	an adverb used with some verbal forms: "not"
mellomen	"we are going to"
memphomai	"to find fault or complain"
mimêtai	"imitators"
mnêmoneuete	"you remember"
mochthos	"labor"
moicheia	"sex" with a respectable woman
monoi	"alone"
nekroi	"corpses" or "the dead"
nêpioi	"infants"
oidate	"you know"
oligon kairon	"a short time"
opsontai	"they will see"
orgê	"rage"
oun	"then," "therefore"
pais	"child," "slave"
parangelô	"I command"
parousia	"arrival"
pathontes	being on the receiving end of an experience
pathos	"suffering," "experience"
parakaloumen	"we encourage"
parakalountes	"encouraging"
paramythoumenoi	"encouraging" or "cajoling"
Peri de	"Now concerning"

perileipomenoi	"who are being left behind"
peripatein, peripateite	"to walk"
perisseusai	"make to overflow"
philadelphia	"love of brothers"
philia	"brotherly love"
phonê	"voice"
phylê	"voting block"
pistis	"belief," "faith," or "trust"
pleonasai	"fill"
pleonektein	"take advantage of," "be greedy," "cheat"
polis	the seat of government: "city" "state"
porneia	"fornication" or "sexual immorality"
pragma	"business"
proelegomen hymin	"we were continuing to tell you"
propathontes	"having been badly treated"
prôton	"first"
phylos	"tribe"
pros kairon hôras	"long enough"
salpigx	"war trumpet"
skeuos	"thing," "tool," "vessel"
skeuos ktasthai	as a calque from Hebrew: "to acquire a wife." Literally "to posses a tool / vessel"
sôthôsin	"might be saved"
stêrizô	"to steady"
symphyletos, symphyletoi	singular and plural forms of "fellow citizens," "countrymen"
synagogê	"synagogue"' but "gathering together" or "assembly" is better
têreô	"to keep under guard"
theodidaktoi	"God-taught"
theos, theou, theôi, theon	(forms of the word "god")
theou huios	"son of god"
thlipsis / thlipses	"trouble" or difficulty
thymos	"soul," "heart"
to	a singular form of "the"
tôi	a singular form of "the"

toiôn	"similar things"
to mê hyperbainein kai pleonektein	"not to trespass against and cheat"
tou apothanontes hyper hêmôn	"who died for us"
touto	"this"
touto gar	"for this"
toutôn	"these things"
xenos	"guest," "host," "foreigner"
zêsômen	"{so that} we might live"

BIBLIOGRAPHY

Donald Harman Akenson, *Surpassing Wonder: The Invention of the Bible and The Talmuds* (Chicago, University of Chicago Press, 1998).

Donald Harman Akenson, *Saint Saul* (Oxford: Oxford University Press, 2000).

William Baird, "One against the Other: Intra-Church Conflict in I Corinthians," in Robert T. Fortna and Beverly R. Gaventa, editors, *The Conversation Continues: Studies in Paul and John: In Honor of J. Louis Martyn* (Nashville: Abingdon Press, 1990).

Ferdinand Christian Baur, *Paul: the apostle of Jesus Christ, his life and works, his epistles and teachings; a contribution to a critical history of primitive Christianity,* 2 Vols. 2nd ed. translated by Dr. E. Zeller (London: Williams and Norgate, 1873).

Marcus Borg and John Dominic Crossan, *The First Paul: Reclaiming the Radical Visionary Behind The Church's Conservative Icon* (New York: Harper One, 2009).

Raymond E. Brown, S.S., *An Introduction to the New Testament* (New York: Doubleday, 1996).

Gilbert I. Bond, *Paul and the Religious Experience of Reconciliation: Diaspora Community & Creole Consciousness* (Louisville, KY: Westminster John Knox Press, 2005).

Charles Buck and Greer Taylor, *St. Paul: A Study of the Development of His Thought* (New York: Charles Scribner's Sons. 1969).

Ron Cameron and Merrill P. Miller, eds., *Resdescribing Christian Origins* (Atlanta: Society of Biblical Literature, 2011).

Richard J. Cassidy, *Paul in Chains: Roman Imprisonment and the Letters of St. Paul* (New York: Crossroad Publishing Company, 2001).

Bruce Corley, ed., *Colloquy on New Testament Studies: A Time for Reappraisal and Fresh Approaches* (Macon, GA: Mercer University Press, 1983).

John Dominic Crossan, *The Historical Jesus: The Life of a Mediterranian Jewish Peasant* (New York: HarperSanFrancisco, 1991).

John Dominic Crossan and Jonathan L. Reed, *In Search of Paul: How Jesus' Apostle Opposed Rome's Empire with God's Kingdom* (San Francisco: HarperSanFrancisco, 2004).

Frederick William Danker, *The Concise Greek-English Lexicon of the New Testament* (Chicago: University of Chicago Press, 2009).

W. D. Davies, *Paul and Rabbinic Judaism: Some Rabbinic Elements in Pauline Theology* (London: SPCK, 1958).

Arthur J. Dewey, Roy W. Hoover, Lane G. McGaughy, and Daryl D. Schmidt, *The Authentic Letters of Paul: A New Reading of Paul's Rhetoric and Meaning: The Scholar's Version* (Salem, OR: Polebridge Press, 2010).

Karl Paul Donfried, "The Cults of Thessalonica and the Thessalonian Correspondence," *New Testament Studies* 31 (1985) 336-56.

Chalmer E. Faw, "On the Writing of First Thessalonians." *Journal of Biblical Literature* 71. (1952): 217-25.

Elisabeth Schüssler Fiorenza, *In Memory of Her: A Feminist Theological Reconstruction of Christian Origins,* Tenth Anniversary Edition, (New York: Crossroad, 2000).

Harry Gamble, "The Redaction of the Pauline Letters and the Formation of the Pauline Corpus," *Journal of Biblical Literature* 94 (1975): 403-418.

Jonathan A. Goldstein, *I Maccabees,* Anchor Bible 41 (Garden City, NY: Doubleday & Company, Inc., 1976).

Edgar J. Goodspeed, "The Canon of the New Testament," *Interpreter's Bible,* Vol. 1 (Abingdon Press, 1952).

Kyle Harper, "*Porneia*: The Making of a Christian Sexual Norm," *Journal of Biblical Literature,* 131, No. 2 (2012): 363-383.

Louis F. Hartman, C.SS.R and Alexander A. Di Lella, O.F.M., *The Book of Daniel: A New Translation with Notes and Commentary,* Anchor Bible 23 (Garden City, NY: Doubleday, 1978).

Martin Hengel, *Judaism and Hellenism* (Philadelphia: Fortress Press, 1974).

John C. Hurd, Jr., *The Origin of I Corinthians* (New York: Seabury Press, 1965).

John.C.Hurd, Jr., "Pauline Chronology and Pauline Theology" in *Christian History and Interpretation: Studies presented to John Knox*, W.R.Farmer, C.F.D.Moule and R.R.Niebuhr, eds. (Cambridge: Cambridge University Press, 1967).

John C. Hurd, Jr., *The Earlier Letters of Paul – and Other Studies* (Frankfurt am Main: Peter Lang, 1998).

Robert Jewett, *The Thessalonian Correspondence: Pauline Rhetoric and Millenarian Piety* (Philadelphia: Fortress Press, 1986).

E. Elizabeth Johnson, "A Modest Proposal in Context" in *The Impartial God: Essays in Biblical Studies in Honor of Jouette M. Bassler,* Calvin J. Roetzel and Robert L. Foster, eds. (Sheffield Phoenix Press, 2007).

George Kennedy, *The Art of Persuasion in Greece* (Princeton: Princeton University Press, 1963).

John Knox, *Chapters in a Life of Paul* (New York: Abingdon, 1950).

John Knox, *Marcion and the New Testament: An Essay in the Early History of the Canon* (Chicago: The University of Chicago Press, 1942).

John Knox, "On the Pauline Chronology: Buck-Taylor-Hurd Revisited" in Robert T. Fortna and Beverly R. Gaventa, eds., *The Conversation Continues: Studies in Paul and John: In Honor of J. Louis Martyn* (Nashville: Abingdon Press, 1990).

Helmut Koester, *Ancient Christian Gospels* (Philadelphia: Trinity, 1990).

Helmut Koester, "The Memory of Jesus' Death and the Worship of the Risen Lord," *Harvard Theological Review* 91 (1998): 335-350.

Amy-Jill Levine, *The Misunderstood Jew: The Church and the Scandal of the Jewish Jesus* (San Francisco: HarperOne, 2006).

Liddell and Scott, *A Lexicon Abridged from Liddell and Scotts Greek-English Lexicon* (Oxford: Clarendon Press, 1891).

William Loader, *The New Testament on Sexuality* (Grand Rapids, MI: Eerdmans, 2012)

Gerd Luedemann, *Paul, Apostle to the Gentiles: Studies in Chronology*, English translation by F. Stanley Jones (Philadelphia: Fortress Press, 1984).

Abraham J. Malherbe, *Social Aspects of Early Christianity*, 2nd ed. (Philadelphia: Fortress Press, 1983).

Abraham J. Malherbe, *The Letters to the Thessalonians: A New Translation with Introduction and Commentary*, Anchor Yale Bible, 32B (New Haven:Yale University Press, 2000).

Wayne A. Meeks, *The First Urban Christians: The Social World of the Apostle Paul* (New Haven and London: Yale University Press, 1983).

Margaret M. Mitchell, *Paul and the Rhetoric of Reconciliation: An Exegetical Investigation of the Language and Composition of 1 Corinthians* (Louisville, KY: Westminster/John Knox Press, 1991).

Margaret M. Mitchell, "Paul's Letters to Corinth: The Interpretive Intertwining of Literary and Historical Reconstruction" in Daniel N. Schowalter and Steven J. Friesen, eds., *Urban Religion in Roman Corinth: Interdisciplinary Approaches* (Cambridge: Harvard Theological Studies, 2005), 307-338.

Arthur Darby Nock, *St. Paul* (London: Thornton Butterworth, Ltd., 1938).

Kirk Ormand, *Controlling Desires: Sexuality in Ancient Greece and Rome* (Westport, CT: Praeger, 2009).

Elaine Pagels, *The Gnostic Paul: Gnostic Exegesis of the Pauline Letters* (Harrisburg, PA: Trinity Press International, 1975).

Philip B. Payne, *Man and Woman, One in Christ: An Exegetical and Theological Study of Paul's Letters* (Grand Rapids, MI: Zondervan, 2009).

Norman Perrin and Dennis C. Duling, *The New Testament: An Introduction: Proclamation and Parenesis, Myth and History* (New York: Harcourt Brace Jovanovich, 1982).

Richard I. Pervo, *Dating Acts: Between the Evangelists and the Apologists* (Polebridge Press, 2006).

Richard I. Pervo, *The Making of Paul: Constructions of the Apostle in Early Christianity* (Minneapolis: Fortress, 2010).

Earl J. Richard, *First and Second Thessalonians* (Collegeville, MN: The Liturgical Press, 1995).

Amy Richlin, *The Garden of Priapus: Sexual Aggression in Roman Humor* (New York: Oxford University Press, 1992).

David Syme Russell, *Between the Testaments* (Philadelphia: Fortress Press, 1960, 1965).

Paul Schubert, *Form and Function of the Pauline Thanksgivings* (Berlin: Verlag Von Alfred Töpelmann, 1939).

Gerd Theissen, *Social Reality and the Early Christians: Theology, Ethics, and the World of the New Testament,* trans. by Margaret Kohl (Minneapolis: Fortress Press, 1992).

Joseph B. Tyson, *Marcion and Luke-Acts: A Defining Struggle* (Columbia, SC: University of South Carolina Press, 2006).

François Vouga, "La première épître aux Thessaloniciens," *Introduction au Nouveau Testament: son histoire, son écriture, sa théologie,* Édité par Daniel Marguerat, Troisième édition mise à jour (Paris: Labor et fides, 2004).

O. Larry Yarbrough, *Not Like the Gentiles: Marriage Rules in the Letters of Paul,* SBL Dissertation Series (Atlanta, Georgia: Scholars Press 1985).

APPENDIX 1

PAUL'S LIFE, AS PREVIOUSLY RECONSTRUCTED FROM THE LETTERS ALONE.

A S mentioned in Part I, chapter 1, Knox, Riddle, Buck and Taylor, Hurd, and Luedemann attempted to reconstruct the history of Paul's life based on information in the letters, without using Acts as a historical frame. In the broadest terms, a scenario of Paul's life, constructed out of the letters, runs like this:

In the first two chapters of Galatians, Paul spoke of his conversion, of his two visits to Jerusalem, and of an argument between him and Cephas. He said he was persecuting the ecclesia (Gal. 1:13) when he received the gospel by revelation (Gal. 1:11) and that he went immediately into Arabia. Paul did not tell us how much time he spent in Arabia; it might have been a few days, or it might have been a longer period. It is quite possible, as Knox points out, that Paul made a lengthy sojourn in the desert.[213] Then he returned to Damascus. Furthermore, as Knox notices, Paul chose the word "returned," as if one "returned home."[214] The word means that Paul was not, at that moment, on a journey from Jerusalem to Damascus, but that he had begun his journey in Damascus and then went back to the place from which he had begun. Paul's point in describing his travels in this way is that he did not go to Jerusalem at the moment of his conversion,[215] and as we shall see, he did not go there in order to be instructed in the gospel by the apostles. The gospel

---

213. John Knox, Chapters in *A Life of Paul*, (Abingdon, 1950), 77.

214. Knox, *Chapters*, 37.

215. Knox, *Chapters*, 51-52. Luedemann, Apostle, 39.

Paul preached was not of human origin, nor did he receive it from a human source (Gal. 1:11-12), particularly not from the apostles in Jerusalem (Gal. 1:17-2:10).

Paul said that he went to Jerusalem for the first time "after three years" (Gal. 1:18). He used the word epeita ("then"), which indicates a temporal sequence, so that it is clear that his first visit to Jerusalem came after some other event.[216] It is not clear whether Paul meant that it was three years after he received the revelation or three years after he returned from the desert to Damascus. It also is not clear whether "after three years" means "in the third year," which could be as short a time span as two years and a day, or "after three full years," which would mean three full years or more. The Greek is inexact about the span of time.

Paul did not say anything about that visit except that he met Cephas and James, the brother of the Lord (Gal. 1:18-19). He made it explicit that he did not meet anyone else, and certified the truth of what he said with an oath (Gal. 1:20). This oath and the statement it supports contribute to our understanding that Paul's reception of the gospel and calling were independent of the apostles in Jerusalem.[217] This statement came in response to an accusation.[218] Apparently ministers who came to Galatia accused Paul of not being a fully qualified apostle, of being subordinate to those in Jerusalem, and not knowing the full truth of the gospel. His successors were teaching the Galatians that they needed to be circumcised and that Paul was a subordinate, derivative evangelist, which Paul here denied. Although it is possible, in view of the accusation, that Paul was thinking of some very narrow distinction and not telling the whole truth, nevertheless he asserted that he was a fully qualified apostle, not subordinate to the leaders in Jerusalem. As Luedemann says, there was one matter on which Paul absolutely needed to be telling the truth, if he was to retain any credibility, and that was the number of times he had been to Jerusalem.[219]

After that first visit Paul went to the region of Syria and Cilicia. Paul, however, did not mean that the region of Syria and Cilicia was the only place

---

216. Luedemann, *Apostle*, 63.

217. Hurd, *Origin*, 20.

218. Luedemann, *Apostle*, 19.

219. Luedemann, *Apostle*, 39.

he went. It is possible that he was thinking that he went to that region when he left Jerusalem, and then after that he went other places; his statement does not imply that this region was the only place he had been. Those other places, in that case, were not relevant to the point which he was trying to make, which is how few trips he made to Jerusalem and how independent he was of the Jerusalem authorities.[220]

Sometime after that first visit to Jerusalem, Paul crossed into Europe and, over a period of years, evangelized Philippi and Thessalonica in Macedonia and Athens and Corinth in the Greek province known as Achaia. Paul's first mission to Europe came within this fourteen year period and before Paul's second visit to Jerusalem.[221]

Also, after that first visit, and probably soon before his second visit, Paul had an argument with Cephas. Luedemann observed that in the first two chapters of Galatians while Paul was describing events that happened one after another in sequence, he used the word epeita ("then"), a word which conveys the temporal sequence. However, when Paul introduced the story of this argument, he used the word hote ("when"), which does not imply a temporal sequence.[222] Although Paul described his argument with Cephas after he talked about his second visit to Jerusalem, the argument came before the visit.

The argument concerned table fellowship between Jews and non-Jews. Because of their customs of kosher food preparation, Jews in the First Century generally did not eat with non-Jews. However, as others were admitted to the body of followers of Jesus, the barrier was being broken, and Jews and non-Jews were beginning to share table fellowship. When Cephas first came to Antioch, where Paul and Barnabas were, he ate at the same table with non-Jewish members of the movement. When some Jewish followers of Jesus arrived from Jerusalem, however, they began to eat separately from the gentiles, and Cephas withdrew from the gentiles and joined the Jewish separatists. Paul then rebuked Cephas in a difficult and complex statement (Gal 2:14-20), which introduces the rest of the letter. Luedemann noted that Paul

---

220. The point he was trying to make was his independence as an apostle. Knox, *Chapters*, 51-52. Luedemann, *Apostle*, 39.

221. Knox, *Chapters*, 79. Buck and Taylor, *St. Paul, passim*, especially 82 and 106. Hurd, *Origin*, 19-21, especially 21 footnote 3. Luedemann, *Apostle*, 23.

222. Luedemann, *Apostle*, 19, 56, 62, 63.

would relate this event out of historical sequence because it is not pertinent to his statement of his independence from Jerusalem and it is pertinent to the rest of the letter, which it introduces.[223]

The incident with Cephas means Paul's thinking and ministry was oriented toward including non-Jews in the Jesus movement, even to the extent of eating with them without distinction. Paul said that he himself was advanced in Judaism beyond his peers (Gal 1:14). His commitment to include non-Jews represents an extraordinary change. He asserted that he had been entrusted with a ministry to other people (Gal 2:7) and that the revelation given to him was his call to that ministry (Gal 1:15). This orientation is precisely what is on display in his argument with Cephas.

After he described his first visit to Jerusalem, Paul said that his second visit to Jerusalem came "after fourteen years" (Galatians 2:1). He again used the word epeita, indicating that this visit, like the first visit, came in a temporal sequence. Like the earlier time frame of "after three years," "after fourteen years" is ambiguous whether Paul meant that it was in the fourteenth year, or whether fourteen full years had transpired. It also is not clear whether Paul was counting fourteen years from his conversion or from his return to Damascus, so that the total period would be fourteen years, or if he was counting fourteen years from his first visit, the total years from his conversion would be seventeen years. Paul's intention in the passage was to illustrate his independence of Jerusalem over a long period of time, and his statement clearly accomplished that intent.[224]

The scene with Cephas puts into perspective that something needed to be done to clarify the status of gentiles in the Jesus movement, and so Paul went up to Jerusalem to lay out in front of the acknowledged leaders the substance he had been preaching. He said he went up to Jerusalem because of a revelation (Gal 2:2). Paul had established all-gentile congregations in Europe and now, because of his argument with Cephas, Paul realized that there might be something controversial in his admitting non-Jews to the fellowship.

In Jerusalem, meeting privately with the acknowledged leaders, Paul set before them the gospel that he preached among the gentiles (Gal 2:2), that is, the gentiles in Macedonia and Achaia. According to Paul, when he told them what he had been preaching, James and Cephas and John accepted that he was

---

223. Luedemann, *Apostle*, 20.

224. Knox, *Chapters*, 51-52. Hurd, *Origin*, 20-21. Luedemann, *Apostle*, 62.

correct in not requiring circumcision or kosher tables (Gal 2:3-10). Not only did they not add anything to the substance of what Paul preached, they also did not compel Titus, a Greek who accompanied Paul during this trip, to be circumcised. Their action, thus, was consistent with Paul's verbal report of the approval they gave him.

Paul said that the pillars of the church made only one requirement of him, that he remember the poor.[225] Paul said that, at the time they made the requirement, he was already eager to do that (Gal 2:10).

Paul spoke of this meeting in Jerusalem and of his commitment to remember the poor, in the past tense. Knox makes much of this past tense that Paul used to say that he was eager to do this.[226] Subsequently to that requirement, Paul put a great deal of energy into raising funds for the poor. This project of his is known as the Collection, assuming that five passages (1 Cor 16:1-3; 2 Cor 8; 2 Cor 9; Romans 15:25-27; and Gal 2:10)[227] all refer to the same event. Because Paul spoke in Galatians of the beginning of the Collection as being in the past, we conclude that Galatians was written some time after that beginning.

First Corinthians both refers to a Previous Letter that Paul had written to them (1 Cor 5:9) and to a question about the Collection that the Corinthians raised in their letter (the "Corinthian Reply") (1 Cor 16:1-3). Probably, Paul announced the Collection in that Previous Letter.[228] Probably, in the Corinthian Reply, the Corinthians asked for specific instructions on the manner of gathering the Collection.[229] In First Corinthians, Paul told them to put a little aside each week, so that there would be no last-minute hassle.

---

225. Although Paul consistently speaks of this task as "remembering the poor," it may well have been a euphemism for "send money." It will be more appropriate to discuss this issue fully in a separate book.

226. Knox, *Chapters*, 56.

227. The insight that 2 Cor 8 and 2 Cor 9 are separate letters and separate references to the Collection arose subsequent to Buck's studies. He consistently refers to them as part of the same reference to the Collection. See Margaret M. Mitchell, "Paul's Letters to Corinth: The Interpretive Intertwining of Literary and Historical Reconstruction" in Daniel N. Schowalter and Steven J. Friesen, eds., *Urban Religion in Roman Corinth: Interdisciplinary Approaches* (Harvard Theological Studies, 2005), 307-338.

228. Buck and Taylor, *St. Paul*, 32, 44. Buck's reconstruction is that 1 Cor 16:1-4 is a specific response to a question that came as a response to Paul's announcement of the Collection in the Previous Letter.
Hurd, *Origin*, 200.

229. Hurd, *Origin*, 233.

Because in Galatians Paul indicated that the decision to take up the Collection came out of his second visit to Jerusalem, it is clear that the Previous Letter was written after that visit. The Collection began after Paul's second visit to Jerusalem, itself some years after the beginning of Paul's European Mission.

Second Corinthians includes two references to the Collection (2 Cor 8 and 9). Both of them urge the Corinthians to finish what they have begun.[230] The tone of Second Corinthians 1-9 is very different from the tone of First Corinthians. Buck attributes this difference to a change of heart. After writing First Corinthians, Paul had been imprisoned and received a sentence of death (2 Cor 1:8-10). Buck speculated that this near experience of his own death led Paul to a change of heart.[231] Therefore, we can date these Second Corinthians some time after the beginning of the Collection, and establish that the first nine chapters of Second Corinthians, even if they are made up of more than one letter, were written after First Corinthians.

In Romans Paul spoke of the Collection as completed and said that he was taking it to Jerusalem (Rom 15:25-26). Therefore Romans is the last in the sequence of these three major letters.[232] Paul also said in Romans that he had finished his work in the East and that he hoped to travel to Rome and that they would help him to go on from there to Spain (Rom 15:23-24, 28).

Because in Galatians Paul spoke of the Collection as having begun in the past, we know Paul wrote Galatians some time after he wrote the Previous Letter. Buck argued that Galatians was written close to the same time when Romans was written, on the grounds that Galatians and Romans have very similar content.[233] Buck added a second argument based on Paul's use of the antithesis between faith and works. Paul did not mention this antithesis in First Thessalonians or First or Second Corinthians; but he used it in both Galatians and Romans. Buck argued that Paul came upon the antithesis while he was writing Galatians and used it from then on, making his point

---

230. Mitchell, "Paul's Letters to Corinth," 324.

231. Buck and Taylor, *St. Paul,* 59.

232. Knox, *Chapters,* 85-6. Buck and Taylor, *St. Paul,* 27-29. Luedemann, *Apostle,* 22-23, Hurd, *Earlier Letters,* 39. In the chapter on "The Sequence of Paul's Letters," Hurd also reviews arguments for this sequence based on doctrinal development, literary affinity, the Judaizing crisis, as well as the collection.

233. Buck and Taylor, *St. Paul,* Chapter 6, 82-102. See also Hurd's review of the arguments in *Earlier Letters,* Chapter 2, "The Sequence of the Letters," 31-46.

that Galatians was written shortly before Romans.[234] Buck saw Galatians as contributing to the broader, more developed expression of justification by faith in Romans, as if Paul learned from writing Galatians and was able to improve his statement when he wrote Romans.[235] Knox was unconvinced by this argument, thinking that Paul might have written Galatians after he wrote Romans, as a brief summary.[236]

The sequence of events is:

- Paul received a revelation from God.
- He went to Arabia.
- He returned to Damascus.
- After three years he went to Jerusalem for fifteen days.
- He went to the region of Syria and Cilicia.
- At an unknown time, he crossed into Europe and founded churches in Thessalonica and Corinth.
- Within a fourteen year period, he had an argument with Cephas about table fellowship.
- After fourteen years, he went to Jerusalem to lay his gospel before the authorities.
- He began the Collection and wrote the Previous Letter to the Corinthians.
- The Corinthians sent him the Corinthian Reply.
- Paul responded in First Corinthians.
- Paul was imprisoned and given a sentence of death.
- Paul wrote Second Corinthians 1-9.
- Paul wrote Galatians, in the midst of the Circumcision Crisis.
- Paul wrote Romans.

---

234. Buck and Taylor, *St. Paul*, 88-89. Hurd, *Earlier Letters*, 39-40.

235. See Buck and Taylor, *St. Paul*, see all of chapter 6, 82-102, but especially 87.

236. Knox, "On the Pauline Chronology: Buck-Taylor-Hurd Revisited" in Robert T. Fortna and Beverly R. Gaventa, editors, *The Conversation Continues: Studies in Paul and John: In Honor of J. Louis Martyn*, (Nashville: Abingdon Press 1990), 258-272, 263.

THE SCHOLARS WHO RECONSTRUCTED THE HISTORY FROM PAUL'S LETTERS

T HESE six scholars show a dialogue over a fifty year period. The earlier ones inspired and set agenda for the later ones. They agree in some broad outlines of the project, and yet are quite independent one from another.

John Knox

John Knox published *Chapters in a Life of Paul* in 1950. In *Chapters*, Knox wrote a biography of Paul. He titled it *Chapters* in order to indicate that it was only a partial biography. Knox concentrated on the events Paul discussed in Galatians 1:13-2:10, where Paul discussed his two visits to Jerusalem before he wrote that letter. Acts, however, reported several more visits. Knox devoted much of the energy of *Chapters* in an attempt to reconcile the visits in Paul's letter with the visits in Acts.

Chapters summarizes work that Knox had previously published in two journal articles.[237] His work on two other early-career books had led him to think of Acts as a second century product, at least in its final form.[238] This perspective enabled him to think critically about Acts. Knox thought that

---

237. The two journal articles are Knox, "Fourteen years later: A Note on the Pauline Chronology," *JR* 16 (1936): 341-49, and "The Pauline Chronology," *JBL* 58 (1939) 15-29.

238. Knox's two previous books include his study of Philemon (*Philemon: Among the Letters of Paul*, St. James's Place, London: Collins, 1960 [reprint. original version 1935]) and his study of the relationship between Marcion and the creation of canonical Luke and the Book of Acts (*Marcion and the New Testament: An Essay in the Early History of the Canon* [The University of

Acts was based on sources no longer available to us, but since he thought that the same author had used source material responsibly in the composition of the Gospel According to Luke, he thought that Luke probably used his sources for Acts responsibly as well.[239] The difference, however, was that Knox saw Paul's letters as themselves primary sources for historical research.

Donald Riddle

Donald Riddle published *Paul, Man of Conflict* in 1940.[240] The subtitle identified the work as a biographical "sketch," anticipating Knox's comment about the paucity of data. Riddle relied on Paul's letters and placed a lower value on data from the Book of Acts, on the grounds that "it was not [Acts'] purpose to recount the life of Paul."[241] Riddle made the distinction between the letters as primary source material and the Book of Acts as secondary source material, but observed that "almost all biographies of Paul" make a synthesis of material from the two sources.[242] Riddle, however, built his slim biography of Paul on what Paul says in his letters, such as his saying that he was a Pharisee of the tribe of Benjamin (Philippians 3:4b-6).

Riddle found conflict to be the key to reconstructing the history of Paul's ministry. The conflict over circumcision, a problem contemporary with the writing of Galatians, marks a turning point in Paul's career. Riddle separated Paul's letters into those that were written before the Circumcision Crisis, those that were written during the crisis, and those which were written afterwards. This grouping placed Galatians close in time to the composition of Romans. However, Riddle addressed the sequence of the letters only in an appendix.[243]

Charles Buck and Greer Taylor

Chicago Press, Chicago, Illinois, 1942]). Neither of those books speaks to the history of the Jesus' movement in the thirties, forties, and fifties.

239. Knox, *Chapters*, 15.

240. Donald Wayne Riddle, *Paul, Man of Conflict: A Modern Biographical Sketch* (Nashville: Cokesbury Press, 1940). Although this book of Riddle's precedes Knox's book by ten years, Knox's two Journal articles preceded publication of Riddle's book. I discuss Knox first because the articles were earlier.

241. Riddle, *Man of Conflict*, 7.

242. Riddle, *Man of Conflict*, 14-16.

243. Riddle, *Man of Conflict*, 204-206.

Charles Buck's ideas were published in 1969, after Buck had retired from teaching, in Buck and Taylor, *St. Paul: A Study of the Development of His Thought*.[244] Buck's primary interest was Paul's thought rather than his biography or the history of the early church. It is a part of biography to trace how people's thought changed during their lifetimes; Buck's interest was to understand Paul by understanding how his thinking developed. Consequently, his interests were served by attention to the letters. It is the letters that show the nuance of Paul's thought.

Buck relied on the letters as evidence for historical analysis, but did not argue extensively for this procedure. Although he thought the author of Acts was Paul's companion on the later journeys and an eyewitness of the latest events in Acts,[245] he recognized that the author was not an eyewitness of the earlier events. "As a historical document, Acts is clearly a secondary source," he said, and there are possibilities of inaccuracy.[246] To rely on Acts for the history and explain away the differences in Paul's evidence "belies the canons of sound practice in historical research . . . . [and that it] has failed to yield satisfactory solutions . . . is evident to every serious student in the field."[247] He was, nevertheless, cautious and said, "If it is a mistake for a biographer of Paul to treat [Acts] as a primary source, it is just as serious a mistake for him not to treat it with respect."[248] Consequently, this book devotes a lengthy chapter accounting for how the author of Acts introduced inaccuracies.

Buck placed First Thessalonians early in the sequence of the letters, primarily on the general agreement among scholars, and secondarily on comparisons of the letters' differences in theology. For example, Paul's treatment of the resurrection of believers in 1 Thess 4:13-18 is much less developed than his treatment of the same subject in 1 Cor 15.[249] Buck infers that in the Previous Letter, Paul presented a statement of the resurrection of believers

---

244. In the preface, Buck and Taylor claim their contributions were mutual. Taylor's original contribution may have been on Paul's changing perspective on the law given to Moses. There is a verbal tradition that Taylor provided the impetus to get the book written—from a conversation with John Hurd, January 2011.

245. Buck and Taylor, *St. Paul*, 5, 208.

246. Buck and Taylor, *St. Paul*, 5.

247. Buck and Taylor, *St. Paul*, 6.

248. Buck and Taylor, *St. Paul*, 7.

249. Buck and Taylor, *St. Paul*, 53-54.

similar to that in First Thessalonians, and that the Corinthians objected in the Corinthian Reply. Paul's thinking about the resurrection took new form as he responded to their objections.[250]

Buck presented the hypothesis of a Previous Letter and a Corinthian Reply as a conversation that preceded First Corinthians. Buck found that at least six[251] of the issues in First Corinthians came out of that previous conversation. Paul wrote First Corinthians as a continuing discussion.[252]

If any part of Buck's reconstruction of the history of this conversation is correct, it is an important piece of the history of the very early Jesus movement. Scholarly agreement has tended to shy away from this reconstruction, but in general it has done so by maintaining the Acts-based history. Buck cast too wide a net and presented radical perceptions on too many facets of New Testament scholarship, so that his work was easily dismissed. However, his insights into the historical process of the development of Paul's theology deserve further consideration.

John Hurd

John Hurd published *The Origin of I Corinthians* in 1965. Although this work was published before Buck and Taylor was published, Buck was Hurd's teacher and inspired Hurd to do graduate work on Paul's letters.[253]

The thrust of *Origin* was to work backwards from what Paul said in First Corinthians to speculate about what the Corinthians might have said in the Corinthian Reply.[254] Proposals by various scholars range from sycophantic requests for clarification addressed to the respected and beloved teacher to provocative argument with the Paul's position. In general Hurd concludes that the issues in the Corinthian Reply were rather argumentative.

Then, in a second and even more speculative step, Hurd considered what

---

250. Buck and Taylor, *St. Paul*, 39-42.

251. The six issues are: associating with immoral persons, marriage and sexuality, meat offered to idols, ecstatic spirituality, the resurrection, and the collection. Buck and Taylor, *St. Paul*, 44.

252. Buck and Taylor, *St. Paul*, Chapter 2, pp. 31-45.

253. Hurd, *Origin*, xi-xii.

254. Contrary to Buck's list of six issues, Hurd found nine issues were discussed in the Previous Letter and the Corinthian Reply: immoral men, marriage, celibate persons, idol meat, spiritual men, the veiling of women, bodily resurrection, the collection, and a request for a visit from Apollos, *Origin*, 213-237.

Paul might have said in the Previous Letter that would have brought forth the response in the Corinthian Reply. Although Hurd was explicitly[255] aware that the first step, estimating the Corinthian Reply, was speculative, and that therefore the second step, approximating the contents of the Previous Letter, was building speculation on top of speculation, he nevertheless found correlation for the content of the Previous Letter, in some resemblances between First Corinthians and Acts. If Hurd is correct in the reconstruction of this conversation leading to the writing of First Corinthians, this is critically important information about the history of the very early church.

Gerd Luedemann

Paul: Apostle to the Gentiles is the major work by Gerd Luedemann available to English readers. Published in 1983, it is the translation of the book originally published in German in 1980. In the forward, John Knox commends the book as "the first full length, full bodied and fully documented study of Paul's apostolic career which is based solely on the letters."[256] Luedemann says on the first page that his work was evoked by the writings of John Knox and Donald Riddle, whose findings had remained unknown in the world of German New Testament scholarship or had been reported in a distorted form. In later footnotes, he also mentions Hurd and Buck and Taylor as having been ignored by German New Testament scholars.[257]

Luedemann concentrates a great deal of his interest and energy on Gal 1-2. After noting that previous commentators had not been exacting enough, he uses rhetorical analysis to shed light on Paul's meaning. Luedemann uses these two chapters to establish the basis of his chronology for Paul's life.

After that beginning, Luedemann sequenced First and Second Corinthians and Romans according to the references to the Collection, and then placed First Thessalonians and Philippians into their correct positions in the sequence in which Paul wrote them. This sequence of the letters, then, is the backbone of Luedemann's chronology for Paul's ministry.

These six scholars are closely related to each other. Charles Buck inspired

---

255. Hurd, *Origin*, 213.

256. John Knox, "Forward," in Gerd Luedemann, *Paul, Apostle to the Gentiles: Studies in Chronology* (Philadelphia: Fortress Press, 1984), xiii.

257. Luedemann, *Apostle*, 2 footnote 2-5, printed on page 29-30; 17 footnote 65 printed on page 38; and many others.

John Hurd, and Buck, Hurd, Donald Riddle and John Knox all contributed to creating Gerd Luedemann's interest.[258] They all worked to establish a chronology based on the historical evidence of the letters. Most other New Testament scholars, however, have not followed them.[259]

258. Luedemann comments that he first read Knox's books because his professor, an Englishman, warned him of their excessive scepticism. Bruce Corley, ed., *Colloquy on New Testament Studies: A Time for Reappraisal and Fresh Approaches* (Macon GA: Mercer University Press, 1983), 314.

259. Hurd, *Earlier Letters*, 12, 104, 114-115, 164-165. An example of scholarship that follows the Acts-based history is Malherbe, *Letters*. The Anchor Bible series represents mainstream Protestant scholarship. Malherbe presents First Thessalonians as having been written in Corinth a very short period, such as six months, after Paul's founding of the ecclesia in Thessalonica, exactly as the Acts-based history would have it.

APPENDIX 3

THEIR CRITICISMS OF ACTS

THE literature on a letters-based history of Paul's ministry includes criticism of the conventional Acts-based history. It was not possible for these scholars simply to say that Paul's letters are primary historical data and that New Testament scholarship should focus on Paul's letters in order to develop a chronology of Paul's ministry. New Testament scholars have been deriving the history of Paul's ministry from some combination of material from Paul and from the Book of Acts for centuries. Therefore, it has been necessary for those who argue for a letters-based history to find reasons to criticize Acts-based history. These scholars have criticized Acts because it is secondary evidence, because its chronology is vague, because there is biographical material in the letters which Acts ignored, because Luke-Acts made a number of mistakes regarding world-history and therefore Acts is not to be trusted, because there are difficulties with those passages where the Acts data conflicts with the letters data, and because Acts has some other agenda than to write history.

It is probably the criticisms Knox expressed of Acts that have given him and *Chapters* the reputation of being radical. His most significant criticism is that Acts represents Luke's reworking of his sources, which makes Acts secondary historical data. Paul's references to historical events are the testimony of an eyewitness, which makes them primary historical data.[260]

Hurd argued against the historical reliability of Acts in the first chapter of *Origin*. Hurd expressed the difference between primary and secondary evidence even more clearly two years later, in an article written for Knox's re-

---

260. Knox, *Chapters*, 15.
Donald Harman Akenson, *Saint Saul* (Oxford University Press, 2000), 140, likens Knox's thesis to telling the Emperor that he has no clothes.

251

tirement.[261] In that article Hurd made a clear statement that we need to base our reconstruction of the history on the letters as if Acts did not exist. Only after the letters have been thoroughly mined and the evidence evaluated on its own merits will it be appropriate to turn to Acts and fit its evidence into this structure.

Acts chronology is vague. Rather than precise dating, Acts uses phrases such as "about that time" (12:1 and 19:23), and "in these days" (6:1 and 11:22). The period Paul refers to as "after three years" is referred to in Acts as "several days" (Acts 9:19) and then Acts has Paul going up to Jerusalem "after some time had passed" (Acts 9:23).[262] Likewise, Paul said that his second trip to Jerusalem was "after fourteen years," which means that even by the shorter reckoning there had to have been at least eleven years between trips. Acts does not account for that long a period between trips, "whichever way these years are counted."[263]

Hurd also observes that there is a lot of biographical information in the letters that does not appear at all in Acts. Hurd lists fourteen items, including Paul's having been whipped and beaten, having been shipwrecked three times, having been imprisoned many times (2 Cor 11:23-25), having been under a sentence of death (2 Cor 1:8), and having organized a collection for the saints. Hurd concludes that these omissions weaken Acts' credibility as a biography of Paul.

After the Roman Empire became overwhelmingly Christian, it became possible to date events by a single calendar, using B.C. or B.C.E. dates for years before the birth of Christ and A.D. or C.E. for years afterwards. Before that convention was adopted, however, historians dated events by the number of years since the first Olympic games or by the reigns of important political figures, such as "in the fifteenth year of the reign of the Emperor Tiberius" (Luke 3:1). The author of Luke and Acts made several such historical references; however, his references were often incorrect. Knox mentions an error

261. John Coolidge Hurd, Jr., "Pauline Chronology and Pauline Theology" in *Christian History and Interpretation: Studies presented to John Knox*, W.R.Farmer, C.F.D.Moule and R.R.Niebuhr, eds., (Cambridge: At the University Press, 1967), 225-248. This article is reprinted in *Earlier Letters*, 9-30, along with Hurd's essay on "The Sequence of the Letters" 31-46, which he originally intended to be published with the article in the Festschrift.

262. Knox, *Chapters*, 48. Hurd, *Origin*, 22. Luedemann, *Apostle*, 7. The use of quotations from Acts illustrating vague specifications of time are very similar.

263. Hurd, *Origin*, 23.

regarding the census when Jesus was born (Luke 2:2) and the order in which Gamaliel mentions two historical figures (Acts 5:34-39).[264] Luedemann says that Luke was "often incorrect"[265] about such dates, but then he provides an exhaustive critique. He might as well have said that Luke makes some error in every one of his references to world history.[266] If this is the case, then, we should be very careful in following Acts regarding any matter of history.

The traditional construction of Paul's history attempts to match up events in both sources. However, closer examination reveals problems with the match-ups.

In Acts, Paul makes five trips to Jerusalem.[267] Since the fifth of these is Paul's final trip to Jerusalem, intended to deliver the Collection and culminating in his arrest, and in Galatians Paul spoke of two trips to Jerusalem, both prior to that final trip, the problem is to reconcile four trips with two. There is a rough correspondence between the second of the visits in Acts (11:29-30) and Paul's description of his first visit. Furthermore, the fourth visit in Acts (15:1-29) and Paul's version of his second visit both deal with requirements for gentile converts. The most glaring difference is that Paul says that the Jerusalem authorities added nothing to his gospel, whereas the Acts version looks more like a compromise formula.[268] Beyond that, Paul presents himself throughout this passage as independent of the Jerusalem authorities, but Acts presents him as under their authority and as using Jerusalem as the home base for his missionary ventures.

Acts includes a story that Jews in Corinth complained to Gallio, the proconsul in Achaia. When Paul appeared before him, Gallio dismissed the charges (Acts 18:12-17). We now know from archaeological evidence that Gallio was proconsul in Corinth in 51-52 C.E.[269] Acts assigns the appearance before Gallio to Paul's first visit.[270] However, that makes Paul's first visit to

---

264. Knox, *Chapters*, 81.

265. Luedemann, *Apostle*, 9.

266. Luedemann, *Apostle*, 8-12.

267. Knox, *Chapters*, 61-62. lists Acts 9:26-27; 11:29-30; 15:1-29; 18:22 and 21:15ff. Luedemann, *Apostle*, 5, discards 9:26-27 as unhistorical.

268. Knox, *Chapters*, 62.

269. Knox, Chapters, 81-82. Buck and Taylor, *St. Paul*, 194, 213-15. Hurd, *Origin*, 31. Luedemann, *Apostle*, 17-18.

270. 1 Cor 1:14-16 and 3:6 refer to the founding visit. Acts reports that Paul visited Corinth

Corinth come late in time, in comparison with the letters-based chronology.
Buck and Hurd note that "although Paul may visit a city several times, his
adventures occur only on one of his visits, usually his first."[271] This tendency
to group events suggests that Acts is not credible regarding the chronology
of those events. We really do not know whether Paul appeared before Gallio
during his first time in Corinth or during a later visit.

Acts says that when Paul arrived in Corinth the first time, he met Priscilla
and Aquila, who had recently been expelled from Rome by Emperor Claudius (Acts 18:2). Dating the expulsion of the Jews in 49 c.e. (in the ninth year
of the reign of Claudius, as a fifth century historian said) matches up nicely
with an appearance before Gallio in 51 or 52. However, both Knox and Luedemann think it more likely that Claudius expelled the Jews from Rome, to
whatever extent he actually did so, in 41 c.e.[272]

Acts said that when Paul left Thessalonica to go to Athens and then on to
Corinth, Timothy stayed behind in Beroea (Acts 17:13-14), and later Timothy rejoined Paul in Corinth (Acts 18:5). Paul, however, says that he sent
Timothy on a fact-finding mission from Athens to Thessalonica (1 Thess
3:2), and then says that Timothy had "just now" returned (1 Thess 3:6). The
most natural reading of First Thessalonians would be that Timothy rejoined
Paul in Athens. So it hardly seems that Acts and Paul are talking about the
same set of Timothy's movements.[273]

For the past several centuries, scholars and others have identified Acts as a
book of history, the history of the very early church. The question, however,
is whether Luke intended to write history when he composed this volume. If
Luke had some other purpose in mind than to provide an accurate historical
account, then it behooves us to recognize what that purpose was and then

---

three times; the letters may refer to more than three visits: 2 Cor 2:1 refers to a painful visit. Rom
15:26 appears to place Paul in Corinth and about to leave for Jerusalem. The appearance before
Gallio may have occurred on one of Paul's later visits to Corinth, and there is some probability
that it was during his last visit there. See particularly Buck's argument, 192-94.

271. Buck and Taylor, *St. Paul*, 192-94. The quotation is from Hurd, *Origin*, 30. Luedemann,
Apostle, 17-18.

272. Knox, *Chapters*, 82. In footnote 5 Knox reports a reflection that Claudius' edict was too
harsh and proved to be unenforceable. Luedemann, *Apostle*, 9-10. In addition to arguing for a
date of 41 c.e. for Claudius' edict, Luedemann suggests that there were too many Jews in Rome
for Claudius to have expelled all of them.

273. Hurd, *Origin*, 25.

to evaluate that purpose in terms of how it contributes to Acts' credibility as history.[274]

In addition to citing Knox and Riddle as the figures who evoked his own work, Luedemann also mentions the work of Philip Vielhauer. According to Luedemann, Vielhauer demonstrated that Paul's speeches in Acts do not resemble the theology of the letters.[275] Luedemann concludes that if Luke is not dependable for theology, then he is not dependable for history.[276] There is a missing step to this argument; perhaps Luke did not intend to present a historically accurate account. If Luke did not intend to present a historically accurate account, then we cannot count on him to present the chronology correctly.

Luedemann claims this insight as the wellspring of his own study. It seems to me that in this, Luedemann has made an important contribution to the conversation about Luke and Paul. If Luke did not intend to be a historian, then we should not read him as a historian. In that case, we really should base our historical analysis on Paul's letters.

To round out the argument that Luke did not intend to write history when he wrote Acts, Luedemann offers the point that journey is a theological motif in Luke's two volume work. When Jesus turned in Luke 9:51 to go to Jerusalem, he began a journey that dominates that Gospel; the journey from Galilee to Jerusalem is the theological motif of the Gospel. Acts presented Paul's three missionary journeys as circles gradually widening toward Rome, the ultimate destination, and take up more than half the book. Thus the journey from Jerusalem to Rome is Acts' theological motif. Along with this theological motif, Acts refers to the fellowship of Jesus' followers as the Way. Paul's journeys, as presented in Acts, fit so well with this geographical theology that we ought to suspect that they were never intended as a historical account.[277]

Knox noted that the Book of Acts has its own agenda. In *Chapters*, he

---

274. In particular Joseph B. Tyson, *Marcion and Luke-Acts: A Defining Struggle* (Columbia, SC: University of South Carolina Press) is a very helpful discussion of the intention and purpose behind Luke's work.

275. Luedemann, *Apostle*, 21. Although Luedemann attributes this insight to Vielhauer, it was stated earlier by Ferdinand Christian Baur, *Paul: the apostle of Jesus Christ, his life and works, his epistles and teachings; a contribution to a critical history of primitive Christianity.* 2nd ed. by Dr. E. Zeller. (Williams and Norgate, London and Edinburgh, 1873). Vol. 1, *passim*.

276. Luedemann, *Apostle*, 21.

277. Luedemann, *Apostle*, 13-15

stated Acts' agenda as a tendency to emphasize Jerusalem and the authority of the apostles there and to present Christianity as politically harmless. Officials of the Roman Empire regularly find no fault with the Christians.[278] Acts presented Christianity as the legitimate successor of Judaism.[279] Knox's point, here, is that since Acts had a different purpose than to present the chronology of Paul's ministry, we should not trust Acts for that chronology.

In an earlier book, Knox presented quite a different purpose for the Book of Acts. Acts was published, Knox argued, in order to answer the heretic Marcion, who had taught in Rome in the early decades of the second century out of a "book" of scripture known as "Gospel and Apostle." Marcion's "Gospel" was a version of Luke's Gospel, missing some strategic pieces, and his "Apostle" was several of Paul's letters, again missing some strategic passages. Marcion was later identified as a heretic, and Paul's letters were associated, by some, with the heresy. Knox suggested that the Book of Acts was compiled in order to rescue Paul from the tint of Marcion's heresy. The other three Gospels and the Pastoral Epistles were added to this "book" and the result was most of the canon of the New Testament. This New Testament, with four Gospels and ten letters by Paul, was able to compete handsomely with Marcion's "book."[280] Thus the composition of Acts contributed to the formation of the New Testament.

It is indeed unfortunate that these scholars, whose intent was to establish a letters-based history of Paul's ministry, had to criticize Acts as part of their program. To those people who regard Acts as sacred scripture, such criticism had to be offensive. That offense has likely contributed to the failure of New Testament scholarship generally to accept the logic that the history of the very early church must be constructed from the primary data of Paul's letters.

Nevertheless, the insight of these six scholars that Paul's letters contain primary historical data is true and significant. It is for this reason that it is necessary to mine Paul's letters exhaustively for what they can tell us about the early history of the developing Christian faith.

---

278. Knox, *Chapters*, 24-28.

279. Knox, *Chapters*, 36.

280. Knox. *Marcion*. Recently, Joseph B. Tyson has taken up parts of this reading of Acts in his book on *Marcion and Luke-Acts*.

INDEX